SOUTHERN LITERARY STUDIES

Southern Literary Studies

LOUIS D. RUBIN, JR.
EDITOR

The Poetry of Randall Jarrell

ISBN 0–8071–0941–X
Library of Congress Catalog Card Number 78–166971
Copyright © 1971 by Louisiana State University Press
All rights reserved
Manufactured in the United States of America
Printed by The TJM Corporation, Baton Rouge, Louisiana
Designed by Charlotte Owens

811.09
F

Quotations from the poetry of Randall Jarrell are used through permission of
the following publishers:

Farrar, Straus & Giroux, Inc., for *The Complete Poems*, by Randall Jarrell
(copyright © 1935, 1936, 1937, 1940, 1941, 1942, 1944, 1945, 1946, 1947, 1948,
1949, 1950, 1951, 1952, 1965, 1966, 1967, 1968, 1969 by Mrs. Randall Jarrell).

The Macmillan Company, for *The Lost World*, by Randall Jarrell (copyright
© Randall Jarrell, 1948, 1961, 1962, 1963, 1964, 1965).

Atheneum Publishers, Inc., for *The Woman at the Washington Zoo*, by Randall
Jarrell ("The Girl Dreams That She Is Giselle," copyright 1949 by Randall
Jarrell, appeared originally in the *Nation*; "A Ghost, a Real Ghost," copyright
1945 by Randall Jarrell, appeared originally in *Kenyon Review*; "Cinderella,"
copyright © 1960 by Randall Jarrell; "Windows," copyright © 1954 by Randall Jarrell, appeared originally in *Poetry*; "The Lonely Man," copyright ©
1954 by Randall Jarrell, appeared originally in *Poetry*; "The End of the Rainbow," copyright © 1954 by Randall Jarrell, appeared originally in *Kenyon
Review*; "The Woman at the Washington Zoo," copyright © 1960 by Randall
Jarrell, appeared originally in the *Times Literary Supplement*; "Jerome," copyright © 1960 by Randall Jarrell; "Jamestown," copyright © 1957 by the *Virginia Quarterly Review*; "Nestus Gurley," copyright © 1956 by the *Virginia
Quarterly Review*; "The Bronze David of Donatello," copyright © 1960 by
Randall Jarrell, appeared originally in *Art News*.)

The quotation from Rainer Maria Rilke, "O this is the creature that does not
exist," *Sonnets to Orpheus*, M. Herter Norton, trans. (copyright 1942 by W. W.
Norton & Company, Inc.; copyright © renewed 1969 by M. D. Herter Norton),
is used by permission of the publisher.

To John Crowe Ransom

Acknowledgments

I SHOULD LIKE to express sincere gratitude to the Academic Senate of the University of California at Santa Barbara for the grants that enabled me to use the Jarrell Collection of the University of North Carolina at Greensboro and paid for the typing of the manuscript. My thanks are also due to the staff at the Walter Clinton Jackson Library of the University of North Carolina at Greensboro, and its former director, Charles Adams, for making my work there so pleasant and efficient.

At various points in preparing the study, I have been encouraged and informed by a number of correspondents: Mackie Langham Jarrell, John Crowe Ransom, Robert Penn Warren, Robert Lowell, the late Donald Davidson, and, most of all, by Mary von Schrader Jarrell, whose memories and generous spirit have enriched all the book, but especially the last two chapters.

I am extremely grateful to Professor Louis D. Rubin, Jr., and the editorial staff of the Louisiana State University Press for their considerate and intelligent handling of the manuscript. Special thanks are warranted for Sister M. Bernetta Quinn and Professor Walter B. Rideout, whose painstaking readings and illuminating suggestions have much enhanced the final version.

I would also like publicly to thank my husband: who first put the notion of such a book to me, and has been unflagging in his moral and intellectual support and indefatigable in running errands, reading and rereading the manuscripts, and typing revisions.

Contents

Illustrations

The Poetry of Randall Jarrell

both present a strongly idiosyncratic vision of a world uniquely their own. Even when writing of historical or public figures, Lowell sees them as a part of his own experience, and in showing their reality for himself makes them real to readers who are able to share his experience through the vitality of his characteristic rhetoric.

Karl Shapiro wrote of Jarrell, soon after his death, that what kept him from being a great poet was that he "lacked the sense of power," [1] which can mean at least in part that Jarrell had not the necessary egotism to suppose his own personality of sufficient importance to justify a body of poetry. He sought a universal experience and tried to define it as truly and exactly as possible; he believed others needed to know themselves and mankind generally much more desperately than they needed to know Randall Jarrell, and through his poetry he tried to teach all he saw of human needs and modes of fulfillment in contemporary society. Strongly influenced from his adolescence by Freudian analytical psychology, Jarrell attempted in his poetry to show how men's conscious motives and actions, and the largely unconscious imagery of fulfillment in their dreams and literature, spring from one primal need—inevitably frustrated in the phenomenal world—to feel secure in their loves and lives.

Jarrell's compulsion to teach his readers about their world resulted in a poetic rhetoric oriented toward the presentation of that world rather than the presentation of a "poet." His style is distinctive, but it is characteristically a colloquial, even homely style, blending the syntax of ordinary American discourse with the romantic color of American dreams. Except for its extravagant allusiveness and wit, it uncannily imitates plain American speech. His imagery, too, enforces attention to the subject rather than to itself; what lingers in the mind after reading Jarrell is rarely the verbal icon, more often it is a picture, tellingly detailed: a girl asleep in a college library; a woman at a zoo staring in horror at the vulture which has flown down "for the white rat that the foxes left"; a boy, a dog, and a woman gliding along Sunset Boulevard in a glassed-in electric automobile. When, near the end of his life, he came to write about his own childhood, that too was ob-

[1] Karl Shapiro, *Randall Jarrell*, Library of Congress Lecture (Washington, D.C., 1967), 23.

jectified, a world that every child growing up has lost and later tried to recover. The setting of "The Lost World" is Hollywood; not just the home of Randall Jarrell's grandparents, but the wellspring for much of America's fantasy life for more than three decades, until television and other less amusing products of modern technology combined to displace its lovely, naïve illusions.

If the personal quality of Jarrell's rhetoric is in part deliberately neutralized by his urge to visualize and explain the world of men in the middle of the twentieth century, the honesty and seriousness of his vision come through with strongly personal conviction. His voice, as he tells the truth about people and things, is anything but objective; it is tender, querulous, astonished, sardonic, outraged, amused, even at times frightened. Although he became famous as a poet of the Second World War, a great part of his work presents the lives of his civilian peers—middle-class, middle-income, moderately intelligent, moderately neurotic, moderately good; those whom American politicians call "the silent majority," who are born, grow up, get jobs, get married, have children, grow old, and die; they make neither trouble nor joy outside their immediate environment. They are downtrodden not by poverty or physical suffering or any obvious oppressor, but only by the ordinary psychological hazards of living in the modern world. But the poems, even those about the war, are not, and will not be dated, for they continually link the lives of their characters to the permanent needs, desires, and predicaments of mankind through the dreams, fairytales, and mythology—Germanic, Classical, Judaeo-Christian—that men great and small by a common impulse have created to help themselves confront the threats and temptations of the mutable world. A study of Jarrell's poetry, consequently, will not be primarily concerned with the development of a highly individual style, or with biographical or historical or even, usually, aesthetic contexts, but with the nuances of attitude and understanding Jarrell displays toward the characters and themes encompassed in his vision.

In the six chapters of this book I have treated chronologically the six separate volumes of Jarrell's poems, beginning with *Blood for a Stranger*[2] (1942) and ending with *The Lost World* (1965), and have

[2] All but one of the poems from "The Rage for the Lost Penny," twenty poems

attempted to trace the development of his major themes and subjects through comparative analysis of individual poems. Since Jarrell culled over and rearranged the poems of the first four volumes for *Selected Poems* (1955) and because these earlier editions are relatively hard to find, the chronological arrangement helps to make clear the interlocking chain of Jarrell's sequence of interests and attitudes, beginning with his apprehension of the general causes of men's cruelty and misery in acquisitiveness—"Trade"—and moving in the major work to close consideration of individual experiences of loneliness, loss of youth or of love, and the reality of death, in war or peace.

His themes are relatively few and closely related as they evolve through his thirty-year writing career: in the poems of the thirties, the "great Necessity" of the natural world and the evils of power politics; in the poems of the early forties, the dehumanizing forces of war and ways to escape or recover from these through dreams, mythologizing, or Christian faith; in the poems of the fifties, and continuing into the sixties, loneliness and fear of aging and death, again opposed by the imagination in dreams and works of art; and in some of the last poems, the defeat of Necessity and time through imaginative recovery of one's own past. The one overriding theme that links and illuminates the others is change, the change that aims toward transcendence. The subjects of the poems are almost always human: men, women, and children in war and peace, sickness and health, sorrow and joy; dreaming, meditating, justifying, consciously resisting the trouble of their lives or seeking some escape from it.

While my analyses are primarily given in order to define precisely the qualities of Jarrell's vision in the specific contexts of individual poems, they are also offered as aids to understanding difficult poems or passages. Of the "levels of meaning" in his poetry, Jarrell wrote in 1950:

> It is better to have the child in the chimney-corner moved by what happens in the poem, in spite of his ignorance of its real meaning, than to

which appeared in a joint collection, *Five Young American Poets* (Norfolk, Conn., 1940), 81–123, were republished in *Blood for a Stranger* and are treated in chapter 1. The authority for all dates of publication up to 1960 is Charles M. Adams, *Randall Jarrell: A Bibliography* (Chapel Hill, 1958), and its supplement, published in *Analects*, I (Spring, 1961), 49–56.

have the poem a puzzle to which that meaning is the only key. Still, complicated subjects make complicated poems, and some of the best poems can move only the best readers; this is one more question of curves of normal distribution. I have tried to make my poems plain, and most of them are plain enough; but I wish that they were more difficult because I had known more.[3]

Although after the very earliest ones, Jarrell's poems are usually straightforward in syntax, the subtleties of his world view, especially in the light of his omnivorous reading of other authors, occasionally create problems of understanding for the uninitiated reader. My explanations are rarely meant to be exhaustive, although I have tried to make them complete enough to show how the parts of the individual poems relate to their wholes.

In selecting poems for discussion I have tried to represent Jarrell by the most significant and characteristic poems from each period of his development, guided largely by Jarrell's own choices for the *Selected Poems* and the two subsequent volumes, *The Woman at the Washington Zoo* and *The Lost World*. For the interested reader, *The Complete Poems*, made available early in 1969 through the impeccable and tireless efforts of Mary von Schrader Jarrell and Michael Di Capua of Farrar, Straus, & Giroux, is invaluable in showing the full scope of Jarrell's poetic career. Unless otherwise noted, however, I have generally based my analyses on the original published versions of the poems, and the quotations may vary somewhat from the *Selected Poems* and *Complete Poems* texts.

Besides an introduction and a guide to Randall Jarrell's themes and to his most important poems, this book is meant to be an appreciation, not altogether uncritical, but predominantly admiring and grateful, of a body of poetry that has taught me and many others— "plain folks" as well as students of literature—"so much about so many things" in our shared world: if not "to change, to change," at least to better understand and to love.

---

[3] Randall Jarrell, "Answers to Questions," in John Ciardi (ed.), *Mid-Century American Poets* (New York, 1950), 183.

1· Early Poems

"The Rage for the Lost Penny" (1940)

Of the twenty poems that were published in "The Rage for the Lost Penny," Jarrell's portion of *Five Young American Poets* (1940), only "A Story" and "For an Emigrant" appear in the *Selected Poems* (1955), where the second is much altered. Both of these poems display some of the postures and rhetoric characteristic of Jarrell's mature poetry, but "The Rage for the Lost Penny" as a whole shows a surprising anonymity in style and content. Many of its poems are all but indistinguishable from the work of a number of competent young poets of the late thirties, many of whose budding reputations did not survive the years of war. Influenced chiefly by Auden, but also by Allen Tate, Hardy, and perhaps even A. E. Housman—about whose poetry Jarrell had written his Vanderbilt M.A. thesis in the early thirties—these poems have a curiously sociological approach to the human condition; only in a few poems does one find the typical strategy of Jarrell's poems about the war: that is, the projection of general human suffering through intensive treatment of the individual case. Rather, both situations and characters are generalized in imagery that is concrete without being specific, and in extended personifications that dramatize abstract conditions of love and suffering.

The subject of most of the twenty poems is the imminent and apparently inevitable self-destruction of man and his civilization through his inward indifference and solipsism, or his lust for useless, meaningless power. In several of these poems the central image is a monster, bloody and terrible, but in itself innocent: man's creature and destroyer, perhaps related to Yeats's "rough beast" heralding apocalypse or to Crane's "blood-swollen God," War, in *The Red Badge of Courage*. In "1789–1939" the monster is a "child,/ Fathered by Reason . . . / Who once like an idol overstrode/ The streets that glittered with his blood . . ." This horror now

> . . . lifts his huge head
> To see with helpless and darkening eyes
> The tyrant standing among his torturers.

"The Automaton" envisions a "great shape . . . / The slave and remnant of the slain" on a battlefield among huddled corpses, waiting for the command to destroy that cannot ever come from "the ruined and strengthless dead." Literally, the automaton with its "senseless limbs" and "powerful . . . lifeless head" may be an enormous gun of some sort, but it represents

> Unconquered, inexhaustible
> The genius of a world's desire
> And cast at that world's judgment
> Into the world-consuming fire—.

In "The See-er of Cities," a "great Gestalt" appears in the penultimate stanza, to be described in the last as "black with the blood of the imposer's breast,/ The sure and treacherous and final sum/ Of sea, soul, city." This "shape" is identified with the "I" of the poem, the "See-er" who sees that because of man's self-centeredness—his own included—all lands and cities are "the same senseless ground." In the final stanza the "I" reports that

> . . . from Dan to Omsk
> I walked this planet and found
> Nothing but my own footsteps on the ground.

This monstrous figure becomes "Love" in the poem "Love, in Its Separate Being," but it is a perverse self-love, deified by men; he is at once the god, the welcomed hero, though earlier, before he was "grown giant, gracious," he was "the exposed child." The diction of the poem suggests Christ, as well as Eros and the various legends of heroes who were abandoned to the elements in childhood, but the image is a distorted one, created by men in their own grotesque image. The poem ends threateningly, for after being established among his people, "Love laughs and is not magnanimous."

In poems where the monstrous shape is not a literal presence, its general significance is often felt. The enigmatic epigraph to *Blood for a Stranger*, taken from Beethoven's F Major Quartet (Op. 135), "Muss es sein?/ Es Muss Sein!/ Es Muss sein!" established Jarrell's own preoccupation with the "Kingdom of Necessity" he found in the work of his friend Robert Lowell. The true horror of Jarrell's monster, like that of Yeats's "The Second Coming" or of Tennyson's "The Kraken," is that its advent is inevitable, in Jarrell's view not because there is any external decree or mover, but because men refuse to see anything but their own footsteps on the ground.

In the poem "For an Emigrant" [1] the idea of the destroying monster is embodied in the Statue of Liberty, with its eyes "absolute in their assurance/ Of power and of innocence."

> And what looks timidly from their clear depths
> Is the child's loneliness, his passionate rejection
> Of his own helplessness and pain, the man's
> Denial of the knowledge he cannot endure.
> The mouth says: "I made me, I shall last, be sure.
> Time is my will.
> Surely the tears are iron within my eyes.
> Look, and find life here about my lips—
> Who has not loved me? I shall never die."

The statue's eyes are those of the child, the emigrant to whom the poem is addressed, but eyes and gesture both are those of Hitler, explicitly named in this early version of the poem. He is, strangely, "the Accuser, the Appeaser, the inhuman Judge." The victim is one with the victimizer because "there is guilt enough for all: existence is guilt enough." The Christian doctrine of forgiveness is seen as a sop to conscience, a lie, a sin of omission. The poet advises the child, "Forgive no one./ Understand and blame"; and when she protests, "But I am all of them. That face, that world is mine," she is told to change, so that when she is finally, inexorably destroyed by those others, they will have to cry, not Baudelaire's "mon semblable, mon frére," but "You stranger, you damned stranger!"

The bitter, anguished outburst of the 1939 version is effaced in the

[1] First published version, not the revised version in Randall Jarrell, *Selected Poems* (New York, 1955).

Selected Poems' "To the New World," which omits nearly all of the second section of the poem, from which the passages quoted above come. Hitler appears, unnamed, but in "his trench-coat," writing "his big book," as in the early version. At the end of the revision "He" appears again, but inside the child herself, watching her own arrival in America "in accusation, in acceptance." The poem concludes, "You escaped from nothing: the westering soul/ Finds Europe waiting for it over every sea," lines which appear near the beginning of the second section of the 1939 poem. By avoiding the name "Hitler" in the *Selected Poems*' version, Jarrell broadens the thematic range; there have been, and will very likely be, others who wear a trench coat (or black shirt, or brown shirt, or any coat or hat or uniform), and write a big (or little) book explaining or excusing themselves. They will attract followers because other men will find in themselves the faces of the leader, "the Accuser, the Appeaser, the inhuman Judge." What men share, in Europe and America, is the conviction of the statue and the child: "Who has not loved me? I shall never die." In the later version of the poem, the meanings are less explicit than in the first, and the conclusion is both more muted and less hopeful than the earlier. The possibility of change, which would leave the dying child a "damned stranger" to the evil of the others, is not even broached.

The "Necessity" that is opposed to human desires, and therefore gives rise to the psychological devices of wish-fulfillment, is one of Jarrell's continuing subjects, from these earliest poems to those of *The Lost World*. The concept seems to have been amalgamated out of Jarrell's early reading of Freud and Spinoza, for it is both naturalistic and metaphysical; Necessity springs from man's own nature, as in Spinoza, and his nature is to gratify himself, as in Freud. The ongoing process of history records the working out of Necessity. The idea is often found in conjunction with two of Jarrell's most characteristic motifs: the child and the fairy tale, especially in its folk origin—the German *Märchen*. Both of these motifs appear in "For an Emigrant," where the child is the protagonist, forced by the Necessity momentarily embodied in Naziism to flee with her family from Vienna, then Prague, then Europe. In both published versions of the poem, she is directed by the poet, presumably against her own wish, to find her persecutor within herself, because she represents all mankind, innocent and guilty. She is called "Beauty" in the second section of the original poem, and told that she "must wake" to the meaning of her human destiny, unlike the Beauty who transcends her own death in the enchanted castle by means of a Prince's kiss. No Prince will come for this Beauty; Necessity itself will waken her.

The fairy tale, though already understood as symbolic wish fulfillment, is introduced sparingly in "The Rage for the Lost Penny"; aside from the hint of Hansel's situation in "A Story," and the obscure, generalized theme of the exposed child who returns as a hero in "Love, in Its Separate Being," all the references (four) are to "Sleeping Beauty" or "Snow White"; in either case it is the possibility of being found and awakened from death-masking sleep that Jarrell seizes upon for his images. The most explicit reference occurs in the last two lines of "The Ways and the Peoples," another poem that sees the fatal Necessity overcome through wish-fulfillment. The five-quatrain poem moves through a series of contrasting images: trees in the wind; the hero "among his dead"; the "skinny digger" in excavations; the shard on which the digger perceives a leopard among deer; a seedling in the wind (returning to the opening image of trees); and finally,

> ... the helpless love
> Of the dwarfs in the forest for the glittering virgin
> Who is dying and glass on her marvellous bier.

The poem as a whole is obscure; none of the images except the last yields its full burden of meaning, none is sufficiently developed, and the relations among them are vague. However, the image of love, the wish of the dwarfs that causes them to keep the body of their princess in a hope that is against all reason, becomes a powerful symbol of man's deep longing for transcendence of nature through strong, if irrational, feeling: the desire for survival.

The motif of the child, in particular the child's way of experiencing the world, is slightly more prominent in the volume than that of the fairy tale; besides the monstrous child of "1789–1939" and related poems, an image that sees the child's innocent, amoral self-centeredness as characteristic of destructive mankind in general, there are actual children. They are generally sufferers, individual, as in "For an Emigrant," and communal, as are the dead children of "The Refugees." In "A Story," one of the two poems Jarrell retained in *Selected Poems*, a child tells of his being sent away to school, where he is lonely and fearful; he finally decides to disappear, so as to make those who left him there sorry.

The poem is distinctively Jarrellian in its use of colloquial diction, realistically portraying the defensive rhetoric of the child, with its naïve dependence on simple and incremental repetition. The rhyme scheme is a perfect sestina,[2] except that there is no envoi. The form, with its unusual stress on repeated rather than rhymed end-words, naturally emphasizes the words so repeated: "empty," "lost," "boys," "say," and "day." In the case of "their," the remaining end-word, attention is forced onto the noun that follows, beginning the next line. Dreams, both daydreams and sleeping dreams, are used to express the child's sense of loss on being, as he thinks, abandoned; the lost boy he hears about is a projection of himself.

The new place, because it is not home, is to the child "empty," nowhere. The anonymous buildings, with empty halls, empty beds; the faceless matron, the unknown boys, the dean, the stranger of stanza five; the railroad trestle, all the roads and signs leading away; *all* are blanks so far as the boy is concerned, for they no longer relate him to his home and family. In spite of, or perhaps because of, its verisimilitude in conveying boyish responses ("They love their new friends better"; "When I feel better they'll . . . find"; "I don't like these boys. . . . I don't care, I like these boys . . .") the poem tends to cuteness; attention shifts from the sense of loss to the sense of childishness.

Jarrell was to use the child's point of view in later volumes, in such poems as "The Child of Courts," "The Truth," "The State," "Protocols," "Gunner"—in which the speaker is a soldier, but like some other Jarrell soldiers, a child at heart—and finally, triumphantly in "The Lost World." The danger of lapsing into preciosity is in some of the poems averted by the seriousness of the situation: in

---

2 "The Refugees," also in "The Rage for the Lost Penny," is an even more amputated sestina.

"Protocols," the death of children in concentration camps. In "The Lost World," a poetic memoir on its literal plane, the concreteness of evocation justifies and enriches the child's vision and rhetoric.

The one other poem in "The Rage for the Lost Penny" which uses a child narrator, "A Little Poem," merits brief attention, for it suggests a parody of the early Dylan Thomas;[3] the speaker is at first inside the womb with his brother, where he sees himself as both a fish and a pig. After birth, the brothers make mud pies:

> My brother patted on his silted knee
> A dumb wish budding into wives, a house
> Where children coiled like smoke around a hearth . . .

His deeper awareness of the tragic deceptions of their childish dreams makes the speaker unable to share his brother's satisfying illusion of joy; his reluctance takes the rather unfortunate image of "unpopped corn." The poem ends with a grotesquely Thomas-like series of images:

> The heart in his oiled breast was dumb as Time
> And his skull crackled with its empty blood.

Because Jarrell's critical statements about Thomas were ambivalent, particularly with reference to overcharged rhetoric, it is difficult to accept this farrago of Thomas' mannerisms, even though the poem seems to treat some of Jarrell's serious concerns. It is possible that, as in the more or less close imitations of Auden and Tate,[4] Jarrell was attempting to discover his own style by exploring styles already developed in modern poetry.

In his rather grudging preface to "The Rage for the Lost Penny," Jarrell enumerated the characteristics of "modernist" poetry:

[1] very interesting language, a great emphasis on connotation, "texture"; [2] extreme intensity, forced emotion—violence; [3] a good deal of obscurity; [4] emphasis on sensation, perceptual nuances; [5] emphasis on

[3] One of Jarrell's uncollected poems, "The Country Was" (1942), is an explicit parody of Marianne Moore's poetry. See Randall Jarrell, *The Complete Poems* (New York, 1969), 432–33.

[4] See below, pp. 17–18.

details, on the part rather than the whole; [6] experimental or novel qualities of some sort; [7] a tendency toward external formlessness and internal disorganization . . . ; [8] an extremely personal style . . . ; [9] lack
of restraint—all tendencies are forced to their limits; [10] . . . a good deal
of emphasis on the unconscious, dream-structure, the thoroughly subjective; [11] . . . anti-scientific, anti-commonsense, anti-public [attitudes]
. . . ; [12] poetry is primarily lyric, intensive—the few long poems are
aggregations of lyric details; [13] poems usually have, not a logical, but
the more or less associational structure of dramatic monologue; and so
on and so on.[5]

Of the thirteen characteristics, Jarrell's own poems reflect seven very
plainly,[6] and two or three more in some degree, curiously, because
in the essay Jarrell shows himself to be impatient with, even slightly
hostile to the "advanced stage of romanticism" to which, he says, the
characteristics belong. His list of "modernist" poets includes Pound,
Eliot, Crane, Tate, Stevens, Cummings, and Marianne Moore, but
neither Auden, whose influence is so general in the subjects, attitudes,
and rhetoric of "The Rage . . ." nor Thomas, perhaps the most romantic of all modern poets, whose markedly personal style Jarrell imitated
in at least one poem. Jarrell ends his preface with a declaration that
is wryly ambivalent: "During the course of the article, the reader
may have thought curiously, 'Does he really suppose he writes the
sort of poetry that replaces modernism?' Let me answer, like the
man in the story, 'I must decline the soft impeachment.' But I am
sorry I need to." [7]

Unlike the later critical essays of *Poetry and the Age* which were
so carefully polished, "A Note on Poetry" has the air of being
hastily written,[8] tossed off, almost, under the pressure of the publisher's desire for a uniform format. It is possible to regroup and
condense the characteristics Jarrell lists under three general head-
ings: form (or what Ransom called "structure")—numbers 5, 7, 10,

---

[5] Jarrell, "The Rage for the Lost Penny," 87–88.

[6] Nos. 1, 2, 3, 9, 10, 12, 13. His "personal style" (No. 8) of cultivated simplicity
in diction and structure was established by 1944 and signaled the disappearance of
several of the other characteristics of "modernist poetry."

[7] Jarrell, "The Rage for the Lost Penny," 90. The identity of the man in the
story is obscure. Mrs. Malaprop, in Sheridan's *The Rivals* (V, iii) owned up to
a "soft impeachment."

[8] It was rewritten and published as "The End of the Line," *Nation*, CLIV
(1942), 222–28.

12, 13; language (Ransom's "texture")—numbers 1, 3, 4, 6, 8; and subjects and attitudes—numbers 2, 3, 6, 9, 11. Although some of the last have counterparts in structure and texture—lack of restraint in attitude is evinced in extravagance of language, for example, and dreams are a structure as well as a subject—these simplified categories seem viable for discussion of Jarrell's own early poetry.

Structurally, young Jarrell's poems in some ways fulfill his descriptions, in others, not. The associational structure of monologue, the poet's as well as his characters', is often the basis of the conceptual form (as differentiated from the verse form). Only a few of the poems have "plots" as structural bases—"A Story," "For an Emigrant," "Che Faro Senza Euridice"; more have implied or pseudo-plots—"A Little Poem," "On the Railway Platform," "The Winter's Tale," "The Ways and the Peoples," "The Bad Music," etc.; others are pure descriptions—"The Refugees," "A Description of Some Confederate Soldiers." Two seem to be dreams—"A Little Poem," "Che Faro . . ."—but others seem to move back and forth between dreams and reality—"The Bad Music," "The Winter's Tale," "A Story."

In verse structure, Jarrell defies his description (No. 7). Though most of the poems have a very free iambic line varying from four to six feet long, most are further divided into stanzas of four to eight lines. Two poems use the difficult sestina form, while most of the others are rhymed. Some poems begin with a regular rhyme scheme, then abandon it. Though they are hardly dull, metrically, neither are the poems of "The Rage for the Lost Penny" particularly innovative. While Jarrell was not really interested in the strictly rhymed and metered forms advocated and practiced by Ransom, Frost, and (sometimes) Auden, he was not a disciple of free verse. One of the most marked stylistic elements of Jarrell's later poetry, repetition of individual words and phrases within a poem, appears only sporadically in "The Rage . . ." and in several instances it occurs in the rigid traditional rhyme scheme of the sestina.

In their language, generally, these early poems lack great distinction. They display a slightly higher level of abstraction than Jarrell's later poems, and, in keeping with their subjects, a good deal of violence; the poems are full of tyrants, oppressors, and tormentors;

wrenching, crackling, stuffing of Earth, bodies, skulls; rejection, loss, pain, anguish, arrogance. Violence seems often to be imported into the poems gratuitously. Like the world of *King Lear*, Jarrell's is a tough rack that breaks men before it kills them.

Unlike Ransom, Jarrell avoids unusual words; "gibbous" is by far the strangest word in all the poems. Their obscurity lies in their syntax and imagery; modifying phrases in particular are often ambiguous. The reader has to supply logical connectives in many cases and assign the significance of the various symbolic figures such as the "monstrous child" of "1789–1939." Although connotation is important, as in other "modernist" poetry, there is little of the word play—punning—that became more and more prominent, even in some of the poems of *Blood for a Stranger*. The style is eclectic rather than personal; some poems are strikingly Audenesque—"Because of Me, Because of You," "When You and I Were All"—several echo Hardy's irony in their tone, and others recall Allen Tate—"The Winter's Tale," "A Description of Some Confederate Soldiers." This last poem seems almost a debunking of Tate's "Ode to the Confederate Dead."

> . . . the hunters came, and kneeling there
> Lifted you, and saw covering your face
> Man's choice, and man's magnificence
>
> Grow monstrous, and unclouded by
> The empty measure of his breath.
> How can the grave hold, a statue name
> Blood dried in that intolerable glare?[9]

Not surprisingly, in the last stanza of the poem these Confederate dead become symbolic of another era, like our own, toppled by a Necessity that is in this case man's own brutal nature.

> They stand like shattered and untopped columns,
> The barbarous foliage of an age
> Necessity instructed and destroyed.
> There is no hesitation in those eyes.

---

[9] Compare Tate's "Ode," ll. 35–40, 45–47, 78–80.

The violence of language and the structure of dreams, also noted in Jarrell's list of modernist characteristics, are intrinsically related to a content of violence and dreams, and both occur in his poetry. Jarrell diverges, however, from the complex of "anti-scientific, anti-commonsense, anti-public" attitudes that leaves the poet "essentially removed" from his society. Although Jarrell judges his society severely, he never stands apart from it. In such poems as "The Bad Music" and "Che Faro Senza Euridice," the poet speaker is himself the cold-hearted destroyer, while in others he addresses himself in pained sympathy to the victims of the world's cruelty, as in "For an Emigrant" and "The Refugees." In still other poems, he is one of the sufferers: "On the Railway Platform," "The Winter's Tale," "A Little Poem."

If one may draw any conclusion from the way Jarrell's poems in "The Rage for the Lost Penny" correspond to his description of modernist poetry in its preface, it might be that Jarrell, perhaps under the influence of his teacher and friend, John Crowe Ransom, thought of himself as moving away from certain undesirable characteristics of the preceding generation of modernists: their external formlessness and internal disorganization, anti-public attitudes, and purely lyrical intensity. On the other hand, he retains some qualities because they seem an inevitable part of his world: violence, lack of restraint; others because they are essential to his deepest personal concerns: dream structure, emphasis on the unconscious, the associational structure of monologue.

While it is clear that the twenty poems of "The Rage for the Lost Penny" [10] are poems of a young man striving intently and only rarely successfully for a distinctive voice and style, they also show a consciousness and a conscience too aware of suffering and destruction to keep still. Though there is no single poem that is in the first rank of modern lyrics, there is none that is trivial, either in conception or execution. They are apprentice poems, to be sure, but they come from an apprentice convinced of the vital importance of his calling, and able to learn, with astonishing celerity, the skills of his masters.

---

[10] The title, taken from an early Beethoven piano rondo, suggests both the recurrent themes and methods of the collection, and a certain humorous detachment.

Blood for a Stranger (1942)

Jarrell added twenty-seven new poems to the nineteen he retained from "The Rage for the Lost Penny" in his first separately published book, *Blood for a Stranger*. Where only two from the earlier collection were published in *Selected Poems*, eight of the added ones were chosen, indicating Jarrell's proportionately greater satisfaction with these newer poems. Although the general subject matter and attitude is the same as that of "The Rage for the Lost Penny," and although many of the poems are stylistically indistinguishable from the earlier ones, some are distinctly better poems, their images more powerfully individual, their statements more convincing and moving. The range of expression has broadened to include the polished, sardonic tone of "The Blind Sheep," with its echoes of Hardy and perhaps Ransom; the mysterious dream vision of "The Skaters"; the first of Jarrell's several "library" poems; and the remarkable symbolic monologue, "90 North."

Despite its title and date, *Blood for a Stranger* is not a book of war poetry. The book is arranged in four sections of eleven to twelve poems each, and the sections seem to develop different aspects of man's responses to modern society. The first section contains poems of questing; the second, poems of self-discovery; the third, generally, poems of a depersonalized world on the verge of breakup; the last, poems of man's longing and betrayal. The first section begins with "On the Railway Platform" and ends with "For an Emigrant," both from "The Rage . . . ." The most striking poem of this group is "90 North." It is Jarrell's first fully characteristic poem, and one of his best.[11]

The quest in "90 North" is a quest for ultimate meaning in life,

[11] Malcolm Cowley, in "First Blood," a review of *Blood for a Stranger*, *New Republic*, CVII (1942), 718, first suggested that "90 North" is indebted to Spender's "Polar Exploration." It seems possible that Jarrell derived from it the basic idea of the polar voyages as symbolic quests for meaning, though Spender's is a simpler, finally a different kind of poem. See also the last ten chapters of Poe's *Narrative of Arthur Gordon Pym*, and Auden's "Journey to Iceland." Cleanth Brooks, in Brooks, *Modern Poetry and the Tradition* (Chapel Hill, 1939), 125–28, discusses Auden's use of "ice age" imagery to convey the moribundity of modern society.

which man—a child in the poem—fondly thinks he can discover by a voyage of exploration. Only a few years before Jarrell's birth, in the "real" world, explorers had made voyages to both poles, not for any practical scientific object, but for the pure glory of achievement against physical obstacles. The geographic poles, although they do mark the ends of the earth's axis, are largely symbolic objects; at the North Pole, of course, there is no land, much less a "pole." Unlike the magnetic north, which can be located physically by a magnetic compass, the geographic pole is determined mathematically, and must be located either by reference to the sun and stars or by analogy with a gyrocompass, whose accuracy is mathematically established. Although the earth's axis moves about, the North Pole is arbitrarily fixed on maps and globes. To the individual it has only conceptual existence, for it cannot be perceived by the senses; one accepts its existence on faith: faith in post-Copernican astronomy and physics.

It is literally the "end of the line," the end of all lines of longitude, the end of latitude; it is also, by the same rule, the beginning of all lines, the beginning of "meaning," since one locates oneself on earth by relation to it. Although zero degrees latitude is the equator, as a symbol of beginning or ending it is not viable; it is too obviously at the center of things. Moreover, man on the equator is somewhere in relation to longitude. Even 0° longitude at the equator has greater reality for men than 90° north latitude; the latter is nowhere, nothingness. Despite this apparent negative symbolism, the polar expeditions had for their time the same magical meaning as space exploration has at present; men and boys too might dream of such conquest; and it is difficult not to think of the actual explorers, Peary, Amundsen, Scott, as men whose capacity for pure wonder remained childlike in a Wordsworthian sense.

The child in "90 North" dreams of discovering the pole, but in his dream the pole symbolizes meaning. Once achieved, however, the pole reveals its ultimate knowledge, "worthless as ignorance . . . pain." The first three of the eight quatrains are densely concrete. The child describes his night journey, not terribly different, at first, from that described in Stevenson's "My Bed Is a Boat" or "Northwest Passage," both in *A Child's Garden of Verses*.

At home, in my flannel gown, like a bear to its floe,
I clambered to bed; up the globe's impossible sides
I sailed all night—till at last, with my black beard,
My furs and my dogs, I stood at the northern pole.

There in the childish night my companions lay frozen,
The stiff furs knocked at my starveling throat,
And I gave my great sigh—the flakes came huddling;
Were they really my end? In the darkness I turned to my rest.

Here, the flag snaps in the glare and silence
Of the unbroken ice. And I stand here,
The dogs bark, my beard is black, and I stare
At the North Pole. And now what? Why, go back.

The boy wears a warm nightgown, sees himself, crawling into the cold bed, as a polar bear "clambering" to its ice floe. His journey takes place not on a "real" sea, but up the sleek, "impossible" sides of a globe. His grown-up image has a black beard, furs and dogs, as a polar explorer should. In a striking use of misplaced epithet, his night is "childish," but he is alone in it; his companions being frozen, he too expects, like the ill-fated Scott, his own death. The last sentence is ambiguous. Does the child dream his death, or is he able to avoid that image by turning away into the polar darkness which is really the darkness in which he sleeps?

Although the imagery of the third stanza repeats and continues that of the child's dream, the change of tense from past to present and the spatial change from "there" to "here" signal the change from childhood to adulthood. The dream is *recurrent*, but for the adult it has a new ending. Where the child was satisfied, and could turn to rest after his achievement, the adult is puzzled. He has planted the flag which gives resistance and sound to the "glare and silence/ Of the unbroken ice," but unlike Stevens' jar in Tennessee, the flag cannot give order to its setting, perhaps because the surroundings are not wilderness but nothingness. In changing the punctuation for *Selected Poems*, detaching "And now what? Why, go back," from the four-square quatrain of *Blood for a Stranger*, Jarrell gave added emphasis to the adult's baffled expectation of some tangible result beyond just reaching 90° North.

The fourth stanza is transitional; its imagery is more abstract than that of the preceding stanzas, and it prepares for the explicitly allegorical imagery of stanzas five through seven.

> Turn as I please, my step is to the south.
> The world—my world spins on this final point
> Of cold and wretchedness: all lines, all winds
> End in this whirlpool I at last discover.

Adapting a line from "On the Railway Platform" which in turn echoes *Richard II* (I, iii, 206–207), the speaker finds all paths leading him away, back to warmth, comfort, mankind. But his world, newly discovered, is a "whirlpool" spinning in a "final point/ Of cold and wretchedness." Here all the lines drawn by man, and all the winds of the natural world, end.

The bare statement that opens stanza five is amplified in the rest of the poem:

> And it is meaningless. In the child's bed
> After the night's voyage, in that warm world
> Where people work and suffer till the death
> That crowns the pain—in that Cloud-Cuckoo-Land
>
> I reached my North and it had meaning.
> Here at the actual pole of my existence,
> Where all that I have done is meaningless,
> Where I die or live by accident alone—
>
> Where, living or dying, I am still alone;
> Here where North, the night, the berg of death
> Crowd to me out of the ignorant darkness,
> I see at last that all the knowledge
>
> I wrung from the darkness—that the darkness flung me—
> Is worthless as ignorance: nothing comes from nothing,
> The darkness from the darkness. Pain comes from the darkness
> And we call it wisdom. It is pain.

Having "returned" from his dream voyage, the child found himself once again in a "warm world," a "real" world where ordinary men "work and suffer" as they move toward their goal, "the death that crowns the pain." This "real" world, where men can imagine that their pain will be rewarded at death, is a Cloud-Cuckoo-Land of dreamers. Only in such a world, real as the world of Plato's cave is real to its inhabitants, can a man reach his goal—discover his North— and find it meaningful.

In the fifth stanza the child's dream and the adult's are juxtaposed. In the child's dream North "had meaning," but in the adult's it has none: that is the revelation adulthood has brought. Moreover, the adult is conscious that his dream of 90 North is the true symbol of a newly discovered real world (not the wish-fulfilling daydream of the Cloud-Cuckoo Land, which is illusory).

In his dream the man is at the "actual pole" of his life. Here, in sleep, where no rules of behavior or morality apply, where the soul is free, beyond "lines" and "winds" (bonds and forces), all actions are meaningless. Just as the polar explorer lives and dies by accident, though he may believe he controls his fate, the man lives or dies in the chance of his dream. At this dark center of his unconscious, he is alone, an Everyman with the knowledge of nothingness; the symbols of his voyage of discovery—the pole which is absolute North, the dark night, the iceberg which is death itself—reveal the "meaning" of existence: ironically, meaninglessness. Such knowledge is "worthless" in the sense that it is negative, uncomforting. Paraphrasing Lear, Jarrell clarifies the terrifying vision which forms the climax of the poem. At the end of one's journey one finds nothing, for an end is the end of something, and when something ends, nothing is; "Nothing comes of nothing." Where there is no *thing* to order, there can be no order, hence, no meaning. The darkness itself is ignorant, for it has nothing to convey. What *is* present in the arrival at the pole, is pain: physical pain for real explorers, mental anguish for the explorers of the unconscious. Back in Cloud-Cuckoo-Land, we call the knowledge of meaninglessness "wisdom," but in reality it is only pain.

In two other poems written around the time of "90 North" (first published in April, 1941), Jarrell develops the symbol of cold as a destruction that reveals the meaninglessness of life's illusion: "The Iceberg" (Summer, 1941), and "The Skaters" (Winter, 1942). In "The Iceberg," not reprinted in *Selected Poems*, Jarrell uses the berg itself as a paradoxical symbol both of death ("evil") and of mankind. As in "90 North" the opening lines establish a real scene: here a diver, "steel beetle" in his gear, is let down to explore the lower part of the berg. He is supplied for life by tubes with light and air, though in descending into the depths he has already left life behind. In the poem, "There is nothing neglected for his ignorance." Safety and comfort, so important in our scientific explorations of space and the sea, are wryly seen by the poet as simple ignorance, inability to comprehend the implications of our actions. The diver is an innocent about to discover evil in the darkness; his report is factual:

> "There is no sign of any end," the diver phones.
> "Already motion is impossible, and life
> Extinct by our standards: the abyss
> Affords no air, heat, food, or light."

But his experience reveals a symbolic, surrealistic truth beyond the facts, as the iceberg takes on faces and "gapes in the thousand looks of men." Their "iron" frown is "great Necessity," and the diver is stupefied by "the sick ambiguous wisdom of the sea." Returning to the surface, he finds the faces appearing on the upper part of the iceberg, too. As it melts in the sunlight "thought runs like water." The deceptive, "mitigating" sunlight "carves in air/ Skills, legend, cultures, a morality." Man's whole achievement is an illusion, for the iceberg is the same above as below, "grim Necessity" moving inexorably toward the man's death. At this point, Necessity is the simple physical reality of all the natural world. The diver, dying of the bends or perhaps of his new knowledge, is now capable of judging between "the conscious and witty evil of the air,/ The witless and helpless evil of the sea."

As in "90 North," the discoverer finds a terrible wisdom in the cold and darkness. Like his prototype, the man who leaves Plato's cave, he finds reality—of a less hopeful sort than Plato's explorer—compared with which, the world he leaves behind, and its values as well, are false and deluded. In "The Iceberg," the world is all one, but its true nature cannot be known without the descent into the darker world beneath the surface; both higher and lower worlds are evil, but one is "conscious and witty" where the other is simply "witless and helpless." The play of connotations about the word "witty" extends from the old sense of "wisdom" or "knowledge" to the notion of humorous commentary. In contrast, the sea lacks both, and is humorless, senseless, stupefying.

Where "90 North" and "The Iceberg" begin developing their metaphors in realistic situations and then move to abstraction, "The Skaters" is frankly expressionistic. Even less than Crane's "The Dance," to which Malcolm Cowley compared it,[12] does the poem draw upon our experience of the actual world. Although it is included in the *Selected Poems*, "The Skaters" is anything but characteristic of Jarrell. Written in trimeter quatrains, with partial rhymes ending the second and fourth lines, it speeds along like the Skaters themselves, and the reader, like the speaker and victim of the poem, is swept onward in the wake. The theme of "The Skaters" is modified from that of the two other poems; although the images of ice and darkness are again central symbols, the quest is a search for love and freedom. The Skaters, like Keats's Belle Dame sans Merci, enthrall their mortal victim, luring him on into death, in Jarrell's poem, "the abyss where my deaf limbs forget/ The cold Mouth's dumb assent." The poem is unusual in its powerful synesthetic images: "the iron's dazzling ring, the roar/ Of the starred ice"; and insistent images of motion: "I flowed," "I sped," "Love wreathed," "speed stiffened," "we skirred," "flickering gaze," "whirl," "flicker," and so forth. Finally, however, its lack of correspondence to a real world seems damaging. The narrator is a shepherd in the first stanza; perhaps he is to be associated with the Judean shepherds to whom the Christ child was announced, but if so the nexus is vague and undeveloped. If not, it is difficult to understand the significance of his occupation. Literary pastoralism seems even more remote from this poem than Christianity.

An even greater difficulty lies in the apparent identity of the Skaters with the speaker himself. Jarrell's iceberg had a thousand faces, but the Skaters have a million, all "bent" to the speaker's gaze "in the stars/ Of one obsessing face," which turns out to be his own reflection. The meaning seems to be that narcissistic man loves in others only what he sees there of himself. The poem further implies that because of his self-love he is doomed to self-destruction. He who follows the Skaters cannot pause "at man's last mark . . . / To block

12 Cowley, *New Republic*, CVII, 718.

from the eternal ice/ Our shelter from this endless night." [13] Unlike the polar explorer, who can at least go back physically to his former place, the follower of the Skaters is plunged into a "long descent," surrounded by skaters flickering "like swallows."

The dream structure and imagery of "The Skaters" is exceptional; in other poems using dreams Jarrell projects a real world as backdrop for the dream. One might call the poem surrealistic if it were not so obviously contrived and rigorously organized. The symbols of cold and darkness which dominate the three poems, "90 North," "The Iceberg," and "The Skaters," do not occur again in Jarrell's work with explicit relation to the polar regions, but the cold is an important symbol in such later poems as "The Snow-Leopard" (1945) and several of the poems about flyers in World War II. The cold symbolizes death in these poems as in the earlier ones, and again it is a death in suspension, giving the victim an opportunity to know his own "grim Necessity" before he is annihilated.

The obsessive need to know one's nature, one's fate, is a continuous theme in Jarrell's poetry through the early fifties. While knowledge may come through analysis of experience, either dreamed ("90 North") or real ("Terms"), it may also come from history ("The Memoirs of Glückel of Hameln") or from books. Jarrell's avidity as a reader has been frequently mentioned by those who knew him. Robert Penn Warren, who taught the Vanderbilt sophomore literature course Jarrell took as a freshman in 1931–1932, recalled that even then, "he had read everything, and remembered everything." [14] John Crowe Ransom, speaking of Jarrell's years teaching at Kenyon, wrote, "He read more books from the library than any student we had, and they were of wider range than any professor would have chosen." [15] Librarian Charles Adams, of the University of North Carolina, Greensboro, has commented that Jarrell was probably the most regular and exhaustive reader that library has ever known. One result of Jarrell's long familiarity with libraries is the extensive allusiveness of his poetry and his prose. Another, less predictable effect is a group of poems about libraries, in particular about children in

[13] To block is both to bar and to plan or cut in blocks; perhaps to build an igloo (compare l. 23).
[14] *Alumni News* (University of North Carolina, Greensboro, Spring, 1966), 23.
[15] *Ibid.*, 8.

libraries: "Children Selecting Books in a Library," (December, 1941), "The Carnegie Library, Juvenile Division" (Winter, 1944), and "A Girl in a Library" (April, 1951).

All three poems consider the value of art to humans, a value that too often only children acknowledge. Stories, like dreams, minister to men's need to transcend the suffering, the Necessity of the real world. Sister M. Bernetta Quinn, in an essay that remains after almost twenty years the best introduction to an important aspect of Jarrell's poetry, fixes upon the theme of metamorphosis, or transformation, as the key to Jarrell's heavy dependence on dreams and fairy tales for subjects and imagery. She writes, "Jarrell has been attracted to *Märchen* as a means of objectifying modern man's psychological position, since these continue to be part of a common heritage, at least during the brief space of childhood. . . . [The idea of transformation, so prominent in folk tales,] is an attempt to go back to that principle of change, natural to the child and common in dreams, in order to live more adequately our mortal measure of years." [16] What Jarrell's children seek in the library is that elusive knowledge of how to change.

Looking at the first two collections of Jarrell's poetry, one sees the theme of transformation only gradually emerging. As if the burden of wisdom gained in the dream voyages of "90 North" and "The Skaters" and the real voyage of "For an Emigrant" had been too painful even for the poet to bear, Jarrell seems to seek a way out, a release from Necessity through change. As early as "For an Emigrant," we see him urging the child, somewhat cruelly, given the circumstances, to "Change, then," so that when the world—Necessity in man's nature—kills her, it will at least not recognize her as its own. In "Children Selecting Books in a Library" Jarrell sees the children as attempting to change, not themselves, but the world. Even though the *Selected Poems'* version is substantially revised from the one in *Blood for a Stranger*, the theme, that children in the library "seek a cure" for their own and the world's ills, remains constant. The early version is clearer, more overtly moralized than the later, and it lacks some of the specific richness of the *Selected Poems'* version. Only

---

[16] Sister M. Bernetta Quinn, *The Metamorphic Tradition in Modern Poetry* (2nd ed.; New York, 1966), 168, 206.

the third stanza remains unchanged, and it bears the central meaning in both versions.

The first two stanzas set the scene: the "little chairs and tables" (*Blood for a Stranger*, l. 1), the wall mural with its beasts and gods ("weapons" in *Blood for a Stranger*), the children engrossed in their search. In *Selected Poems*, the child's head is "food-gathering" as it moves along the shelves, introducing the idea of nutriment that is further developed in the early version as well. In *Blood for a Stranger*, the poet comments on grownups' illusion that the childrens' lives are fortunate, "blanched with dew." Their language is, to their elders, unintelligible; "Their cries are those of crickets, dense with warmth." If we dip into memory, however, as Siegfried dipped into Fafnir's blood, the cries of the children, like the cries of birds to Siegfried, will be once again meaningful. Once more we will be sensitized to the meaning of tales and legends; our ears, like theirs, will "Burn with the child's peculiar gift for pain."

The third stanza explains the inexorable appeal of the stories:

> Their tales are full of sorcerers and ogres
> Because their lives are: the capricious infinite
> That, like parents, no one has yet escaped
> Except by luck or magic; and since strength
> And wit are useless, be kind or stupid, wait
> Some power's gratitude, the tide of things. . . .

In the grown-up world, as in the children's world, Jarrell believed, "Strength and wit are useless"; neither man nor child can really control his destiny. In the *Märchen*, it is not the clever sibling who wins the prize, but the foolish one, who is merely kind or patient, or simply lucky.[17]

The children hunting along the shelves for books are seen as dogs hunting medicinal grasses, in the *Selected Poems*' version finding "one cure for Everychild's diseases/ Beginning *Once upon a time there was* . . ." In *Blood for a Stranger*, they simply take "four cures for their one need," referring to the custom of allowing each child

---

[17] See for example, the Grimms' tales, "The Three Feathers," "Old Mother Hulda," "The Youth Who Could Not Shiver and Shake," "The Three Little Men in the Wood," "The Golden Goose," "The Golden Bird," "The Devil with the Three Golden Hairs," and so forth.

four books at a time (compare "Carnegie Library . . . " l. 17). In
the early poem the children's cures are useless for grownups' "diseases," because the grownups cannot understand how "these games
and giants lure them/ To be clerks or us or crazy? To be great?" The
poet responds in the final stanza that books do not show the children
how to enter the grownup world directly, but parabolically.

> They are not learning answers but a method:
> To give up their own dilemmas for the great
> Maze of The World—to turn in all their gold
> For the bank-notes of the one unwithering State.[18]

The tone becomes ironic, and a kind of sarcasm pervades the image
of the "bank-notes of the one unwithering State." Although this
State is obviously meant to express an ideal world of fulfillment and
satisfaction, it also suggests an analogy with the relation of grownups to their State; in childhood, one exchanges one's real life for
stories that are more satisfying, though they are only "paper," but in
adulthood, one exchanges "real" life for the promises and deceptions
of occupations and nations: states that do not wither away but get
more and more inhuman and cumbersome. The analogy is clever, but
it tends to devalue the books, and that may be why in revising the
poem Jarrell omitted the image and developed another full stanza to
conclude the poem. Besides introducing more concrete, comple-
mentary images to convey the values of literary experience, Jarrell
stressed the ideas of escape and change. In addition, he linked the
last part of the poem more closely with the earlier sections by introducing a dewy-eyed goddess, "Change," to complement the grey-
eyed goddess, "Care," of the revised first stanza; "Change" is the
only cure for that disease of selfhood, from which the only escape
is imagination.

The necessary function of art, to the psyche, is "trading another's
sorrow for our own; another's/ Impossibilities . . . for our own."
What literature offers is change; both exchange and transformation.
"Children Selecting Books in a Library" helps us to understand fur-

---

[18] Straight or inverted, Marx's image of the state that will wither away was a
favorite with Jarrell. In *Pictures from an Institution* he assigns this predilection to
the composer Gottfried Rosenbaum.

ther the motifs of the child and the *Märchen*, introduced in "The Rage for the Lost Penny" and developed in every succeeding volume, reaching a peak in *The Seven-League Crutches*. The child's capacity for suffering and change is simply buried in grownups' deeper levels of consciousness,[19] and the *Märchen* objectify the suffering and relieve it through formalized wish-fulfillment.

Besides those poems already mentioned in the discussion of "The Rage for the Lost Penny," *Blood for a Stranger* has two poems dealing with children's consciousness—"90 North" and "Children Selecting Books . . ."—and one, "The Christmas Roses," in which the speaker is an adult, although because of his illness he becomes both childish and childlike. He cries out pitifully to someone who might equally be a lover or mother:

> . . . And now I know you never meant
> The least letter of the poorest kiss
> You thought about and gave me; you and life were tired of me,
> You both thought—quickly, quietly, in a dream—
> To kill me, to be rid at last, for good, for good,
>
> Of that blind face that still looked up to you
> For love, and then pity, and then anything.

The narrative tone, if not the diction, is indistinguishable from that of "A Story," and the psychological situation is very similar.

The fairy tale motif is central to two other poems in *Blood for a Stranger*: "Jack" and "Variations," the latter of which appears unchanged in *Selected Poems*. In "The Rage for the Lost Penny" Jarrell had limited his use of fairy tales primarily to the image of the death-like sleep and awakening in "The Sleeping Beauty" and "Snow White," but in "Jack" he develops the later life of "Jack and the Beanstalk." Grown old, Jack examines the past as "pieces . . ./ Of a puzzle that, once joined,/ Might green again the rotting stack." But the puzzle cannot be solved, Jack "can never regain/ The land the harp sang so loudly." Jack's wish-fulfillment is all in the past, in

---

[19] The woman at the Washington Zoo, the woman of "Seele im Raum," and many of Jarrell's soldiers are grownups who reach back to the child's world to change themselves.

his childhood; aging, he cannot recover the key to his own story.

"Variations" is an even more somber poem behind its witty surface. The first variation is about the deaths of Punch and Judy, appallingly violent but supposed to be tremendously amusing. ("Clap," said the manager; "the play is over.") The second variation is loosely mythological, blending an indeterminate far eastern setting with a vaguely Christian rhetoric. The "son of God" brings fertility to the earth, but when winter comes no one remembers: "Who spared his charcoal for the son of God/ The vain wind failing at the pass to Hell?" Variation three is a melange of "The Three Bears" and "Hansel and Gretel," plus a real world with a dead mother and a cruel nurse. The last variation has a child speaker in the first five lines, identified in the sixth as "The white, the yellow, the black man." He tells of death and oppression. But "the world," in the last five lines, tells him, "Child, you will not be missed./ You are cheaper than a wrench, your back is a road;/ Your death is a table in a book."

The extension of the theme of suffering through a series of images, from the popular art form of the Punch and Judy through myth and fairy tale to sociology, marks "Variations" as an early poem. Where in the later poems Jarrell concerns himself more and more with the individual soul in its mortal predicament, the early poems are more often directed at the world, at civilization and its failures. The numinous figures of the early poetry—Newton, Leibnitz, Mandeville, and Pope in "The Memoirs of Glückel of Hameln"; Beethoven in "The Head of Wisdom" and "The Boyg, Peer Gynt, the One Only One"; Galileo, Newton, and Bruno in "The Emancipators" (the last two in *Little Friend*)—are public figures who in some way influenced the thought or destiny of generations of mankind. In *Blood for a Stranger* there are more poems about the external, political world, about "lives" in general than about individuals; but already in the war poems of *Little Friend, Little Friend* and *Losses*, the individual life is central, the external world significant only as it affects the one life.

The crucial link between the individual and history is developed in "The Memoirs of Glückel of Hameln," one of the most interesting and appealing, and one of the most serious, of the poems in *Blood for a Stranger.* Except for the final stanza, which is so changed in *Selected*

Poems as to alter the direction of the poem, the *Blood for a Stranger* version is substantially the same.

The *Memoirs of Glückel of Hameln* was one of the earliest books written and circulated in Yiddish, in the early eighteenth century. Glückel was a Jew of a mercantile family, and his memoirs provide just such a record of life in eighteenth century Hameln as Jarrell describes: accounts of business transactions sanctioned or foiled by a "too-immediate" God, the coming of age and marriage of Glückel's children and grandchildren.

The poem begins as a general meditation upon history and our relation to it. "We are all children to the past," says the poet, and we wish to see how it is relevant to us. Our knowledge is insufficient; we despise, or carefully avoid the luxury of despising, ordinary historians because they deal only with dry facts; what we seek are hypotheses, the "touch of insight [that] makes the ages kin," but the poet wryly warns that "nothing helps like ignorance to apply it" (the insight). The second stanza develops the idea of the historians' search for facts that, in the early version "rather astonish than inform."

> But if one learns little from them, still
> One emerges, sometimes, skeptical
> Of a little one has known before.

The "facts" of Glückel's memoir cause just such skepticism; they test the hypothesis that the eighteenth century was an age of reason and enlightenment. Unfortunately, Glückel's mass of information is not graced with tasteful selection and arrangement; for the reader he is mostly boring:

> The deals all ended in a gain or anguish
> Explained and disregarded with a text;
> Money and God were too immediate,
> The necessities that governed every act.
> To marry and have children who get married
> Is bad enough to do, and worse to hear:
> In time, the amount of every dowry
> Came to be, almost, more than I could bear.[20]

---

[20] The later version, with its facetious allusion to St. Paul, is weaker than the first.

However, the reader is forced to think of Glückel in the context of "those progressive years,/ Of Newton, Leibnitz, Mandeville, and Pope." They were theoreticians, generalizers; sentimental Glückel gives "body to the thought," forces the reader to revise his conception of the history. A single particular image is recalled: "I hear you in the plague: 'See, see, she plays/ And eats a buttered roll, as nicely as you please.'" Such memories are *real*, like those of our own lives; they are intractable, cannot be explained away. If we must choose between Newtonian theory and Glückel's "fact," our own lives will give the edge to Glückel.

The final stanza of the early version concludes that the value of Glückel's memoirs is that they help us to see how we as individuals are ignorant and indifferent to the "history" of our own time.

> Glückel, Glückel, you tell indifferently
> To ears indifferent with Necessity
> The torments and obsessions of our life:
> Your pain seems only the useless echo
> Of all the evil we already know.

As he also shows in revisions of "For an Emigrant" and "Children Selecting Books . . . ," in the *Selected Poems* version of "The Memoirs" Jarrell has become less obsessed with a rigid, abstract concept of Necessity. In his revision of "The Memoirs," he ignores Necessity to contemplate the function of vicarious experience in the relation of our lives to individual lives of the past.

> The one thing missing in your book is you;
> But how can we miss it, we who never knew you?
> But we miss it, somehow; and, somehow, we knew you.
> We take your place as our place will be taken.
> The butter is oily on the roll, and the child plays
> As nicely as you please—as nicely as we please.

Glückel's life not only gives "body" to the history of the eighteenth century but provides the same sort of perspective most humans have on their own experience, self-centered, but not self-conscious in any positive way. Every reader takes Glückel's place—his point of view— in reading the memoirs and in constructing his own memories, which are "useless" (l. 44), but persistent and significant to him. Thus the *Memoirs* provide not simply an insight into history, but into the workings of the individual heart.

To look outward is to see the facts, whether of one life or of many, but man must look inward as well, and find a bond between the self and the outer world, the world of history. The *Memoirs*, because they are not art, but unselective like our own memories, provide insights of their own into the ties between the individual and his culture.

The achievement represented in the forty-six poems of *Blood for a Stranger* is not insubstantial, even though the poet himself rejected more than three-fourths of them in his 1955 *Selected Poems*. Like the poems of many precocious and well-read young men, the *Blood for a Stranger* poems show rather too much reliance on a kind of median poetic fashion. Too shrewd to imitate the mannerisms of the most individual poets of the preceding generation—Yeats, Eliot, Frost —Jarrell wrote his earliest poems in a style that seems a blending and watering down, mainly of Auden and Tate, but with echoes of Hardy and at times Wallace Stevens, Hart Crane, or even Dylan Thomas. In some half-dozen of the poems, however—"90 North," "Children Selecting Books in a Library," "Variations," "A Story," "The Christmas Roses," "A Picture in the Paper," "The Memoirs of Glückel of Hameln," perhaps a few more—Jarrell's distinctive voice and stance are present in the conversational style and rhythm, with frequent repetitions of significant words, particularly nouns and modifiers; the speaker who apostrophizes and exhorts his characters to understand themselves, to change themselves; the images drawn from fairy tales and children's fantasies, laid open to expose "Everychild's diseases," for which they supply remedies.

Most of the poems of *Blood for a Stranger* continue to develop the themes of "The Rage for the Lost Penny"; more than half of them are about the destruction that threatens man's world because of what one might call innate depravity (selfishness, inability to love), which is seen in the poems as neo-Spinozan Necessity. Suffering and anguish are present in the love poems, another substantial group, as well as in the poems about Europe, and often for similar reasons; such as they are, these poems are all about lost love or frustrated love, not happy love.

Many of the poems are quests: literal journeys, dream journeys, journeys of the mind into itself, into the past, the future. But, as Jarrell says in "On the Railway Platform," "journeys end [not in Shakespearean "lovers' meetings," but] in/ No destinations we meant"; nearly all Jarrell's quests end in nothingness and death.

The weakness of the poems generally is the lack of specific situation, lack of an identifiable "objective correlative" for the feelings of despair the poet wishes to express. The best poems of the volume have specificity, do create a situation in which the reader can participate. Obscurity, too, is a problem in some poems, although most will yield at least a general sense to patient explication; the difficulties stem from a sometimes deliberately ambiguous use of pronouns and prepositions, and sometimes from quasi-surrealistic imagery. Unlike the early, obscure poetry of Dylan Thomas, in which, because of Thomas' consistent rhetoric, the obscurity of a particular poem can almost always be resolved by cross-references to others, Jarrell's early poems are eclectic in their imagery, too shifting in associations for such unraveling. Perhaps Jarrell's obscurity was a part of his idea of fashionableness, because it does not seem to result from the attempt to say something new and difficult, as does Stevens', but from an idea that it is all right, maybe even a good thing, for poems to be difficult.

Even more strongly than "The Rage for the Lost Penny," *Blood for a Stranger* exemplifies the qualities of penetration and seriousness coupled with wryly sardonic wit that would characterize Jarrell's next two volumes. It took, not the war in general, for that had already broken out well before most of the poems of *Blood for a Stranger* reached a finished form, but Jarrell's insight into the experience of the soldiers to give him focus for his obviously considerable gifts of language, intellection, and feeling. With the soldiers, Jarrell could look at the individuals and the world at the same time; he could dramatize in terms of specific human lives man's universal guilt and suffering.

2·Little Friend, Little Friend

ALTHOUGH THERE ARE foreshadowings in *Blood for a Stranger* of the directions Randall Jarrell's style and thought were taking, it would have been difficult to predict from that book the immediate consistency he achieved in his second volume of poems, *Little Friend, Little Friend*. Between 1942 and 1945, a series of impulses, primarily aesthetic and worldly rather than personal, I believe, coalesced to set for once and ever the course of Jarrell's career. It would be rather dreadful to say that a world war was necessary to bring Randall Jarrell to poetic maturity, yet to some extent that is true. His first-hand experiences with planes and men as a flight instructor and Celestial Navigation tower operator at a B-29 base in Arizona became the specific material for several striking poems—"2nd Air Force," "Losses," "A Front," "Mail Call," as well as some lesser ones; while his indirect, vicarious experiences through reading reports of the war, in particular the sensitive, human accounts of Ernie Pyle, provided some of the key insights for the poems of actual warfare: "A Pilot from the Carrier," "The Dream of Waking," "Siegfried," and a number of the poems of *Losses* (1948).

In conjunction with the new subject, an important shift in Jarrell's poetic strategy occurred in the years between *Blood for a Stranger* and *Little Friend* . . . ; where only a small proportion of the earlier poems have specific situations or incidents as a structural basis, nearly all of the poems in *Little Friend* . . . do. The influence of Auden, in the style, unlocalized settings and generalized characters of so many of the *Blood for a Stranger* poems, appears in only two or three, notably "The Wide Prospect," while the influence of Hardy and Ransom, both of whom developed specific plots and characters to deal with thematic abstractions, looms larger, though in a rather general way. Gone, too, are the generalized, swingy love poems, also influenced by Auden, which formed nearly a quarter of the total in the earlier volume. Jarrell had become wholly engrossed in the soldiers and victims of the war.

A majority of the poems in *Little Friend* . . . are written in blank verse; Jarrell also continued to use unrhymed iambic pentameter stanzas, most often quatrains, in many successful poems, thus keeping a modicum of metrical order without the rigor of rhyme. His characteristic device of repeating words in close juxtaposition is more pronounced.

> And you are home, for good now, almost as you wished;
> If you matter, it is as little, almost, as you wished.
> If it has changed, still, you have had your wish
> And are lucky, as you figured luck—are, really, lucky.
> ("Siegfried")

A dominant theme of the first book, Necessity, is modified in *Little Friend* . . . . In two poems which most resemble the earlier ones, "The Emancipators" and "The Wide Prospect," a specific sin, rather than general depravity, is assigned as cause of the world's distress: the obsession with Trade. In "Siegfried," however, Necessity is simple: "It happens as it does because it does." Siegfried's personal guilt is absorbed in his suffering. He is not asked to change, like the little girl in "For an Emigrant"—whose personal guilt, we assume, is less than that of Siegfried, the bomber pilot—but only to "understand." The idea that "It happens as it does because it does" might be said to characterize the attitudes of the soldier-victims of Jarrell's war poems. Their bafflement at their situation is a result of self-protective spiritual blindness coupled with the military training that is imposed on their civilian consciousness. In "Soldier, [T.P.]" ("T.P." stands for "Title Pending"), not included in *Selected Poems*, the unidentified, unidentifiable soldier learns to "bear and be silent."

> To do what I must, as I must: that is, to die.
> .   .   .   .
> Here what they teach is other people's deaths;
> Who needs to learn why another man should die?
> Who has taught you, soldier, why you yourself are dying?
> And there is no time, each war, to learn.

The need to know about one's destiny, which dominates such poems as "90 North" and "The Iceberg," appears modified in the war poems of both *Little Friend . . .* and *Losses,* whose emphasis rests strongly upon the theme of learning, or understanding, that which ultimately is illogical, chaotic, unknowable: why men desire and inflict death upon each other. Three of the best poems of *Little Friend*—"2nd Air Force," "Losses," and "Siegfried"—demonstrate three aspects of this new concentration on knowledge.

"2nd Air Force" is the first poem in *Little Friend, Little Friend,* and it is one of the earliest poems for which manuscripts are extant and available in the University of North Carolina, Greensboro, library collection. One interesting aspect of the work sheets is that the brilliant opening lines of the poem originally came from another poem which was never finished, and which was much more in the vein of the earlier poems of generalized characters and action, though the setting is fairly specific. It is made more specific in "2nd Air Force" by a unifying point of view, that of a mother who has come to visit her son at an airbase. Her character is not developed, only her vision. The first verse paragraph (ll. 1–24) is primarily setting. At first all the mother sees—with her outer eye and her mind's eye—"Busses and weariness and loss, the nodding soldiers," are simply the way to her son, "a pass to what was hers." After the meeting and her grief-heavy recognition that her son has grown up, she is able to see around her "a world" in precise detail, from "the bubbling asphalt of the runways," to the "dim flights moving over clouds like clouds," [1] and the men, "armorers in their patched faded green,/ Sweat stiffened, banded with brass cartridges." The planes seem awkward birds or even insects at first, "all tail . . . wrong and flimsy on their skinny legs," but in air the "green, made beasts" are at "home." The men, clumsy as the grounded planes in their flight equipment, are beasts within beasts, bears in a cave—in other poems, babes in a womb. The section ends as it began, with an image of peculiar force, conveying night and mystery where the opening image presented daylight and summer's heat: ". . . hour by hour, through the night, some see/ The great lights floating in—from Mars, from Mars."

The second verse paragraph (ll. 25–45) focuses on the mother's new knowledge of her son. When the flight has gone out and silence

---

[1] A typical Jarrell image; compare "They look back at the leopard like the leopard," in "The Woman at the Washington Zoo."

has returned to the base, the woman's mind draws back to the immediate scene. The afternoon shadows lengthen into a "forest," the strange light of early evening "washes them like water"; the entire scene is drowned, so to speak, in twilight: a "long-sunken city." In this fantastic setting, this "last dreaming light," the mother sees the soldiers "pass like beasts, unquestioning." Like the "long-sunken city" they have been enchanted into their present state. Through her perception of the scene the mother has an access of understanding. Still looking with her outward eye at the men who are now not even beasts but "shadows learning in their shadowy fields/ Their empty missions," she inwardly envisions another scene, a scene of war for which the learners, including her son, are preparing. Perhaps she has read, or heard over the radio the account of an escort fighter pilot whose bomber had been damaged by enemy fire. The "story," or a fragment of it, forms the epigraph to *Little Friend, Little Friend*:

....Then I heard the bomber call me in: "Little Friend, Little Friend, I got two engines on fire. Can you see me, Little Friend?"
    I said "I'm crossing right over you. Let's go home."

In the poem, the woman hears the call, but sees, in imagination, "the ragged flame eat rib by rib/ Along the metal of the wing into her heart." The flyers bail out in their parachutes: "The lives stream, blossom, and float steadily/ To the flames of the earth." The flames are physical reality to the airmen, but they haunt the minds of all men; like the planes at twilight above the peaceful airbase, the flames "burn like stars above the lands of men," not from Mars, alas, but Earth itself.

In the brief last stanza, the mother's attention returns to her immediate situation. "From the twilight that takes everything" the mother's eyes "[save] . . . a section[2] shipping, in its last parade," while she imagines the flyers above, unseen "in the steady winter of the sky." Still bears, in a sense, they "tremble in their wired fur." No longer solely preoccupied with her son, she "feels for them the love of life for life."

Her newfound compassion leads her into new bafflement. The

---

[2] Changed to "squadron" in Jarrell, *Selected Poems*.

flyers in their fur, like their bombers, are "hopeful cells/ heavy with someone else's death" (the enemy's, they hope), "cold carriers of someone else's victory" (the governments', certainly, and not a personal victory for the flyers who must kill and be killed). This significance "gropes" into the woman's mind, passing the significance of their lives as individual human beings. Her son, like all the other sons who leave this base, must become one of the killers, a beast within his beast, and perhaps one of the victims.[3] For her, who has raised a child to manhood, there is complete frustration, "bewilderment" in the meaning she has sensed on her visit: "The years meant *this?*" The poem then ends with a shift in the point of view. There is no resolution to the mother's dilemma, only the hopeless response of the poet-narrator: "But for them the bombers answer everything." For their own sanity they dare not think as the mother does. They only do what they are told.

"2nd Air Force" and its companion poems cry out harshly against the senseless destructiveness of warfare, yet Jarrell was not in a strict sense a pacifist. Unlike his friend, Robert Lowell, Jarrell consented to induction; though he did not fight he trained others. His poems about the concentration camps show deep awareness about why Americans *had* to fight in World War II. Hating war, he participated in it. Not only his conscience but his sensibility hurt him. The war dispatches of Ernie Pyle display the same frustrated awareness of the brutalizing effects of warfare on essentially gentle, simple men. In writing of Pyle, soon after his death, Jarrell seemed to describe himself: "Pyle is always conscious of the shocking disparity of actor and circumstance, of the little men and their big war, their big world. . . . For Pyle, to the end, killing was murder: but he saw the murderers die themselves." [4]

The learners in "Losses," unlike the simple soldiers at the training base in "2nd Air Force," do learn about their own deaths but, like the mother in "2nd Air Force," they cannot fathom *why* they must kill and die. Part of their problem is to recognize death as personal, as their own:

---

[3] Compare Kipling's treatment of a similar perception in "Mary Postgate," one of the stories Jarrell selected for *The Best Short Stories of Rudyard Kipling,* ed. Randall Jarrell (Garden City, 1961).

[4] Randall Jarrell, "Ernie Pyle," *Nation,* CLX (May 19, 1945), 574–75.

> It was not dying: everybody died.
> It was not dying: we had died before
> In the routine crashes—and our fields
> Called up the papers, wrote home to our folks,
> And the rates rose, all because of us.
> We died on the wrong page of the almanac,
> Scattered on mountains fifty miles away;
> Diving on haystacks, fighting with a friend,
> We blazed up on the lines we never saw.
> We died like ants or pets or foreigners.
> (When we left high school nothing else had died
> For us to figure we had died like.)

The tone of astonishment in this first stanza marks the poem as Jarrell's. Surely, these soldiers think, it cannot be our death when we crash accidentally, on training missions; surely, the casualty rates cannot rise "all because of us"! Even that homely record of useful and irrelevant facts, the almanac, cannot record us properly! These deaths mean no more, have no more point, than the commonplace, unheroic deaths of ants (aunts, in *Selected Poems*), pets, or foreigners; surely, the soldiers believe, their deaths will be of moment and significance.

In the second stanza, the crews are sent to war; "[We] turned into replacements and woke up/ One morning, over England, operational." Strangely enough, death is the same as before.

> It wasn't different: but if we died
> It was not an accident but a mistake
> (But an easy one for anyone to make).
> We read our mail and counted up our missions—
> In bombers named for girls, we burned
> The cities we had learned about in school—
> Till our lives wore out; our bodies lay among
> The people we had killed and never seen.
> When we lasted long enough they gave us medals;
> When we died they said, "Our casualties were low."
> They said, "Here are the maps"; we burned the cities.

It is still impossible to recognize one's own death in such a context. No longer accidents, the crashes are now "mistakes," or at least they seem so. Where there is no actual visual contact with an enemy, it seems incredible that someone might deliberately, successfully, shoot down one's plane. Moreover, the flyers' lives go on essentially as they had in the training camp. The cities are no more "real" than when the missions were only pretense, than when the flyers learned about them in high school; the people in the cities are simply foreigners, dying as before.

The commonplace feeling that, if a flyer only flew enough missions, he was almost certain to be shot down, is expressed in terms of lives' being used up, worn out, like commodities. Jarrell speaks explicitly of the soldiers' lives as commodities in "The Wide Prospect," "The Sick Nought," and "The Soldier." If a life lasted longer than usual it was rewarded with a medal, but if consumed at the normal rate it became part of a statistic, the "rates" of stanza one.

The four lines of the final stanza all conclude in some verbal form of death, as all the possibilities of warfare ultimately resolve in death.

> It was not dying—no, not ever dying;
> But the night I died I dreamed that I was dead,
> And the cities said to me: "Why are you dying?
> We are satisfied, if you are; but why did I die?"

The flyers' inability to recognize and accept dying blurs as death approaches; the individual, "I" at last, not "we," dreams his death, and at last accepts the deaths of the cities, personified—abstractions still, but real. The continual shifting of pronouns in the last two lines resolves from plural to singular, second person to first person. Although syntactically it is the cities who must say "Why did I die?" psychologically it is the flyer who asks the question about his own death. In the poem, the cities of foreigners (and pets and ants/aunts) become one with the flyers, and all the flyers coalesce into a single individual who cannot relate his death to any logical cause. Like Jarrell's more famous ball turret gunner, the flyers of "Losses" have fallen into a State that gives its citizens a "dream of life," but no explanation of death.

"Losses" is a less successful poem than the best of *Little Friend, Little Friend*, partly because it lapses into a generalized rather than a specific point of view, and partly because the reader accepts only with difficulty the naïvety of the speaker(s). Even for men so remote from the gore and misery of heavy casualties as bomber crews, death cannot have been quite so obscure, or so the grounded reader supposes. Cities may well be simply "maps," but one's companions are more like oneself. Obviously, Jarrell attempted a difficult, communal point of view and psychology in the poem, and a certain kind of exaggeration was necessary to make his point, even as a certain flatness of diction was necessary to establish the speaker(s)' character. The poem seems to collapse under the strain of so many conflicting demands.

"Siegfried" is a more complicated poem about the learning experience, much of its complexity stemming from the introduction of the legendary figure of Siegfried into Jarrell's conception of his protagonist, a gunner in a long-range, level-flight bomber. Even though the Siegfried motif, used mostly ironically, deepens the significance of the poem, it is responsible as well for a serious weakness, for the reader is uncertain how far the poet wishes him to explore the possible analogies between the Siegfried of medieval lay and the World War II flyer.

The elements of Siegfried's story which seem most pertinent have to do with his early victory over Fafnir, the giant who, in the form of a dragon, guarded the hoard of the Nibelungs. Jarrell had used some of the same elements in "Children Selecting Books in a Library." In Wagner's version, derived from the *Volsungasaga* and the lay, "Der Hürnen Seyfrid," Siegfried reforges the shards of his father's sword, Nothung, then fights Fafnir in an attempt to discover fear, ignorant of the great treasure until the dying Fafnir tells him about it. Like Siegfried, the modern hero feels no fear, but, ironically, only because of his psychic barrier against recognition of death, like that of the flyers in "Losses." His mind simply refuses to accept the possibility of its own destruction.

> In the turret's great glass dome, the apparition, death,
> Framed in the glass of the gunsight, a fighter's blinking wing,
> Flares softly, a vacant fire. If the flak's inked blurs—
> Distributed, statistical—the bomb's lost patterning
> Are death, they are death under glass, a chance
> For someone yesterday, someone tomorrow; and the fire
> That streams from the fighter which is there, not there,
> Does not warm you, has not burned them, though they die.

Although it "streams" toward him from the enemies' wing guns, or perhaps from explosions destroying the plane, death is to this Siegfried merely an "apparition," a "vacant fire" which he might ride through, fearlessly, as the other Siegfried twice rode through the magic fire to Brünnhilde. There is no recognizable object—no bride—in his exploit, merely entranced fulfillment of an order that is like destiny to him. This Siegfried is something of a Gunther, too, standing aside to watch as Siegfried performs the heroic deed. Death is a "chance," a statistic, framed, under glass, on display but quite insulated from the gunner:

> Under the leather and fur and wire, in the gunner's skull,
> It is a dream: and he, the watcher, guiltily
> Watches the him, the actor, who is innocent.

As a man of action, the gunner perceives the world outside his plexiglass dome as unreal, an apparition, and he is innocent of the suffering that goes on there, but as a man of conscience, he sees his own actions as guilty, even though he does not choose them. They seem foreordained, as were those of Siegfried. There is no cause, no logic, no reason; the line immediately following those quoted above reads simply, "*It happens as it does because it does.*" Like the earlier Siegfried, this one is used by others who take advantage of his strength to serve their own ends. The bullets that "magically" find their target ("the steel that understands") are similar to Nothung in their invincibility; they "understand" what Siegfried does not wish even to know.

The plane's navigator, or perhaps, because it is a bombing mission, the bombardier, is "the fatal/ Knower of wind, speed, pressure" who finds the target through his knowledge; he would seem to be compared to the Norns, who read, but cannot determine, the future, which remains to them "unvalued facts." Like the gunner confronting his "statistics"—the flak, the bomb's pattern—the navigator, as actor, may only find physical facts divorced from moral responsibility. There is no right or *wrong* in Nature, but by the same token there is no computation of right and *left*; if you impose one, the other follows, Jarrell implies.

In the second verse paragraph, the modern Siegfried seems more remote from his namesake, though (in his plane) he destroys a "dragon," a visual image of mapped Japan. He is part of an "invulnerable" machine, but somewhere inside lurks the frightened, vulnerable man.

> So the bombs fell: through clouds to the island,
> The dragon of maps; and the island's fighters
> Rose from its ruins, through blind smoke, to the flights—
> And fluttered smashed from the machinery of death.
> Yet inside the infallible invulnerable
> Machines, the skin of steel, glass, cartridges,
> Duties, responsibility, and—surely—deaths,
> There was only you; the ignorant life
> That grew its weariness and loneliness and wishes
> Into your whole wish: "Let it be the way it was.
> Let me not matter, let nothing I do matter
> To anybody, anybody. Let me be what I was."

Like Siegfried, the gunner develops a (metaphorical) horny skin to make himself impervious to his conscience. He does not want glory, however, only release from moral responsibility for his unwilled actions. He does not wish to move into the future but into the past, the time before.

The last two verse paragraphs record the fulfillment of his wish. Unlike Siegfried, this hero does not die; he remains "lucky," and returns home. He does not become, as Siegfried did, the agent by whom the *Götterdämmerung* is finally accomplished,[5] but he is simply, individually removed from the scene of battle.

> If it is different, if you are different,
> It is not from the lives or the cities;
> The world's war, just or unjust—the world's peace, war or peace;
> But from a separate war: the shell with your name
> In the bursting turret, the crystals of your blood
> On the splints' wrapped steel, the hours wearing
> The quiet body back to its base, its missions done;
> And the slow flesh failing, the terrible flesh
> Sloughed off at last—and waking, your leg gone ...

---

[5] See "1945: the Death of the Gods," in Randall Jarrell, *Losses* (New York, 1948).

In the last part of the poem, Siegfried comes to terms with his new
life, still governed by blind fate. He is a victim now, not a hero, and
though his release takes place in a "theatre" he no longer acts. His
life is devoted to understanding, or escape from understanding,
through sleep and dreams.

> To the dream, the old, old dream: *it happens,*
> *It happens as it does, it does, it does—*
>
> But not because of you, write the knives of the surgeon,
> The gauze of the theatre, the bearded and aging face
> In the magic glass; if you wake and understand,
> There is always the nurse, the leg, the drug—
> If you understand, there is sleep, there is sleep....

Instead of an invincible weapon, he now has a "clever leg/ of leather,
wire and willow." Contrary to his wish, things cannot again be as
they were, not only for physical but moral reasons. The gunner is no
longer Siegfried, but he cannot get rid of his fatal knowledge: not
the language of birds, which Siegfried obtained by tasting Fafnir's
blood, but the language of death. "You have understood/ Your world
at last: you have tasted your own blood."

Jarrell's hero is not of the old order. Unlike the Siegfried of legend,
he is neither fearless nor joyful. He lacks the innate self-confidence
of his namesake, but perhaps because of this, he does not willfully
defy his destiny; and again unlike Siegfried, it is not his fate to die
through his own foolhardiness and trustfulness. Siegfried-like, he
goes to war an innocent, but he does not remain so. This Siegfried is
lucky; he is only maimed, morally and physically, while the other
Siegfried dies and inadvertantly destroys along with himself his whole
culture, including its gods. As in "Losses," innocence and ignorance
are traded for a terrible wisdom.

With such an emphasis on "learning," it is no surprise to find that
many of the war poems of *Little Friend, Little Friend* center upon
children, in years and in consciousness. In "Protocols" two children
of the concentration camps alternate—the voices are differentiated by
use of italics and Roman type—in explaining a common lesson they
learned: "That is how you died." In "Come to the Stone" another

dead child, this one killed in a bombing raid, asks to know *why* he died—like the cities and the flyers of "Losses." "Mother, Said the Child," has the boughs of the trees teaching the buried child about his death, though his dead mother attempts to comfort him. In "The State," the child-victim is not literally dead but insane as a result of his losses. His "State" is a nightmare extension of the possible "state" at war: the "crazy" mother is liquidated as a burden on the state, the sister is drafted, the cat taken "for the Army Corps of Conservation and Supply"—to catch mice, as the child supposes. Left alone, the child thinks of himself as dead, for they were his life, and they are gone.

There are older children in Jarrell's war poems, too; the ball turret gunner is literally grown-up, but in understanding he is newborn as he falls from his mother's sleep into the State. The speaker of "Gunner" is childlike, though he is grown-up enough to have left behind a wife. This brief poem consists almost entirely of questions the gunner asks about his past, his being sent away from his cat and his wife to the army and his death, "all still and grey in the turret." In the last of its three quatrains, he finds one response to his own questions— "How easy it was to die!"—then wonders what became of his past:

> Has my wife a pension of so many mice?
> Did the medals go home to my cat?

The apparently nonsensical questions make as much human sense as any others. Is a pension of money any better substitute for a husband than mice? Is a medal any more use to a wife than to a cat? The implicit question is again that of "Losses": "We are satisfied, if you are; but why did I die?"

One of Jarrell's strongest intuitions about the enlisted men is that they revert to a childlike innocence in times of stress. Pointing up the childlike qualities of the soldiers is the title, *Little Friend, Little Friend*, taken from the book's epigraph, apparently a newspaper account of an escort fighter pilot whose bomber was hit by enemy fire. The fighter's code name, "Little Friend," has complicated and even ironic implications; one common motif of fairy tales and fables is that of the "little friend" who helps the larger, normally more powerful figure to his goal. The bomber pilot's cry is in a sense a prayer, not to divinity but to a *little* friend; the little human friends are man's last hope "in this year of our war" ("Siegfried").

One other poem in the volume besides "2nd Air Force," with its allusion to the epigraph, uses actual reportage of the war, and it, too, stresses childishness. For "The Dream of Waking," Jarrell uses an epigraph written out more fully in the work sheets than in the finished poem. In the manuscript it reads, "At Palan, two marines were lying in the bottom of a boat with their arms around each other. Both were seriously wounded, bleeding in several places. One was crying and stroking the face of the other, who was obviously dying, and saying: 'Come on now, you'll be all right. You'll be all right. Don't die, please.' "

The first two stanzas of the poem relate a dream. In it the wounded man imagines his old teacher comforting him for some long-ago hurt; his cat, curled on his quilt; and his old room at morning. In the last stanza he wakes from the reassuring dream of childhood to the horrid reality of maturity where the teacher and the cat become the anonymous nurse, and the weight on his lap is not "Kitten" but a dying man.[6]

I have already pointed out the "adolescent" imagery of "Losses"; in "A Pilot from the Carrier," Jarrell reaches back even earlier into the child-soldier's history. This poem is one of the most successful in the volume, and I should like to give it close attention. In its basic theme and even its image sources, it resembles "The Death of the Ball Turret Gunner." Where the more famous poem makes its impact through its intense economy and ironic understatement, "A Pilot from the Carrier" develops the character and the particular setting into a more qualified and nuanced statement. The twenty-one-line poem is written in blank verse, always one of Jarrell's best forms for individualized subjects.[7] It falls into three sections, differentiated by tone, as it describes a flier's escape from his burning plane and his parachute descent, during which he sees his carrier also

---

[6] "Kitten" was the name of Jarrell's longtime pet, a very large, fluffy black tomcat.

[7] For some reason, the rhymed poems tend toward generalization, with a few exceptions, notably "The Lost World."

struck and burning. The first section (ll. 1–7) focuses upon the fiery pain of his struggle to freedom.

> Strapped at the center of the blazing wheel,
> His flesh ice-white against the shattered mask,
> He tears at the easy clasp, his sobbing breaths
> Misting the fresh blood lightening to flame,
> Darkening to smoke; trapped there in pain
> And fire and breathlessness, he struggles free
> Into the sunlight of the upper sky—

In spite of the fact that the pilot is literally "strapped" in his seat behind a "blazing wheel," Jarrell has him "at the center," suggesting a vortex in which he is trapped. The "wheel" as a binding force suggests the symbolic wheel of Buddhism or King Lear's metaphorical "wheel of fire," both of which imprison and torture the souls of those who desire too much from their lives. His cockpit is afire, but the flyer's face—visually merely blank flesh—is "ice-white" against his shattered oxygen mask. The mask, like the wheel, seems symbolic as well as literal, for later in the poem the pilot sees his life for the first time without the protective mask, the prepared face men at war make to disguise themselves against their own cognition and conscience.

Even though the clasp of his safety belt is "easy," in his pain and fear he "tears" at it, sobbing. The images of lines 3 to 5 are complex and protean. The flier's blood, not his breath, becomes a mist, presumably on the glass of the mask, but his breath is the agent by which the mist is spread. It "lightens" in color and in the sense that it vaporizes because of the high altitude; because his mask is shattered, his blood literally "boils," and the pain, like the color, is fiery. At the same time, the bright flames and the dark smoke of the actual fire combine with the blood and the internal pain. Perhaps the heat of the fire dries and darkens the misting blood on the mask, too. The three conditions, "pain," "fire," "breathlessness," are reiterated explicitly as the pilot finally "struggles free."

The next five lines describe his freedom.

> [He] falls, a quiet bundle in the sky,
> The miles to warmth, to air, to waking:

> To the great flowering of his life, the hemisphere
> That holds his dangling years. In its long slow sway
> The world steadies and is almost still....

While the images of the first section are chaotic and violent, and the actions described are constricted and desperate, the images of the second section are clear and peaceful; the action is gentle and suspended. In contrast to the confined burning of fire and blood in the beginning lines is the open "sunlight of the upper sky" which lights without heat. After the confusions and struggle of the cockpit, the pilot finds himself "a quiet bundle" in space. He must fall through miles of sky to "warmth, to air, to waking." Like the ball turret gunner, he is figuratively born in his destruction.

The "great flowering of his life" is literally the opening of his parachute, "the hemisphere that holds his dangling years," yet his new consciousness of life is a flowering, too, and "hemisphere" also describes his impression of the sky, open, domelike, above and around him. "Years" is used as a metonymy; it is not merely the pilot's body which dangles, but all the years of this life, past as well as present. By constrast with the parachute's "long, slow sway," the world seems almost still, stabilized in time as well as space. The "years" are translated into eternity.

In the last section, the pilot, old in time but newly born in perception, learns to "read." What he reads in the seafoam is his own death.

> He is alone; and hangs in knowledge
> Slight, separate, estranged: a lonely eye
> Reading a child's first scrawl, the carrier's wake—
> The travelling milk-like circle of a miss
> Beside the plant-like genius of the smoke
> That shades, on the little deck, the little blaze
> Toy-like as the glitter of the wing-guns,
> Shining as the fragile sun-marked plane
> That grows to him, rubbed silver tipped with flame.

A striking quality of the experience is the detachment Jarrell has managed to convey. From the total involvement of the opening lines, the pilot has passed to a state which seems entirely disinterested;

even his approaching death is an illusion, born of appearances and helplessness.

He sees first his carrier's irregular wake; as he recognizes it he is "reading a child's first scrawl." Next, "milk-like" in the foam, he sees the ever-widening circle made by a bomb that missed its target, and beside that, smoke rises like a djinn and a plant, growing and wraith-like to the "child's" eye. The great flight deck, in the new perspective, is little, like the blaze; both are "toy-like," as are the wing guns of the Japanese plane that approaches. The plane is "sun-marked," in its emblems and in the way it reflects sunlight. It, too is like a toy, "fragile . . . rubbed silver," but as it shoots, it is "tipped with flame." It "grows" to him as it gets larger in his sight, but also as it becomes real to his understanding; in a sense, he identifies with it because it is really *his* death. The ferocity of the implied attack on the defenseless flier is in direct contrast to the images of suspension and childhood. Life, death, warfare, peace: all are of equal significance in the quiet of the upper air. The pilot and his ship are equally doomed, equally unimportant to the natural world, which is merely the theater of their tragedy. What the pilot has learned, essentially, is that freedom and death are the same. He has gained release from the "blazing wheel."

The childlike innocence with which the pilot "reads" his death in the sea and in the sky is a consistent theme of the war poems in *Little Friend, Little Friend* and *Losses*. Although the soldiers are in fact guilty of murder and in jeopardy of their own lives, their ignorance to some extent protects their consciences and psyches from the meaning of their own actions. The protection from reality offered by the unconscious is sleep with its wish-fulfilling dreams. In one of the most interesting and characteristic of the *Little Friend . . .* poems, "Absent with Official Leave," a soldier dreams himself back to childhood, to love and acceptance which unfortunately never quite overcome his apprehension of guilt. The poem takes as its basic metaphor the image of the soldier's sleep as his only real life; it suggests that in dreams he lives as he used to before the war, known and loved, while awake, he is merely a cipher (like the wounded man of "The Sick Nought," another *Little Friend . . .* poem). He has neither identity nor true being while he is waking. Asleep, he is absent from the army, though the army unknowingly gives him "leave."

The first quatrain sets the scene: the barracks seen impersonally from outside. As the lights go out—a conventional image of approaching death—the soldier prepares for "all the hours of [his] life." The intermittence of the extinguishing lights is regulated by the "hollows" of the wakeful. "Hollow" is a peculiar word in this context; its connotations are chiefly of two sorts; first, it suggests calling out for recognition or help, particularly if one is lost; second, it is a variant spelling of "hallow," to bless or consecrate. It can also imply that the men are "hollow," or sound hollow, or that they hollow out a place to rest, like bears in their caves.

The first line of the following stanza finds the individual but nameless soldier "composing" his body into "life," and the succeeding four quatrains describe his drifting like smoke—"plumes the barracks trail into the sky"—past his comrades, who are only depicted as "laughs," "quarrels," and "breath." He drifts into dreams, those "ignorant countries where civilians die/ Inefficiently, in their spare time, for nothing," unlike the soldiers, whose business, by implication, is to die.

In this world the roads, unlike the gridiron of the army base, are "curved," and "hopping through the aimless green," an image probably inspired by Tate's "insane green" in "Ode to the Confederate Dead." The indirection "dismays" the soldier, apparently because he has come to expect and need the organization of army life. His dream life is now too free; it alarms him. The scene of his dream is pastoral: "cottages where people cry/ For themselves and, sometimes, for the absent soldier"; "hedges," through which the soldier "inches" in his training for war, but where, in the dream life (a *real* life), "hunters sprawl/ For birds, for birds." The repetition of "for birds" is typically Jarrellian; in this instance it implies reassurance, joyous unbelief that such a frivolous world should be. The soldier dreams himself inside a cottage, turning "his charmed limbs" ecstatically, soothed and "endearing" like those of a small child, before "slow small fires" lit by women: mothers, loving and accepting. At this point the soldier's dream becomes a fairy tale, with the word "charmed" forming the transition. He is a bear in his "enchanted sleep," like the bear sheltered by Snow White and Rose Red in the Grimms' tale, dozing by the fire, having the snow brushed off him by the maidens. In his dream, the snow of the tale is merely blossoms, blown down the chimney, or ashes, transformed by the dream into blossoms.

A disturbing element in the dream is "the unaccusing eyes/ That even the dream's eyes are averted from." The implication is that the eyes have a right to accuse, and that the "dream"—the point of view of the dreamer in his dream—is ashamed to face them. The owner of these eyes is not further identified at this point. However, the last line of the sixth stanza introduces new figures which are developed in the seventh. These are "the grave mysterious beings of his years—/ The causes that mourn above his agony like trees." The beings are ambiguous, though the context makes it fairly plain that they are the opaque "causes" assigned by "States" for waging war: causes which the individual soldier does not understand, but which piously profess to mourn *his* death in their service. Unlike the simple people of the cottages who actually cry for the soldier, they "mourn" hypocritically; in the dream they become beneficent, as the soldier wishes them, granting him a simple face "opening" with love, eyes that can look "without shame even into his." The mysterious beings who are the sources of his agony now grant him peace. He is not accused of evil-doing or even of attempted escape. Even if the man has been transformed into a bear metaphorically, into a soldier really, the face of love, like the women who find his limbs endearing, opens its heart to him. To this face he is an innocent child.

In the last stanza, the dreamer, still a child, awakes. His dream life gone, he finds around him the other soldiers, breathing and sighing, his "dark companions": dark because they are in the dark, because they have mysterious "lives" like his own, and because, like him, they are benighted and guilty. With them, he "labors, sleeps, and dies."

The theme of guilt and judgment which emerges obscurely and is repressed in the soldier's dream surfaces more emphatically in "The Angels at Hamburg," where it has its strongest statement in the volume. In this poem the war is seen in terms of the last judgment and the first sin. Sleep and dreams are the agents of symbolic understanding of man's situation. The point of view is for once neither that of the killer-victim-soldier nor of the innocent child-victim, but of the grown-up civilian. In "The Angels at Hamburg" he is faceless, almost a disembodied collective consciousness; like the soldier of "Absent with Official Leave," he escapes from the "reality" of waking life into the freedom of sleep, his "last Eden"; but in the poem his sleep may be his physical death.

In Hamburg, Jarrell chose a symbolic setting appropriate not only because Hamburg was a great seaport and industrial center heavily bombed in World War II, but because it had been a great trading and cultural center since the Middle Ages, and its people had retained their independence and a republican form of government through several centuries. As Jarrell makes explicit in "The Metamorphoses" and "The Wide Prospect," Trade, the growth of power through money and commodities which ends in men's lives being made commodities, is a primary cause of war and general injustice and cruelty among men. On the other hand, Hamburg was one of the earliest of the German cities to accept the Protestant Reformation, with its emphasis on individual conscience. Consequently, it is a suitable object for meditation on the Good and Evil of the civilization for which man will be judged by history if not by God.

In the first of the three blank verse paragraphs, the "soul" falls asleep, apparently in a bomb shelter that is a kind of cave—once a "spent mine," then a "ruined factory." The notion of the cave with its workers carries suggestions of the dwarfs of German legend, now no fairy tale gnomes guarding ancient treasure, but men hiding from bombs, the "angels" that come to judge and punish in the night. The shelter is a "hive of earth" to the soul (anonymous as a worker bee), which in sleep is freed from the dreadful waking "dreams of Good and Evil, from the fiery judge/ Who walks like an angel through the guilty state/ The world sets up within the laboring breast." Guilt is not simply political and communal, for it is set up in every breast which labors—for bread or for breath. The soul, lapsing into sleep, "falls past Heaven into Paradise" where, no longer a bee, but a silk worm or caterpillar, he spins a cocoon, "his last Eden." The image is clearly one of hope for transcendence: a new life.

The second stanza treats the man's dream. In his Eden of sleep, the real world tempts the man: "*Here is Knowledge*, the bombs tempt fruitlessly." He sleeps on, "estranged from suffering," as his consciousness "floats like a moon above the starving limbs/ Oppressed with remembrance." In his free state, like unfallen man, "He knows neither good, nor evil, nor the angels/ Nor their message: There is no justice, man, but death." This last line embodies a difficulty similar to that of the last two lines of Keats's "Ode on a Grecian Urn," for we must ask "Who says this?"—the poet, or the apparent speaker within the poem: here, the angels? The freed soul "watches the child and the cat and the soldier dying," apparently unmoved, "not loving or hating their judges, who neither love nor hate." These judges are the bombs, impartial because they are inanimate; their judgment is universal death, and the basis of judgment is not individual Good or Evil but proximity. In the last two lines of this second stanza, the dreamer frees himself from social meaning as he has from individual meaning—his indifference to the deaths of the child, the cat, and the soldier; to him "Hamburg is no longer a city,/ There is no more state."

At this point of annihilation of personal and social values, Jarrell depicts a mechanistic apocalypse. The final stanza is the shortest, just eight lines long; only the first two are normal five-foot lines, the others are four-foot and two-foot lines. The short lines, four and six, are given further prominence through rhyming with the first and third lines, in a poem which has only two other rhymed lines. The rhyme words—"night," "light," "desire," "fire"—are important in summing up some of the main images and ideas of the poem. The imagery of the stanza is traditional, even biblical, but the context is only too clearly modern Europe.

> The judges come to judge man in the night.
> How bitterly they look on his desire!
> Here at midnight there is no darkness,
> At day no light.
> The air is smoke and the earth ashes
> Where he was fire;
> He looks from his grave for life, and judgment
> Rides over his city like a star.

As in the day of judgment, normal day and night are suspended. In Hamburg there is no darkness at midnight because of the fires from the bombs. In daytime the light is clouded with smoke, dust, and ashes from the previous night's bombing. As he does in "Losses," Jarrell substitutes for the expected pronoun another that shifts the sense in the final lines: "The air is smoke, the earth ashes," not "where *there* was fire," or "where *it* [the city] was fire," but "where *he* was fire." The dreamer has not escaped the world and its judgment after all. His shelter in the "hive of earth," his dream-spun Eden, was only a grave, from which he "looks for life" (seeks life; looks out, imprisoned "for life"). Now, not his free soul like a moon, but judgment like a star "rides over his city."

The implications of the poem may be baldly stated; where moral Good and Evil cease to have meaning, where men become indifferent to the deaths of others—children, soldiers, even cats—human values disappear and justice as a concept is void, and judgment becomes mere death. In this particular place, this particular war, the judgment is particularly horrible, inflicted by "angels" that are little winged missiles dropped by airplanes whose crews do not discern persons but only, as in "Losses," "maps . . . [of] cities we had learned about in school." Even if the citizen should escape physically by hiding in a shelter, escape emotionally in sleep and dreams of innocence, his whole existence is moral death.

While "The Angels at Hamburg" is not among the best of Jarrell's war poems—there is a marring vagueness about its logical progression, a lack of immediacy in its imagery—it expresses very well his general view of the war: that in war all humans, civilians and soldiers alike, are morally annihilated as they are brutalized—conditioned—into accepting warfare as a normal, acceptable state of being. Despite the fact that "the State" is the villain, men's ignorant acceptance seems to implicate them individually, as in "Eighth Air Force" (*Losses*) where the bomber crews are called "murderers" while the poet himself is characterized as Pontius Pilate. Even confrontation with death does not ennoble these men, as it does in the war poetry of Wilfred Owen. Jarrell's soldiers retreat from heroism even in their wishes, as in "Siegfried"; or in their dreams, as in "Losses" or "Absent with Official Leave"; and they face death with bafflement, as in "A Pilot from the Carrier" or "The Death of the Ball Turret Gunner." A fusion of Jarrell's conflicting attitudes toward the soldiers appears in "1914," a prose poem that looks back at World War I through contemplation of old photographs. The poem ends with a description of a picture of one dead soldier propped against a little hill. "Underneath his picture there is written, about his life, his death, or his war: *Es war ein Traum*. It is the dream from which no one awakes." [8]

The war poems are so predominant in *Little Friend, Little Friend*, that it is something of a surprise to come upon "The Snow-Leopard," one of Jarrell's most frequently anthologized poems, in the collection. "The Snow-Leopard" has close links with "90 North," in *Blood for a Stranger*, but its relation to the early war poems is more interesting. Because the theme of man's hopeless suffering in an indifferent universe is basic to the war poems, its appearance in the context of "The Snow-Leopard" forces us to see the theme as reaching beyond even the cataclysm of war.

At first reading one may speculate that Hemingway's "The Snows of Kilimanjaro" (1936) suggested the fundamental symbol of the poem, the leopard who goes higher among the mountains than any other creature, but it is typical of Jarrell that his leopard is not the mysterious, doomed, romantic leopard of Hemingway's Africa, but the specially adapted Asian snow leopard, who does not "seek" anything at high altitudes, but lives there normally. In the realm of the snow leopard, man is the intruder beyond his element, subject to pain and death as the leopard looks on indifferently. In Hemingway's story, the dead leopard is identified with a man; in Jarrell's poem, the snow leopard symbolizes all that is not man in the universe, "the brute and geometrical necessity" that teaches man his limitations. A closer literary source for Jarrell's poem is probably Blake's "The Tyger"; in a new idiom "The Snow-Leopard" asks Blake's question, "Did he who made the lamb make thee?"

The poem is written in free verse, unusual for Jarrell. The first six lines, a single sentence, impressionistically describe the leopard, "weightless in greys and ecru" watching a caravan which apparently

---

[8] Adapted from Goethe's *Faust*, Part II, 1. 9414.

carries tea across a high pass in the Himalayas. The caravan, as one might expect, turns out to represent primitive trade; here a few men suffer to move a few pounds of tea to a foreign market. In the war poems many men die for a world in which "all men wish is Trade" ("The Emancipators"), and where ultimately "men see men once more the food of Man/ And their bare lives His last commodity" ("The Wide Prospect"). In his lack of interest in the struggling caravan, the leopard, on the other hand, is identified with "the crystals of the cirri wandering/ A mile below his absent eyes."

The second sentence (ll. 7–11) mocks the absurdity of the caravan, heroic though its effort may be, with its "burlaps/ Lapping and lapping each stunned universe/ That gasps like a kettle . . ." These two lines are the weakest in the poem, and they detract from the austere beauty and veiled horror of the opening lines. The humor of the word play is feeble, and the word "universe" is so loosely used to describe either the individual yaks or the humans—perhaps they are wearing burlap?—that it seems almost meaningless. There is a way in which man can be seen as a microcosm, but the poem does not seem to draw upon this common Renaissance metaphor. "Gasps like a kettle" is also a peculiar image, as kettles do not "gasp," a word which implies sudden or spasmodic intake of air, but they exhale, usually continuously, in boiling. Whatever Jarrell had in mind, it is observed by the leopard as "pools in the interminable abyss," rising from which one encounters the abyss of night above.

The next image is an intriguing one, in which the lowland animals, including the men, appear as "raiders of the unminding element," and, in an even more striking image, "the last cold capillaries of their kind." What is strange is that they are said to "move so slowly they are motionless/ To any eye less stubborn than a man's." They are watched by the leopard; is he so uninterested that he does not look at them long enough to see their movements? Does Jarrell imply that *only* another man would care enough to watch them move? Surely a hungry leopard would watch carefully enough. The senselessness of the caravan is reflected in "the implacable jumble of the blocks" of the mountain, where "the grains [of snow] dance icily," "scouring" the breaths of the men.[9] In the hostile environment, life-

---

[9] "The men" is used for the ambiguous "they" of line 20 in several of the manuscripts at University of North Carolina, Greensboro.

sustaining breath is unsustainable, even as it finally is in the lower world, and below as above, the poem implies, men *trade* for their deaths.

The men sense, though they cannot see, the presence of the leopard. He is inherent in the place; he is its symbol; he is death, however beautiful. Behind the known, physical world—"the world their blood sets up in mist"—there lies "the brute and geometrical necessity." The necessity in this case is clearly Spinozan, for it was Spinoza who chose the "geometrical" method of proof from hypothesis to "prove" his philosophical system, at the heart of which is the idea of the necessity of all things in the universe. In the poem, as in Spinoza, Necessity is essentially the working out of Natural Law or Natural process, all that a man in his physical state (Lear's "poor, bare, forked animal") must acquiesce to. The leopard, in this environment, is more free than men. Though an animal, like the men, he is unlike them in being at one with the altitude and the cold which oppose them. He is truly, as the poem says, "the heart of heartlessness."

"The Snow-Leopard" is no more a poem about a cat than is "The Tyger." If anything, there is less attention given to the animal itself. Its appearance is sketched in two lines and the only other physical details alluded to are the "grating purr" and the waving six-foot tail. One has to have seen the snow leopard for oneself, as one has to have seen the tiger, in order to understand its fascination. The issue is not "fearful symmetry" here, but the combination of animal life with mysterious, wraithlike beauty, and fierce, antihuman power. Like the tiger, the snow leopard represents the order of nature which stands aloof from man's desires and needs, the natural order that seems to man to mock his aspirations as absurd, that does doom him to death at last.

As in "90 North" and "The Iceberg," the cold is the destroyer. In the poems of wartime flyers, the cold is often a symbol of detachment as well as death: see, for example, "the steady winter of the sky" in "2nd Air Force"; "The crews cold in fur, the bombers banging/ Like lost trucks down the levels of the ice," in "A Front"; the "belly" of "the State" in which the ball turret gunner's "wet fur froze."

Perhaps the link between the war poems and a poem like "The Snow-Leopard" can be most clearly seen in such a phrase as "They sense with misunderstanding horror, with desire." A very common theme of the war poems is the lack of understanding, the general benightedness in which the soldiers labor and die. Their aspirations are few and simple: "Let it be the way it was," wishes Siegfried; in "Mail Call," "the soldier wishes simply for his name." In "The Sick Nought," the poet speaks pityingly of the wounded soldier's "one theory, to live." They want life and personal identity; as "Absent with Official Leave" and "Eighth Air Force" tell it, they want absolution from guilt. Ultimately, as their dreams show, they want a little love, like the characters of such later poems as "Orestes at Tauris," "The Woman at the Washington Zoo," or "The End of the Rainbow."

Richard Fein, in his essay "Randall Jarrell's World of War," writes that "war, in the poetry of Randall Jarrell, is a masquerade of experience in general, the catastrophe and disasters of war being violent and symbolic extensions of what it simply means to be alive. Constantly confronted by that maze of experience which is permanently threatening, his people are the common and helpless victims of war." [10] While there is basic truth in what Fein says, one can not accept it as the whole truth. Jarrell's fundamental attitudes toward human bafflement and suffering were established before the war poems, and if it had not been for the war, he probably would have continued in his early modes a little longer before turning to the kind of civilian poem one finds in *Losses*—"Lady Bates," for example, or "Orestes at Tauris," which express suffering without the imagery of war. Although the war poems do share themes and certain mannerisms with Jarrell's other poems, their world of horror is also peculiar to war, to one certain war, particularly to flyers in that war. While it is true that Jarrell has a sizable number of poems about the victims of war—children, wounded and dead soldiers, prisoners—the really memorable ones are those about the planes and their pilots, the carriers and the airfields which bore, then lost them. The sense of unreality, of detachment from the human significance of the bombs they drop, in "Losses" and "2nd Air Force," and from the battles that rage about and beneath them, as in "A Pilot from the Carrier,"

10 Richard Fein, "Randall Jarrell's World of War," *Analects*, I (Spring, 1961), 14.

or "Pilots, Man your Planes" (*Losses*), becomes a metaphor for all human detachment in the face of others' sufferings. At the same time, the real brilliance of much of the visual imagery is related directly to the specific subject and setting. The poems are memorable, in short, not because of their ideas, which are rather ordinary in most cases, but because of the unusual vitality of their concrete particulars. What sets them off from the poems in *Blood for a Stranger* is not any marked development in the themes, though Jarrell clarifies and sharpens his thematic statements; nor is there a pronounced development in style, though Jarrell seems to settle upon one style from the mélange of the earlier volume. The difference lies first of all in the new subject, war, next in the important shift in narrative technique, limiting the point of view to one individual, or to the "poet" in debate with an individual in a specific setting, a particular incident. The poems are narrative in the sense that they have "plots" of a sort, but like the most characteristic modern short stories—developed by one of Jarrell's favorite writers, Chekhov—they do not extend in time, but focus upon a single instant, a single, illuminating, psychological experience.

It is characteristic of Jarrell that these experiences of illumination or discovery should be couched so often in terms of teaching and learning; like his mentor, John Crowe Ransom, and other associates of his formative years, Allen Tate and Robert Penn Warren, Jarrell made a career of college teaching, and he took it seriously, as a kind of mission and responsibility. Peter Taylor, writing of Jarrell's graduate years at Vanderbilt, recalls: "Randall held sway, held court, held class—that's the word for it—on a grassy plot outside the student union building either at mid-morning or in early afternoon. . . . It was there that I first heard anyone analyze a Chekhov story. . . . Even then Randall could talk about a story you had read and make you feel, make you realize that you had never really read it before." [11] It was not just the teaching of creative writing, to which so many poets have turned as a means of supporting themselves, but the teaching of literature as vital experience which Jarrell embraced. To this preoccupation we can trace the insistence of the poet-narrator that

[11] Peter Taylor, "Randall Jarrell," in Robert Lowell, Peter Taylor, and Robert Penn Warren (eds.), *Randall Jarrell, 1914–1965* (New York, 1967), 242.

his characters learn to understand themselves and their world. Jarrell's lasting interest in Freudian psychology and in dreams and fairy tales are other manifestations of his obsession with the acquisition of self-knowledge.

Curiously enough, the concluding lines of one of the few poems in *Little Friend, Little Friend* that does not deal with the war seem best to summarize Jarrell's achievement in the war poems and to point up the underlying unity of his themes. In "The Carnegie Library, Juvenile Division," another poem on the subject of "Children Selecting Books in a Library," Jarrell pinpoints the fascination of myths and *Märchen* and of literature generally.

> We learned from you so much about so many things
> But never what we were; and yet you made us that.
> We found in you the knowledge for a life
> But not the will to use it in our lives
> That were always, somehow, so different from the books'.
> We learned from you to understand, but not to change.

The need "to change," first expressed in "For an Emigrant" and "Children Selecting Books . . . ," is explicit in only one other poem of *Little Friend, Little Friend*, "The Soldier Walks under the Trees of the University," but it is implicit in many poems, for the step after learning, after understanding, as "Carnegie Library . . ." shows, is to change: that is, to transcend the guilt and suffering. In *Losses* the movement from simple understanding to metamorphosis accelerates, but in *Little Friend, Little Friend*, knowledge itself is almost unbearable. The lasting value of the war poems of *Little Friend . . .* is that, through the splendid impressionism of their imagery and the pathos of their statements, they bring to life for each reader a heritage of human agony to which we cannot allow ourselves to become indifferent. In stressing his characters' growing comprehension of the specific, individual meaning of their own deaths and of their guilt in the deaths of others, Jarrell exposed the heart of personal experience in war. His images come from a particular war, but the poems are not dated; Jarrell penetrates that outer shell of concreteness he so brilliantly evokes, revealing again and again the universal humanness at the heart of war's inhumanity.

3 · Losses

The real war poets are always war poets, peace or any time.
RANDALL JARRELL

ALTHOUGH *Losses* is usually thought of as a volume of war poetry, a companion to *Little Friend, Little Friend*, only nine of its thirty-one poems treat warfare directly, and another twelve deal with war-related subjects: the concentration camps, hospitals, prisoners, returned soldiers. The remaining ten are poems of civilian life, but from the earliest written, "Orestes at Tauris" (first published in 1943) to the latest, "Lady Bates" (February, 1948), "A Country Life," and "Moving" (first published in *Losses*), these too are poems of strife and loss, and of the attempt to come to terms with loss.

The actual war had ended even before the publication of *Little Friend, Little Friend* late in 1945; as Jarrell wrote in "The Range in the Desert," "the worse/ Ceded at last, without remorse,/ Their conquests to their conquerors." The inner struggle to accept new knowledge about men's capacity for cruelty and agony did not stop, however, with the signing of peace treaties. Some of the poems of *Losses* are close in attitude and method to those of Jarrell's preceding book, but in others, superseding the bitter, outraged questioning of man's apparently endless suffering, there is a sustained, if unsuccessful, effort to reconcile consciousness and sensibility to things as they are. The wife in "Burning the Letters," for example, has reached the end of the line trying to fathom *why* her husband died and has decided to live her own life rather than continually, fruitlessly reliving her husband's death in efforts to understand it. Her acceptance of his death, demonstrated in her act of burning his letters, is the hopeful commencement of change to new life, herald to the "great change" Jarrell called for in such earlier poems as "For an Emigrant" and "The Carnegie Library, Juvenile Division." In their commemoration of death and their search for reconciliation, many of the poems of *Losses* are elegiac; seldom, however, do they achieve any comfortable assurance of transcendence.

Coming to terms with loss involves various stages. As in *Little*

Friend, Little Friend, the first step is recognition and understanding of death or loss of identity: a psychological death in life. In most of the *Losses* poems directly concerned with the war, such as "Pilots, Man Your Planes" and "The Lines," recognition is the main impulse. A second stage, associated exclusively with physical death, is the acceptance of physical dissolution as the change that sets men free; this view is presented in "New Georgia," "The Dead in Melanesia," and "The Subway from New Britain to the Bronx." Christian reconciliation with death is explored and conditionally rejected in such a poem as "Burning the Letters," partly because Christianity as an ethic seems to have failed so utterly; see "Eighth Air Force" and "A Camp in the Prussian Forest." It is an interesting aspect of these poems that, although Jarrell used the Bible as a source of imagery and subject matter throughout his career, only in *Losses* does he treat specific problems of Christian faith, especially the concepts of Christ's saving Grace and His suffering as purgation for men's sins.

For those who go on living, dreams are a means of changing the painful experiences of waking life, and Jarrell continued to explore the "dream-work," tangentially as well as centrally, in a substantial number of poems in *Losses*. Although Jarrell's interest in fairy tales as vehicles of transformation and transcendence culminates in *The Seven-League Crutches* (1951), several *Losses* poems deal with magical, mythical materials, and Jarrell's first major effort to explore the meaning of Grimms' tales, "The Märchen," appears here.

Besides Christianity, few wholly new subjects come into *Losses*, though such a poem as "The Rising Sun," whose setting and character development were suggested by an Army documentary film Jarrell saw, is unique within the larger context of the war poems. *Losses* is also Jarrell's only volume in which one finds poems touching upon the social issue of race; here are three, possibly four. "New Georgia" and "The Dead in Melanesia" are about Negroes in the war, as "The Subway from New Britain to the Bronx" also seems to be. The first poem in the book, one of Jarrell's finest, is an elegy for that "poor little nigger girl," "Lady Bates." In all these poems the implications of racial injustice are secondary to the main subjects, death and dissolution: change from a bad life to a death that is not really worse or better, just different.

In technique, *Losses* is more varied and experimental than *Little Friend*. In spite of the fact that blank verse is still the staple of the longer poems, *Losses* contains a slightly larger number of rhymed poems than *Little Friend*; Jarrell seems to have turned periodically to rhyme as a kind of bracing influence throughout his career. There are several dramatic monologues, "Money," "Burning the Letters," "In the Ward: The Sacred Wood," but in many poems Jarrell retains his characteristic device of speaking *to* the protagonists in his role as poet. One poem formally quite different from Jarrell's other work is the long narrative, "Orestes at Tauris," which ends *Losses*, though it was written earlier than any of the other poems in the volume and first published in *Kenyon Review* in the spring of 1943. Although its subject may roughly be described as loss, its uniqueness seems to warrant separate treatment.

"Orestes at Tauris" is Jarrell's second longest poem: 324 lines of irregular blank verse. As its title implies, it is Jarrell's version of Orestes' reunion with Iphigenia, ending not as Euripides' does, with the flight of Iphigenia, Orestes, and Pylades, bearing away the statue of the Taurian Artemis to Ephesus, but with Orestes' death in Tauris at Iphigenia's hands. She recognizes her brother, but too late to save him. In so changing Euripides' story Jarrell seems to challenge its veracity. For many readers, a weakness in Euripides' *Orestes* is that the happy ending does not seem appropriate to the bloody saga of the family of Atreus. Other flaws might be seen in the lengthy recognition scene, which loses its tension very early, soon after Orestes' recognition of his sister, but long before her acknowledgment of him; and in the dénouement, where Thoas, the Taurian king, is too easily fooled, the escape much too simple. It all seems a fairy tale wish-fulfillment, and Jarrell, for once, rejects the wish and presents what "truly" happened. His Orestes is not the virile, shrewd hero of Euripides; he has been utterly beaten down before the poem begins and is all but mute throughout. Jarrell's Taurians are primitive warriors; their goddess is a crudely hacked wooden image covered with furs and skins, "barked" in the dried blood of its victims, and the shrunken heads of previous sacrifices are hung on poles about the altar. Garbed in skins and plants, the worshippers of this primitive fertility cult perform wild dances. Iphigenia does not merely sanctify the victims by pouring lustral waters upon them, but she wields the fatal sword herself.

The poem, which falls into eleven sections, begins with a description of Orestes' voyage to Tauris, culminating in a shipwreck described in the second section. In the third section (ll. 46–90) Iphigenia appears among the Taurian warriors, "a woman in a dyed cloak, holding a flat wand." Throughout the procession to Tauris, Orestes is silent, resigned and childlike, and even the Furies, who appear only briefly—almost as features of the landscape—are drowsy and patient. The most interesting sections of the poem (ll. 139–204) describe the fertility rituals of the Taurian Artemis. There are maidens dressed as bears, "Old men . . . in fresh washed flax" holding out "green branches, green rye-woven crowns." The rotting heads on the poles have jeweled eyelids that incongruously belie their putrefaction. Finally an old man, apparently the high priest of the cult, appears in a white hooded cloak, under which he seems faceless. After he strips the skins off the "black goddess," revealing her "splintered arms and hacked-out breasts," the maidens prepare Orestes for the sacrifice, decking him with furs and flowers, "long ribbons, leaves, and garlands hanging down."

The relationship between Orestes and Iphigenia is a curious one, almost overwhelmed by the ritual in which they are the principal actors. Draped in flowers and leaves, Orestes looks "more like a bush or some low branchy tree/ Than like a dead man hanging at the side/ Of his own death." Iphigenia, grotesquely painted, peers at him "with a bird's pitiless and gloomy stare," though to Orestes she is fairer than any woman he has ever seen. Only after she has struck the death blow does she recognize her brother, but she has little time for reflection, as the maidens immediately wash the blood off her hands.

The ninth section (ll. 281–314) is a strange appendage to the story; in it Jarrell describes the hypothetical journey of a traveller who *might* have come to see the scene in the previous section, might have returned to Argos to tell the story. He might have sailed the Aegean, might have passed through the Hellespont, coming at last to Tauris. Jarrell's description of this voyage is an attempt—not ineffective—to reproduce one of the characteristic effects of Homeric narrative by linking one story to a contrasting story having the same general subject, here, a far-travelling brother and sister. The place, the Dardanelles, is described by association with the story of Phryxus and Helle, whose death gave the mouth of the strait its name:

> . . . those straits
> Where passed the Boeotian prince, that hungry year
> His mother and her servants parched the seed
> (He from the altar and his father's sword
> Fled on the Ram, to Colchis; out of love for him
> His sister fled, and by the Chersonese
> Fell like a star) . . .

For Orestes at Tauris there is no flying Ram, no Golden Fleece, no loving sister. The supposed traveller, who seems by now "the dying autumn, or some wandering god," passes inland, through the marshes with their birds, to see, at evening,

> Naked and grim among her worshippers,
> The image of the Taurian Artemis.
>
> This was the image Orestes came to take—
> And beside it his head and body lay.

The last lines of the poem make it plain that this is only what a traveller might have seen, for no one really came.

It is clear that Jarrell attempted to let his action and setting develop characters, but without real success. There is an emptiness at the core of the poem. Neither Orestes nor Iphigenia seems to have any very specific or profound responses to the situations, except when Orestes falls into a fit upon recognizing his sister. Both are passive counters in an action that ends in the utter annihilation of spiritual values, ironically, since the fertility ritual is meant to foster such values. In a sense, perhaps, their behavior follows the course of Necessity; like modern man, they lose individual human values in their participation in the perpetually repeated rituals of blood sacrifice, whether to Artemis or Mammon, that so-called "civilized" men engage in. War is, naturally, one of the most familiar of these rituals.

Whether "Orestes at Tauris" is a symbolic vision of man's habitual inability to recognize his brother, or simply Jarrell's attempt to work with what was for him an unusual subject and an unusual mode—imitation of a classical form and subject—it is impossible to say for certain. Jarrell's own uneasiness about the poem testifies to its difficulties. Even though it was probably written several years before its first publication in 1943, it was not included in *Little Friend, Little Friend*. It is not printed in *Selected Poems*, Jarrell hints, because it was too long, yet "The Night Before the Night Before Christmas" is reprinted there, and it is fifty lines longer. While in parts the poem is very striking and often beautiful, in other passages it is flat, and some of the narrative and description seems rather pointless: two haystacks along the road to Tauris, for example, are "like wheaten snowmen/ Standing like glaciers by the flood." One of these similes is bad enough; two are painful. The profuse bird imagery, to take a different kind of example, never comes to a culmination. Its intent appears to be to unify the poem by repetition rather than signification. Even more troublesome is the relationship, never made clear, between the primitive fertility rituals of the goddess, given substantial attention in the poem, and the Orestes story. In spite of its weaknesses, however, "Orestes at Tauris" is an interesting poem in its reworking of an ancient story and theme. For Jarrell, it seems to mark a "road not taken."

More typical of the main body of Randall Jarrell's work are the war poems of *Losses*, which resemble, but are subtly distinguishable from, those of *Little Friend* . . . . The title of the later book is the same as that of a poem in the former, but its significance is broadened to cover not only wartime casualties, but human "losses" in general. The poem called "Loss" in *Losses* is about the death of a baby bird rather than loss through war.

An example of how the theme of loss is modified in *Losses* is "Pilots, Man Your Planes," which has the same basic subject matter as "A Pilot from the Carrier," the loss of a carrier-based fighter plane. It is a much longer poem than the earlier one, ninety-six lines as opposed to twenty-one; while the action itself has roughly the same time span, much more physical detail of the carrier and the enemy encounter is given. The possibility that both poems grew from a single inspiration that split into two centers of attention cannot be discounted,[1] and it is intriguing to see two such different poems grow out of a single donnée. Where "A Pilot from the Carrier" treats the individual's apprehension of his inevitable death, "Pilots, Man Your Planes" focuses upon the strange emotional and physical relationship of the planes and their pilots to the ship, which is seen as a kind of mother to them. Consequently, the catalogue of physical details is full and specific, where that of "A Pilot from the Carrier" was suggestive and impressionistic. The main figure in the later poem is more a technical device for unifying the point of view than a real protagonist, though at the end he "knows, knows at last" the meaning of his experience.

To begin, Jarrell describes the dark interior of the carrier, where a thousand men with their "thousand necessary deaths" sleep, "hunched in the punk of Death"; we see the hangar, the laundries, rockets, "bakeries, war-heads, the steel watch-like fish." At dawn an alarm sounds, and the flyers prepare for counterattack against a Japanese raid, unseen except by the radar which shows the speed and, thus, the type of planes approaching, "a mile in every nine or thirteen seconds." Jarrell kindly provides a note that nine seconds indicates fighters; thirteen, torpedo planes.

The nameless central character, a "boy," girds himself and is "locked at last into the bubble, Hope," with a pun on bubble (a soap bubble and the plexiglass "bubble" of his canopy) and a probable parody of Pope's "In folly's cup still laughs the bubble, joy." [2] Once in the air, he feels still while the world rolls beneath him, an image also used in "A Pilot from the Carrier." The carrier, from this height, is "the little carrier," with "cats' cradle wakes"; the raiders are toy-like, as in the other poem; they have a flaming "kite's tail" as they fall. The descriptions are in the manner of photomontage, shifting quickly between the carrier and the planes in the air. The fighter plane has to attack the torpedo plane through his own supporting

---

[1] Another such case is the poem "Jonah," which, as the work sheets clearly show, originally was part of "Jews at Haifa."

[2] Used again in Jarrell's poem, "Hope," (1948); "In folly's mailbox still laughs the postcard Hope."

flak, and he is hit, first by bullets from the enemy plane, then by what is perhaps one of his own ship's tracers, perhaps simply the one destined for him (compare ll. 45–47). Some of the child's point of view from "A Pilot from the Carrier" remains in his "somersault" into the sea. As the pilot in the other poem had to struggle free into the air, this pilot has to struggle out of his plane under water, but once he has surfaced on his inflated life-raft, it is only to see his carrier mortally hit, the planes that remained unlaunched "flung up like matches from the stern's white burst." The descriptions are intensely visual, flashing one after another, like the explosions they relate, until the ship "sinks home into the sea." The orphaned planes still in the air "fly off looking for a carrier," while destroyers, contrary to their name, seek out "the dead of the carrier," which includes also the injured. Those in the water, cruelly "oil-blackened and fire-blistered. . . . / Cling with cramped shaking fingers to the lines/ Lowered from their old life." The "old life," the safe life of the caring ships, has been superseded by a new life, less secure, less hopeful. That is what the injured, but safe, pilot "knows, knows at last," before he falls asleep. As a vivid description of a raid, "Pilots, Man Your Planes" is unquestionably superior to "A Pilot from the Carrier," but as moral statement it seems to me inferior. What the pilot "learns" from his experience is essentially that one's emotional and physical home, apparently so sustained and sustaining, is perishable, even puny, but the theme does not emerge with a strong, inevitable thrust from the situations. In "A Pilot from the Carrier," though the details are few, they are selected with attention to the greatest possible significance, and consequently the experience seems more, rather than less, real, and though very similar to that of "Pilots, Man Your Planes," it is also more moving and more convincing in the shorter poem.

In trying to expand his statement through extending the descriptions, Jarrell multiplies the concreteness until it goes well beyond the logical structure it was meant to develop. Generally speaking, increased concreteness of physical detail, rather than "story" or character development, or refinement of ideas, is characteristic of Jarrell's longer poems in *Losses* and in later volumes. Where the structure is adequate, these poems are wonderfully successful, as, for example "The Lost World"; otherwise, while they are brilliant in places, the *whole* poems tend to diffuseness, frustrating to the reader.

Another characteristic but quite different type of Jarrell's mature poems, a type almost always brief, is exemplified in "The Lines," a war poem Jarrell liked to read in public.[3] Here the emphasis is on words and word play; imagery there is in plenty, but the images are generalized, almost—if that is possible—abstract. I will quote the entire poem.

> After the centers' naked files, the basic line
> Standing outside a building in the cold
> Of the late or early darkness, waiting
> For meals or mail or salvage, or to wait
> To form a line to form a line to form a line;
> After the things have learned that they are things,
> Used up as things are, pieces of the plain
> Flat object-language of a child or states;
> After the lines, through trucks, through transports, to the lines
> Where the things die as though they were not things—
> But lie as numbers in the crosses' lines;
> After the files that ebb into the rows
> Of the white beds of the quiet wards, the lines
> Where some are salvaged for their state, but some
> Remanded, useless, to the centers' files;
> After the naked things, told they are men,
> Have lined once more for papers, pensions—suddenly
> The lines break up, for good; and for a breath,
> The longest of their lives, the men are free.

In the army, Jarrell was fond of saying as he introduced "The Lines," "you have to stand in line to get killed." The most prominent word in the poem is "line[s]"—queues, lines of battle, lines of grave markers, lines as things-not-humans—but there are other words that are also played upon for fuller signification: files and rows (also kinds of lines), centers, salvage. The theme of the poem is not new; men must be made into "things" in order to be useful to the State in war-time, and as "things" they get used up. The metaphor makes "men" into "lines." The psychology of lines is simple: lines are things; they

---

[3] Jarrell recorded the poem, with commentary, at least three times. See Library of Congress tapes LWO 2689, reel 6 (readings made in 1947 and 1948), and LWO 3558 (October 25, 1961).

teach men to think of themselves as things, or parts of things, rather than individuals. Jarrell speaks of the "object language of a child or states," but the reader may associate the phrase with Swift's Llagado, where the object language is absurd and very funny; the implication is ironic, for when any state turns to the object language of "The Lines"—war—absurdity passes into horror.

At the center of the poem, line 10, when the lines have become battle lines, the things die individually, humanly, "as though they were not things," and once they are dead things they lie "as numbers," their serial numbers inscribed on the crosses that mark the lines of graves. The lucky ones move instead to rows of beds, "lines/ Where some are salvaged," again "things." Those that are useless go back to the files at another center, this time to be discharged, in a looking glass repetition of their induction. Now they must learn to be men again, and as the lines finally disperse, the men have an instant of freedom before being absorbed into other responsibilities and functions. The last two lines of the poem are far from encouraging. The men are at last free from the obvious lines of the armed forces, but what other "lines" will bind them after this "breath" in which they are free?

Although "Pilots, Man Your Planes" and "The Lines" represent two distinct types of Jarrell's poems, many others combine the sardonic wit and shrewd generalization of the shorter form with the vivid concreteness of the longer. These include the best of the wartime and peacetime poems of *Losses*. Such a synthesis of strategies seems to make possible a deepening and broadening of themes as well as texture in the poems. One large group of the war-related poems deals with transformations of humans into things in wartime; along with "The Lines," these include "The Rising Sun," "The Subway from New Britain to the Bronx," "The Dead in Melanesia," and "Burning the Letters." The transformations in these poems come through the deaths, physical and spiritual, of their protagonists.

One poem, "The Rising Sun," typical in its treatment of the theme of transformation through death, is unique in its subject matter; it is about a Japanese boy who learns to fight and die by his country's traditions, as American boys learned to do in "Losses." The poem is full of compassion for the child, although the rituals of his state and its religion, Shinto, are treated with a barely controlled wrath.

The title "The Rising Sun," is loaded; it refers primarily to the emblem of the Japanese flag, the blood-red sun. Chief in the ancient Shinto pantheon or Kami is Amaterasu, the sun goddess, and the sun emblem is associated with her and with the Shinto gods' representative on earth, the "divine" emperor of Japan. Thus the state itself, in its quest for domination of Asia, might well be metaphorically spoken of as a rising sun. Sun is also, in English, a common pun for son; and in Christian literature, a frequent epithet for Christ. In the poem, the little boy is a kind of rising sun (son), as in his dream he floats, "a sun in air, the pure sky gazing down/ From its six-cornered roof upon the world." The Christian links are more problematical, but nonetheless present. Moreover, at least one critic[4] has suggested that the "Rising Sun" is a reference to the explosions of atomic bombs at Hiroshima and Nagasaki. I am not convinced of such a reading, though Jarrell speaks ironically of the bomb in "1945: The Death of the Gods" as the "first human sun." However, in the last verse-paragraph of "The Rising Sun," the language is deliberately ambiguous, and at one level, in referring to death as the "deliverer" from the West, Jarrell may be writing of the atomic bomb. However, he seems certainly to refer to Christ, the "rising Sun" of the prevalent Western religion, as well as to the "Deliverer" from corruption and the "burning" of human desires which is, paradoxically, death in Buddhist-oriented Shinto. Christianity, institutionalized in the Western states more subtly but just as surely as Shinto in Japan, is a part of the war machinery, subnuclear or otherwise, that destroyed Japan, and, to a degree, Shinto as well.

In *Selected Poems*, "The Rising Sun" is the opening poem in a section titled "The Trades." As we might expect, given Jarrell's hatred of "Trade"—which devours life without respect for individual lives—the term here means commerce first, trade winds second. Finally, trades are the exchanges men and states make of life for death: a bad bargain.

The opening seventeen lines of the poem describe the child and his dream, with plenty of apparently harmless local color. Only the

---

4 Glauco Cambon, "Jarrell's War Poems and the Syntax of Eloquence," *Analects*, I (Spring, 1961), 11.

first two lines hint that there is something wrong behind the idyllic existence the dream portrays: "The card-house over the fault/ Was spilt in a dream." "Card-house" is a facetious description of the fragile wood and screen Japanese house, but in the context of World War II, it is also the Japanese empire and its dream of conquest. The fault is an earthquake fault, but also a moral or intellectual fault. The following lines are uniquely pictorial, as they embody typical features of Japanese landscape painting and the life depicted in *Ukiyo-e*, the "floating world" of Japanese wood block prints. In them the mother's good-morning kiss, the cold floor, the warming teakettle of the real world blend with the dream images, the "five-colored cloud," the great fish kite, the sun "from its six-cornered roof upon the world." The room in which the child wakes is seen as having a "bare, old order," foreshadowing the treatment of ritual in the next section of the poem.

As in many of the Nōh plays, restless ghosts move through the poem, part dream, part daydream, part memory. Here they are the masterless feudal warriors of the *Chushingura*, the *ronin*. "These kill, these kill, and have not died"; they have not been punished with ignominious death, but immortalized in drama and story for their bravery and skill, or so the boy thinks. He emulates his ancestors by playing with his wooden sword and wearing his armor, a school uniform patched because of wartime hardships. In his school, the boy learns the intellectual and moral rituals of death.

The last three lines of the passage (31–33) step back from the scene, with its carefully blended elements of reality, dream, and purely picturesque.

> On this stage even a wall is silk
> And quakes according to a will; heads roll
> From the gutted, kneeling sons by rule.

"All the world's a stage," as we know; on this particular stage the stylized dramatic illusion has been totally confused with reality; ritual and real life are so mingled as to give aesthetic distance to real suicide, in the ritual of hara-kiri. The opening images of the poem are recalled in the reference to the silk walls of the stage which "quake"; like the

card-house on the fault, the world represented in this traditional stage
will crumple and, in spite of its ritual support, fall.

Through the hedge of traditions, learned "by rote," men of this
society "are pressed into obedience" to its ethos. The identity of the
child's tormentors is left ambiguous; they seem at first to be tempters
from his own society—their "way" is his—but it seems possible, too,
that the poet has shifted his ground to make the tormentors the enemy,
Western man, who also learns to kill and die by rules; different rules,
but the methodology is all too similar. One recalls the Siegfried of
an earlier poem, who, as an "actor" in the "theater" of war saw himself an "innocent."

The third section of the poem moves to the common theme of
East and West, as Jarrell sees it: Trade. Fortunetelling is done by
bookkeepers. The clerks determine men's lives with an abacus; literally, they compute money accounts, business transactions, but the end
of their endeavors is warfare. Jarrell asks, "Are these the commerce
of the warrior/ Who bowed in blue, a child of four,/ To the fathers
and their father, Strife?" Not literally, but really, these are his "commerce," though he is blinded to the facts by the beauty and efficacy
of his traditions. He and his "fathers," the *ronin*, honor most not the
gentle, life-giving Amaterasu, the sun, but her violent brother,
Susanoo, the storm: Strife.

The last section of the poem treats the outcome of the trades, the
training, the lovely and terrible illusions: death, which has its own
ceremonies. War is the agent of the transformation. It is the deliverer,
but it does not deliver men in the ways that they suppose or hope.
Men are "delivered" from their humanity, from the wish to live,
"into the hope of death." In line 48, the "child" is dead, his ashes
"whirled . . . from the West/ Into the shrine beside the rocks."
From the context, it is clear that this child is no longer a plump
schoolboy but a soldier whose ashes, in a lacquered box, are sent
home to his mother, or wife, who performs the rituals for the dead.
War, which the soldier has learned from childhood, has delivered him.
In the poem war is also the "Way"; Shinto means, "The Way of the
Gods." "The Way" has led "the twitching body to the flame," for
the body recoils from the annihilation which the child has learned
mentally to accept. Unlike the hunting ghosts of the *ronin*, who kill

and have not died, the soldier's ghost is "weak." He was, after all, merely human, and thus he is remembered and mourned, in a ritual still.

Jarrell's attitude toward ceremony and ritual, "the old order," in "The Rising Sun" is basically antagonistic. Unlike one of his long-standing favorites, Kipling, who found ritual and ceremony necessary to man as one of his fundamental safeguards against chaos, Jarrell seems to say that men fool themselves out of their humanity by per-petuating rituals that mask the significance of suffering and death; that cover up man's basic, wicked acquisitiveness with ceremonies of "honor"; that ultimately make men see their actions as pictorial, a play, rather than real. The grownup soldier, because of his traditional conditioning, can no more discriminate between aesthetic illusion and reality than the child of four in his blue school uniform. The constant shifting between the traditional features of Japanese art and real life, the pretty illusion and the real war, sets up a strong emotional ten-sion in the poem, a tension that is released in the closing images of the funeral ritual. The true release is death, which somehow frees the weak, human ghost from the heroic archetypes and rituals that bound his life. Even if death does not bring transcendence, it does give a certain kind of ironic freedom.

A very short poem, only twelve lines long, which also shows death as conferring freedom is "New Georgia," in which a Negro soldier from "old" Georgia, who had been in prison as a civilian, lies "paid, dead, and a soldier" on one of the Pacific islands given new American names in the war. Awakening in the night, while he was still alive, the soldier sometimes confused the branches overhead with the bars of his old cell window, and the creepers beneath him with his prison bed, but now that he is dead, he is liberated at last. Better yet, he has an understanding of his experience: "Who fights for his own life/ Loses, loses; I have killed for my world, and am free." In "old" Georgia, or even as a living soldier in New Georgia, he was a pris-oner, much more circumscribed in personal freedom than the pre-sumably white "prisoners" of such poems as "The Lines" or "Gun-ner." His moralizing of his death is a military perversion, no doubt foisted upon him by his officers or other army propagandists, of Christ's paradoxical words: "Whosoever will save his life shall lose it;

and whosoever will lose his life for my sake shall find it" (Matt. 16:25). Here in New Georgia, the killer is not punished but set free, because he kills for his world, even though not much of it was really his when he was in it. Like the Japanese soldier, he has been deceived by his state's dogma and ritual.

Still another poem which sees the death of a soldier as release, even more ironic than in "New Georgia," is "The Subway from New Britain to the Bronx." This title is a rather gruesome joke, for the only "subway" from the tropical island of New Britain to the Bronx is the dark earth itself, the earth to which the poem's "sparrow" returns by means of his body's dissolution. "The Subway . . . ," like "The Rising Sun," Jarrell includes in "The Trades," and it, too, utilizes the various meanings of "trade" and "exchange." One of the basic images is the orchid, which was used to advertise florists on the subways of New York and grows wild in the rain forests of New Britain. In "the unquestioning Trades of the leaf," the orchid's metabolism, photosynthesis, the "sparrow's" body finds the example for its change back to earth and water. The first three stanzas of the poem all begin with the phrase, "Under the orchid"; in the first, the phrase, continuing "blooming as it bloomed/ In the first black air," seems to describe New Britain, but the following images are clearly about the New York subways, "tiled swarming tubes/ Under the stone and Reason of the states." Conversely, the second stanza has the orchid "flowering from the hot/ Dreams of the car-cards," but makes the supposed subway "break to sunlight in one blinding flame/ Of Reason, under the shaking creepers of the isles." "Reason," the word the Renaissance and the Enlightenment used to describe man's faculty for knowing Natural Law, the earthly reflection of Divine Law, is degraded and perverted to the service of states in pursuit of trade and technology, finally of war. The exotic orchid becomes a symbol of "black desires" and "hot dreams," not so much of sensuality as of lust for superfluous goods (the "black desires" are said to be "coiled like converters in the bowels of trade") stimulated by the advertisements along the walls.

The third stanza clearly sets the scene in New Britain, where the orchid, usually associated with weddings, courtship, and other festive occasions in this country, marks a grave; it is a "rank memorial."

The electrical imagery of the second stanza is continued in the description of the skeleton as an "armature about which crystallized/ A life." The man is the "armature" supporting the coil of "black desires," which generates the qualities of the life, its "tanks, its customers, its Christ," all equal in what passes for Reason in this wartime. The rain forest, too, is without discrimination, for its "tepid siftings leach/ Its one solution." Literally, it makes the man into "solution," and it solves his problems as well, by *dis*solving him. It is a final solution.

The fourth stanza, which varies the verbal formula to "Here under the orchid," clarifies the rather difficult imagery of the preceding stanza by commenting upon the "solution." "A little water and a little dirt/ Are forever urban, temperate: a West/ Dead in the staring Orient of earth."

In the last stanza, the islands seem to take pity upon the man. Although in nature it has no direct link to the earth (or the subway), being epiphytic, the orchid in its fulfillment of natural process by "trading" oxygen for the water and nourishment it gets from the air, seems to "sigh" for the soldier. He is called "sparrow," perhaps a nickname for a drab "bird" out of his element in the land of the orchid, but he is also the bird whose fall is marked by the Lord (Matt. 10:29, Luke 12:6–7). The "sigh" given by the orchid, the trade "of the leaf, of longing, of the isles," is said to be "the same yearning sigh" given by the animals in the Bronx Zoo to "their conquerors" in other times. "Sparrow" was a prisoner, in life, of his "Reasonable" culture, in which zoos exhibit living creatures as curiosities, and exotic flowers are bought and sold to grace the bosoms of girls and matrons on their special occasions. He was conquered, first by an enemy gun, we assume, but then by Natural process, which nonetheless freed him from all the bonds and compulsions of life. "Sparrow's" death "under the orchid" of New Britain has a reasonableness that his life "under the orchid" of the Bronx subway lacked. Conversely, it was the "Reason" of the states that sent Sparrow to New Britain, where he traded away his life. Given the society of the subway, with its hot dreams and black desires, the solution of the isles is made by the structure of the poem to seem inevitable, even attractive.

The elegiac quality of "The Subway from New Britain to the Bronx" is echoed in another poem about the Pacific islands, "The Dead in Melanesia." Here too, Nature receives with equal graciousness the violent and covetous of any race or nation. Trade is once again a main theme; slave trade is its particular form, and in the end the islands receive the white soldiers in trade for "their own black dead." The word "Melanesia," as Jarrell reminds us in his notes, means "the black lands."

The trades, "the old trades" in line two, are trade winds, which made trade possible for the sailing ships of former times. The natives of the islands, "niggers" to the slave traders, cultivated warrior heroes, the "man-god in his outrigger." These fell to the traders, and to Nature their deaths were "fabulous," incredible folk tales.

The second stanza deals primarily with the Japanese warrior heroes of the *Chushingura*, the *ronin* (or perhaps their modern counterparts who sometimes hid in the caves of the islands when the Americans invaded). Nature brings its solution to these men, too: "this world works, grain by grain, into the graves/ . . . its alien genius/ . . . takes uncomprehendingly the kites, the snow—/ Their decomposing traces."

The third group of men to find death in Melanesia are the Americans; they are not by nature or training heroes or warriors. Jarrell says they "hid their single talent in Chicago,/ Des Moines, Cheyenne, are buried with it here," referring to Christ's parable of the talents (Matt. 25:15–30). Jarrell seems to pity them, for like the servant in the parable who hid his one talent, they have it taken away from them. But the land, which had accepted the defeated dead, understandably mistakes these dead "conquerors" for "failures," and accepts them along with the rest. They are seen as missionaries, perhaps bringing salvation to the islands as did earlier missionaries, many of whom also died there. They have crosses, at least for their graves. To the dead, any beachhead is "untaken"; contrarily, they are "taken" by the earth: "And the isles confuse [them] with their own black dead."

The somewhat playful animism of "The Subway from New Britain to the Bronx" and "The Dead in Melanesia" in part draws upon the conventions of pastoral elegy. Of the soldier, Jarrell implies gently, "He is made one with nature"; he is changed, and his sins no longer matter. There are other poems in *Losses* in which reconciliation does not come so easily. Although the ground in "A Camp in the Prussian Forest" "does not yet refuse/ Its usual Jews," the speaker in the poem cannot come to terms with the deaths whose evidence he sees there. Perhaps, too, it is easy to accept the deaths of hypothetical, anonymous soldiers, who died far away, and for us, long ago. For many of Jarrell's dead, who are freed from often intolerable lives or moral dilemmas brought about by their own actions, it is difficult to feel any deep dismay. In "Burning the Letters," a poem first published only a few months after the end of the war, a different attitude is taken. The poem is a fully developed dramatic monologue, in which a widow of a carrier pilot addresses her dead husband as, burning the letters she saved, she tries to find a way to reconcile his death with her life, to reconcile death generally with life.

Jarrell's headnote explains the situation, difficult to discern immediately in the constricted and convoluted stream of consciousness narration: "The wife of a pilot killed in the Pacific is speaking several years after his death. She was once a Christian, a Protestant." The major symbol of the poem, as of several earlier war poems, is fire. Her husband died a fiery death, and now she burns his letters, a second fiery death in her experience. The figure of Christ (sometimes confused in the poem with the figure of the dead husband), whose traditional symbol is "Light of the World," also appears as a flame.

The poem is a powerful one because Jarrell focuses squarely and exclusively upon the paradoxes of life and death in the context of Christian promise. Strangely, the wife does not call to mind scenes of her husband's life, but only his death. The first seven lines of the poem describe the scene of the carrier's sinking, and the burial at sea of the corpses "rescued" by other ships. The next fifteen lines describe the letters which "float" to the woman from her vision of the sea. She also seems to have a photograph, perhaps a newspaper clipping, from which her husband's face "looks home to me, a child's at last." The wife remembers her husband not as a lover or provider, but as a child, growing "younger and younger, as my eyes grew old." By his dying he seems to have rejected her (l. 20), to have changed her into a "troubled separate being." His letters were full of questions, she thought when she received them, but now that she must question the bases—metaphysical and moral—of her whole life and of his death, the letters seem to have questioned "so little."

The second "movement" of the poem, lines 23 to 49, brings to light another phase of the woman's suffering; "she was once a Christian," but her experience has formed a new and terrible context that does not tolerate faith. As a child she could accept the reasonableness of the "savage figures" of the Christian pattern of life attained through death. Jarrell quotes St. Paul, "By man came death," but Christian doctrine teaches that by dying and conquering death Christ gave man eternal life. In the poem, man's spiritual "life wells from death, the death of Man." The imagery at this point gives way to a nightmare sequence in which the Savior is a bird of prey and a flame, hunting out like a tracer bullet "the lives that burrow under the hunting wings of the light of the darkness." But the hunted turn on the hunter, pulling him down "for his unused life/ Parted into the blood, the dark, veined bread/ Later than all law"; as the drowning person pulls down his rescuer to save himself, the faithful seem to destroy God by depending on him. The dreamer sees herself as an "aging" child, clutching at "the peering savior," who perversely seems to be feeding upon himself, "his talons cramped with his own bartered flesh." Like the fire which devours her husband's words and picture, the image of the savior "pales, flickers, and flares out." Afterward in the dark (without faith) she is haunted by the "afterimages of light—/ The dying God, the eaten Life." Like her husband, the God dies and his life is consumed in the flames.

A brief transitional section recalls the scene of sea burial from the opening lines, but also the secretive burial of Christ.

> (The flames dance over life. The mourning slaves
> In their dark secrecy, come burying
> The slave bound in another's flesh, the slave
> Freed once, forever, by another's flesh:
> The Light flames, flushing the passive face
> With its eternal life.)

The imagery in the passage is difficult. Men are slaves to mortality and to their own illusions; Christ came, He said, to free men from mortality, but His triumph may have been just one more illusion by which men are enslaved. Those who buried Christ, those who bury the dead at sea, and the wife who is attempting to "bury" her dead by burning the letters, are equally slaves, as are the dead victims. Christ, the God who borrowed man's flesh, and the husband, whose death "lives" on in his wife, may both be said to be bound in another's flesh; in another way the wife participates vicariously in her husband's death and is bound in *his* flesh. Christ's sacrifice was to have been the all-sufficient atonement, freeing man from death "once, forever"; but the wife, a slave, is freed by her husband's death. The Light of the World reflects from the dead face, as the firelight briefly illuminates the husband's photograph.

The ironic, negative identification of the dead flyer with Christ is completed in lines 49 to 62. Not only her husband, but all the dead soldiers, like the dead conquerors of "The Dead in Melanesia," give their lives, as Christ did, for a victory. The phrase, "their lives are fed," recalls both the sacrament of the Eucharist and Jarrell's notion about the "consumption" of soldiers by the states. But "the ships sink, forgotten," and "the life . . . bought by death," the wife at home, is left alone, " staring westward, passive, to the blackening sea," with the vision of her husband's "charred, featureless" head crying out in "the bestial cry/ Of its pure agony." It is not to Christ, but to her husband that she says, "O death of all my life,/ Because of you, because of you, I have not died,/ By your death I have lived." Her whole awareness of life is terribly centered upon death, and exacerbated by her consciousness of continuing to exist, to grow old, while her husband has died. His life has stopped, in a way so horrible that she has not been able to reconcile herself to it, but has had to contemplate, with her living soul, only his dying.

The passage of time has almost drained her of horror, and as there seems to be no possible explanation of his death, no possible accommodation of it to Christ's promise, the wife has finally decided to try to free herself from his death by burning the letters that recall his life; by giving up what remains of the time when he was. In other words, she may be able to accept his not being, even though she could not accept his dying. In burning the letters, she echoes Christ's last words in his mortal flesh.

> ... Bound in your death,
> I choose between myself and you, between your life
> And my own life: it is finished.

Even though she burns the letters, she carries the memory of the "black body in its shroud/ The dog tags welded to your breastbone," which she has seen with her mind's eye, even as Christians may have a vision of the Savior. Her final prayer (ll. 76–79) is not to God, but to the grave, "the unliving universe in which all life is lost." The husband's life is no longer rejecting as in line 20, or unaccepting as in line 68, but "accepting and accepted." The wife's acceptance, however, is not the Christian affirmation of eternal life, but an almost existential negation of that life coupled with the acceptance of death. Essentially, when she speaks of his "accepted life" she means his accepted *death*: his mortality.

Because of the peculiarly horrible manner of his death, her child's faith in the efficacy of Christ's death crumbled; because for her there could be no reconciliation of Christ's promise with His own painful death and the continuing sin and death of mankind, the only possible course is the acceptance of death as a part of life, though not its whole. She achieves freedom, but the price is dreadful to contemplate. It involves, in Allen Tate's words, "set[ting] up the grave in the house[,] the ravenous grave."

The difficulty of reconciling Christian promise with real life, and particularly with war, is central to other poems of *Losses*. In the final stanza of "A Camp in the Prussian Forest," a poem which up to that point is restrained and even understated, the narrator, who has seen how a last breath of smoke from the crematory "fouls" the pinewood star of David he cut as a memorial, breaks into hysterical laughter at this "yellow joke."

> ... I laugh aloud
> Again and again;
> The star laughs from its rotting shroud
> Of flesh, O star of men!

What is the meaning of Christ's sacrifice, Jarrell asks, when a Christian nation kills six million Jews, and other Christian states remain neutral or act too late to stop it. The treatment of Jewish refugees by the Christian world calls forth Jarrell's wrath, too. In "Jews at Haifa," he poignantly envisions the turning back of a shipload of Jews from the "promised land," to a resettlement camp at Cyprus, where they become prisoners much as they were in the concentration camps. They no longer seek faith, but some reasonable doubt that they are what they seem to be: dead.

> There is no hope; "in all this world
> There is no other wisdom
> Than ours: we have understood the world,"
> We think; but hope, in dread
> Search for one doubt, and whisper: "Truly, we are not dead."

We have seen in Jarrell's early poems, including the early war poems, a tendency to pity individuals for their sufferings and deaths while blaming such abstractions as Trade or the States for the apparently insatiable impulse to aggrandizement that seemed to Jarrell the source of all men's misery. Behind Trade and the State lies Spinoza's Necessity, which takes into account Nature as well as the incidental, cumulative causes men create out of their own nature. At the same time as these poems, concerned with collective causes, Jarrell was writing of the individual soldier's desires for absolution from blood guilt in the wish-fulfillment of dreams and fairy tales. In "Siegfried" (1945) and in "Losses" (1944) the problem of the enlisted men's responsibility for the deaths they cause is important, but not absolutely central. In the poems dealing with the concentration camps, and in such poems as "Eighth Air Force," the issue of guilt becomes crucial; moreover, as in "Burning the Letters," human guilt and suffering are intimately connected with the death of Christ that was to save all men from sin and death, and establish on earth a community of men based on charity. Two thousand years of human history since then seem to hold Christ's sacrifice and His teaching in contempt.

"Eighth Air Force," probably one of Jarrell's two or three best-known poems, uses language and situations from the gospel accounts, particularly St. Matthew's, of the judgment of Christ by Pilate as a context for its judgment of men at war. In World War II, it was the

Eighth Air Force that bombed continental targets from bases in Britain; the speaker of the poem who says he "did as these have done," though he may not actually be one of them, describes a scene at an English base and judges the men as he sees them.

The five-line rhymed stanzas (abcbb) are notable in that the rhyme words recur. "Can," as noun and verb, is used three times to rhyme with "man," used six times. "Man" is the crucial figure of the poem: what "can" be done with him?

The poem opens with a quasi-domestic scene, such as civilian soldiers always make in their off-duty lives. The men of the Eighth Air Force, based fairly safely away from the vicious, day-to-day battling of the infantry invasions, for example, have the opportunity to recover the semblance of ordinary life when they return from their missions. They shave, keep pets, and even, in the poem, cut flowers; but the speaker is unwilling to find them innocent from such evidence.

> If, in an odd angle of the hutment,
> A puppy laps the water from a can
> Of flowers, and the drunk sergeant shaving
> Whistles *O Paradiso!*—shall I say that man
> Is not as men have said: a wolf to man?
> The other murderers troop in yawning;
> Three of them play Pitch, one sleeps, and one
> Lies counting missions, lies there sweating
> Till even his heart beats: One; One; One.
> O *murderers!* . . . Still, this is how it's done:
> This is a war.

The first two stanzas avoid direct reference to judgment or to Christ, but the Christian motif is present in the drunken sergeant's perhaps not fully conscious choice of a song, and perhaps in the card game played by the soldiers in the second stanza, reminiscent of the game played for Christ's garment at the crucifixion. The name "Pitch" may be significant, as it recalls the proverbial test of virtue, to "touch pitch and not be defiled," or perhaps as an epithet of Satan: "Old Pitch." The question raised is a difficult one: Can these men kill without becoming murderers? The speaker calls them "murderers," but they do not behave as do the murderers of folk tales or the movies, or even the newspapers; they play innocently, and at least one fears his own death. Jarrell had used the term "murderers" in writing of Ernie Pyle's ambivalent attitude toward the soldiers (see chap. 2 above, p. 40.) But the judgment and the terminology are dependent on one's point of view. The pilot who has only one more mission to fly[5] before being sent home looks upon it not as a strike against an enemy, he does not judge it as murder, but a terrible risk for himself. Missions are part of a game whose end may be fatal.

The second and third stanzas are linked formally and thematically through the transitional sentence, "Still, this is how it's done: This is a war." Where stanza two accuses, stanza three attempts to excuse, but ends in betrayal.

> This is a war. . . . But since these play, before they die,
> Like puppies with their puppy; since, a man,
> I did as these have done, but did not die—
> I will content the people as I can
> And give up these to them: Behold the man!

These puppies—wolf cubs?—play innocently, endearingly before they go to kill and be killed. The speaker has also played, and perhaps killed, or has at least implicated himself by condoning their killing, but his mission now is to "content the people" by giving them a scapegoat, as Pilate gave Christ to the Jews even though he recognized Him as guiltless. Pilate's words, as reported by St. Matthew, convey significant ambiguity. *Ecce homo*, as the Vulgate puts it: "Behold the man!"

The central event of the Christian religion is Christ's death as a man, His putting off of mortal flesh for spiritual being, at once a sacrifice and an example and promise to His followers. But the context of the words "Behold the man!" is Pilate's delivery of Jesus to those who wished to kill Him. In Jarrell's poem, the words carry analogous meanings. As the last stanza indicates, there is a sense in which these "murderers" are saviors, freeing Europe from an invader whose aim was not only conquest but the extermination of the

---

[5] Pyle comments on the anxiety of those with only a few more missions to fill their quota in *Brave Men* (New York, 1944), 111.

people from which Jesus came: paradoxically, since this genocide would seem to culminate all that belies Christian teaching in nominally Christian society.[6] To "behold the man" is to see him as a simple, loving human soul and as a murderer; as a puppy and as a wolf; as a savior and as a sinner; and finally as a scapegoat for the guilt of other men. Though equally guilty and innocent with the victims—the bomber crews, here—the narrator will, like Pilate, give up the victim[s] to the accusers to do with as they please, to villify as they please, for the bomber crews are mostly dead and will no more defend themselves than Christ did.

In the last stanza Jarrell paraphrases the words of Pilate and his wife as well. The flyers are explicitly identified with Christ, whom Jarrell describes in a note to the poem as "that criminal and scapegoat about whom the gospels were written."

> I have suffered, in a dream, because of him,
> Many things; for this last saviour, man,
> I have lied as I lie now. But what is lying?
> Men wash their hands, in blood, as best they can:
> I find no fault in this just man.

In defending the flyers—"I find no fault in this just man"—the speaker lies, for the faults are only too plain. "But what is lying?": a defense of the spirit, like dreaming, a kind of saving. The juxtaposition of action and meaning in the last two lines is particularly striking. Pilate washed his hands in water to signify his guiltlessness in the death of Jesus, yet in passively allowing the murder, he, too, shared in the guilt. Man has sinned so often, actively and passively, that his attempts to absolve himself are no longer credible; like Macbeth, he incarnadines the seas with his blood guilt, rather than washing it away with water.[7] As Jarrell sees it, men at war attempt to wash their hands (excuse themselves) in blood (literal bloodshed), and they do it as well as can be expected, given the situation. When Pilate, the speaker, utters his judgment, "I find no fault in this just man," the reader has been conditioned to mistrust him by the earlier admission that

[6] Compare "A Camp in the Prussian Forest."

[7] Compare also Lady Macbeth's "A little water clears us of this deed (II, ii, 67)"; and her futile efforts to wash Duncan's blood from her hands in V, i.

the speaker lies to defend his "last saviour, man," and also by the admission that he, too, has washed his hands in blood. The poem has no resolution of the problem, for the flyers are as innocent and guilty as at first, but the speaker and the reader have come to understand that whatever the judgment, they must also share in it. Man is irrevocably both savior and destroyer, and the poise between these poles is an extremely delicate balance.

Perhaps the blackest of all the judgments in the war poems in *Losses* is that of "1945: The Death of the Gods." Here the Gods are envisioned as extensions or archetypes of the world's States, sometimes merely "made" (imagined) by men. In Jarrell's horrid and circular mythology, men create the institutions which in the end destroy them. Men's imagination in the summer of 1945 put to use "the first human sun/ Your wisdom found," the atom bomb, and in so doing dreadfully imitated the mythic action of Prometheus, bringer of fire. These gods, this society, determine "men's last obedience," but the nature of the gods and of society is "determined/ In the first unjudged obedience of greed/ And senseless power." Now, with the creation of this "human sun," the gods have set in motion the machinery of their own annihilation:

> Tomorrow when the rockets rise like stars
> And earth is blazing with a thousand suns
> That set up there within your realms a realm
> Whose laws are ecumenical, whose life
> Exacts from men a prior obedience—
> Must you learn from your makers how to die?

Even as men have died for centuries in obedience to their "warring Deities," the deities must now prepare to die with the men in a manmade holocaust. The Western Gods are doomed along with their Eastern counterparts of "The Rising Sun."

The war poems of *Losses*, with their harsh emphasis on the acceptance of inevitable, terrible death and dissolution, and the insistence that all men must bear the guilt of world war, seem to grow naturally from the poems of *Little Friend, Little Friend*, in which the soldiers, and the readers, learn about the horror and degradation of war and of the world that nurtures war. The outrage that marks the tone of *Little Friend* . . . is sometimes modulated in *Losses* to a quiet desolation and pity for the victims, who are all men, whether guilty or innocent (if there be any of the latter). The new note of infinite compassion and love sometimes assumes overtones of irony or even sarcasm: the weapon of wit fighting back against the intractable misery of the world. Such a complex tone prevails in "Lady Bates," one of the civilian poems of *Losses*, that it is possible for the reader not attuned to Jarrell's voice to find it condescending or even tasteless in its treatment of the protagonist, a dead Negro girl.

Read attentively, however, the poem is one of Jarrell's most sympathetic and profound. In a sense it is a poem of protest, but not the simple protest that Lady, in her lifetime, was denied her civil rights or the benefits of middle-class white economy[8] or even personal dignity. The protest lies deeper than that; it is protest against trifling with human life and hopes, as the world, religion, and even Death "trifle" with little Lady Bates. What if she is only a "trifling ghost," Jarrell asks, should she not have her elegy?

The quality of elegy suggests that perhaps the poem is an ironic inversion of Ransom's "Bells for John Whiteside's Daughter," a very well-known and very brilliant poem about a little lady whom everyone noticed and gave way to in her lifetime, and who fixed everyone's attention by her unexpected death, unlike the forgotten Lady Bates. A more immediate source came from Jarrell's reading of Corbière's *Rondels pour Après*, four of which are translated and published in *The Seven-League Crutches* under the title "Afterwards." There are many echoes of "Afterwards" in "Lady Bates," both verbal —"There're no nights any longer, there're no days" (II, 2); "You're not afraid of being alone, though—poor little thing, are you?" (III, 3–4)—and in the generally teasing tone Corbière's speaker takes toward the dead child of his poems.

Jarrell annotated "trifling" (l. 48) as "worthless, good-for-nothing, no-account . . . often used affectionately." [9] The affection, how-

---

8 One sees these benefits in their true light in "Seele im Raum," "The Woman at the Washington Zoo," and "Next Day."
9 Jarrell, *The Complete Poems*, 5.

ever, is condescending; "trifling" is a word used for inferiors, not equals. To "trifle with" someone is to treat him as one of little worth, a "trifle." Lady Bates has always been trifled with; even her death was an accident, a mistake.

Jarrell's strategy in "Lady Bates" is to describe the setting of Lady's life and some of its incidents: her baptism, the teasing of other girls while Lady helped her stepmother wash clothes. The six work sheets in the University of North Carolina, Greensboro, collection—obviously only a small portion of what must have been a large number —show that the poet had toyed with the idea of giving the details of Lady's death: "Shot in someone else's shooting-scrape . . . poor ignorant bystander in the midst of things"; and of her funeral: "You went to your grave [in a] 1935 Pierce-Arrow." He ultimately rejected these too sordid "facts," describing Lady's death only impressionistically: "The wind has blown you away forever/ By mistake; and they sent the wind to the chain-gang/ And it worked in the governor's kitchen, a trusty for life." He introduces "The Lord God and the Holy Ghost and the Child Jesus," as well as personifications called Night and Day, and Death, all of whom speak to or about Lady. Her own thoughts or feelings, except for her being scared, we never know. Jarrell's choice of point of view and the basic narrative strategy convey the blankness at the heart of Lady's existence; she *is* a ghost, and the reader sees clearly everything in the poem but Lady herself, while a richness of detail fixes each scene around her vague figure in a few dextrous strokes, blending minute particulars with symbolic generalizations.

The seventy-nine-line poem has four irregular stanzas, within which the scene shifts back and forth among Lady's grave, her past life, and a cosmic setting in which the eternal rest of Lady's soul is debated. Although the verse is free, its rhythmic units are almost musical, and qualifying the elegiac elements there is a sense of lullaby, of soothing Lady to sleep after an unpleasant dream.

The first stanza has Lady waking, in her grave, to the lightning of a summer storm, frightened as she was in life, unable to distinguish between the real thunder and that of her bad dreams. In death, the dream and reality are one, as are night and day. The dreams are not only real, but the *only* reality.

The lightning of a summer
Storm wakes, in her clay cave
At the end of the weeds, past the mock-orange tree—
Where she would come bare-footed, curled-up-footed
Over the green, grained, rotting fruit
To eat blackberries, a scratched handful—
The little Lady Bates.
You have played too long today.
Open your eyes, Lady.
                    Is it a dream
Like the ones your mother used to talk away
When you were little and thought dreams were real?
Here dreams are real.
There are no more dreams, no more real—
There is no more night, there is no more day.

The delicacy of the description is almost beyond praise. The grave is euphemistically imagined as a place to play, a clay cave, in an accustomed spot where the mock-oranges, green and inedible but, as Jarrell said, "impressive to children" [10] lie, teasing the feet of the barefoot Lady. The misplaced epithet "scratched" brilliantly condenses an image of Lady's meager berrypicking. The fading of reality into dream forms a transition to the second stanza, where one of Lady's dreams—daydreams, imaginings—becomes real. As she was promised that God the Father, Son, and Holy Ghost would care for her personally after death, so they appear, smiling and singing like a gospel quartet.

When the Lord God and the Holy Ghost and the Child Jesus
Heard about you, Lady,
They smiled all over their faces
And sang like a quartet: "Lady Bates,
Is it you, the little Lady Bates
Our minister, one Sunday evening,
Held down in the river till she choked
In a white dress like an angel's, red
With the clay of that red river? Lady,
Where are the two we sent to fetch your soul:
One coal-black, one high-yellow angel?
Where is night, where is day?

---

[10] *Ibid.*

Where are you, Lady Bates?"
They looked for you east, they looked for you west,
And they lost you here in the cuckoo's nest
Eating the sweet white heart of the grass. . . .
You died before you had even had your hair straightened
Or waited on anybody's table but your own.
You stood there helping your step-mother
Boil clothes in the kettle in the yard,
And heard the girls go by, at play,
Calling to you in their soft mocking voices:
"Lady-Bug, Lady-Bug, fly away home."

Behind the amusing imaginary picture of the Trinity singing "like a quartet" is another picture, a "real" one, in which Lady is baptized, her white dress "like an angel's" unfortunately sullied with the same red clay that makes her grave. Her guardian angels are coal-black and high-yellow; they correspond to night and day, in Lady's vision of the world. Their search for Lady is like a children's game, but the refrain "Look to the East,/ Look to the West,/ Look to the one you love the best" is changed by the dream-work from love found to love lost. The cuckoo's nest is a joke, of course, for the cuckoo's habit of laying its eggs in other birds' nests, from which the baby cuckoos often evict the rightful children, is the source of the cuckoo's bad reputation; the cuckoo is a trifler of the worst sort. The cuckoo's nest is nowhere, and Lady is lost, "eating the sweet white heart of the grass," as she did in life, as many children do. Within the stanza comes another abrupt shift to Lady's lifetime. The narrator pretends to decry the early death that prevented Lady from fulfilling her Negro destiny: to have her hair straightened, to wait on table. The real pathos of Lady's life—the death of her mother, the teasing of the other children who play when she must work—is only hinted at. Even her name, which as a title signifies a position of dignity or honor, is turned to gentle scorn; what is more trifling than the lady-bug, even if her house is on fire?

At the beginning of the third stanza Lady is at home, in her grave, where for the first time she does not have to share a bed.

You are home.
There is a bed of your own

Here where a few stones
Stick up in the tall grass dried to hay—
And one willow, at the end of summer,
Rustles, too dry to weep for you,
And the screech-owl sheers away
And calls, *Who, who*—you are afraid
And he is afraid: who else could see
A black ghost in the dark?
A black, barefooted, pigtailed, trifling ghost
With eyes like white clay marbles,
Who haunts no one—who lies still
In the darkness, waiting
While the lightning-bugs go on and off?
The darning-needles that sew bad girls' mouths shut
Have sewn up your eyes.
If you could open your eyes
You would see nothing.
                    Poor black trash,
The wind has blown you away forever
By mistake; and they sent the wind to the chain-gang
And it worked in the governor's kitchen, a trusty for life;
And it was all written in the Book of Life;
Day and Night met in the twilight by your tomb
And shot craps for you; and Day said, pointing to your soul,
"This *bad* young colored lady,"
And Night said, "Poor little nigger girl."

Here Lady is resurrected as a ghost, frightening the screech-owl, a
bird traditionally associated with death. The nearest Jarrell comes to
physical description of Lady is generalized—"black, barefooted, pigtailed, trifling"—and the one specific detail, "eyes like white clay
marbles" rolled in the dark for fear, is a cliché, though it has the
special connotations in this poem of a trifling kind of toy, since clay
marbles are made and used only by children too poor to buy real
ones. The play motif of the singing games in lines 28, 29, and 37, and
of marbles, is developed further in the work sheets, where a rejected
note reads that she plays jacks "not on pavement squares but drawn
out in dirt," somehow confusing jacks with hopscotch.

The speaker's allegation in lines 55 and 56 that, if Lady *could* open
her eyes, she would see nothing, refers not only to her being dead,
but also to her apparent self-protective intellectual blindness to the

deficiencies of her life. The last part of line 56, "poor black trash," is a value judgment not of Lady's intrinsic worth, but of the world's indifference to her. Poor white trash is lower, socially, than respectable Negroes. What, then is poor black trash? Not even a social class, but a discard from life's card game. The agent of Lady Bates's death is no more personal than the wind which blows her away forever like a scrap of paper, a thing. "And it was all written in the Book of Life," says the poet.

The two angels seem to find Lady at last in lines 61 to 64. In another game, the particular name of which is associated with Negro dialect, they shoot "craps" for her soul.[11] Self-righteous, white (or high-yellow) Day judges Lady severely, but Night, the dark angel, pities her, so that even the term "nigger girl" has a gentleness that Day's "colored lady" merely mocks.

But, alas for Lady Bates, the angels do not take her away to Heaven, or anywhere else. Death is her master, and Death comforts her, teasing a little, lulling her back to sleep.

> But Death, after the habit of command,
> Said to you, slowly closing his hand:
> "You're a big girl now, not even afraid
> Of the dark when you awake—
> When the day you sleep through
> Is over, and you awake,
> And the stars rise in the early evening
> An inch or two over the grass of your grave—
> Try to open your eyes;
> Try to reach to one, to the nearest,
> Reach, move your hand a little, try to move—
> You can't move, can you?
> You can't move....
> You're fast asleep, you're fast asleep."

Lady's efforts at transcendence (reaching to a star) fail, while dream and reality merge once again. As in dreams we find ourselves unable to move, so the dead Lady tries to reach out, but cannot.

"Lady Bates," published in the *Nation* in February, 1948, seems to mark the beginning of a new phase of Jarrell's poetry. The speci-

---

11 Compare the dice game played for the soul of the Ancient Mariner.

fic subject is unique, but the attitudes and techniques are more characteristic of the poems of *The Seven-League Crutches* and *The Woman at the Washington Zoo* than of the war poems. The strain and the sharp irony that toughen the war poems are relaxed and tempered with gentleness. It may be worth noting, too, that while all of the war poems except "Burning the Letters" have as protagonists men or children, many of the best later poems have women or girls as central figures. Even in "Burning the Letters," the woman is not particularly feminine in her reflections, which are basically intellectual, theoretical, qualities usually thought masculine. Like Rilke, Jarrell found a kind of integrity of feeling and a special capacity for suffering in women that seemed to him of greater value than the physical and intellectual virtues of men. One reason Lady is so vulnerable is that she is a girl; moreover, Jarrell can write of her tenderly without fear of sentimentality.

Technically, too, in the greater freedom of its verse from the pentameter line Jarrell had always favored, "Lady Bates" moves in a new direction; though pentameter remains prominent, there are more free verse poems in the middle period than elsewhere in Jarrell's poetry. The echoing of parts of lines in a kind of loose incremental repetition becomes more and more typical.

One of the primary motifs of "Lady Bates" is the interaction of dreams with reality; this motif is recurrent in many of the war poems and also in the poems utilizing fairy tale materials, for, as Jarrell knew, the transformations of the dream-work are inseparable from those which inform the *Märchen*.[12] In dreams Jarrell's characters compensate for the pain and loneliness of their waking lives, as in "Absent with Official Leave" in *Little Friend . . . .* A number of poems in *Losses* use dreams incidentally. Three of the most distinguished, "The Rising Sun," "Burning the Letters," and "Lady Bates," have dreams as an important part of their content. Other poems are so dominated by dreams that dreams and "dream-work" may be singled out as their primary subject.

---

[12] Jarrell sometimes seems to use the term "dream-work" in a simpler sense than Freud, to mean not the complicated process of condensation, displacement, and symbolization of dreams, but simply the change from unpleasant reality to wish-fulfilling images.

The simplest poem, the simplest dream, is that of "The Dead Wingman." In this poem the protagonist is a fighter pilot who searches, again and again, in sleep, for the companion shot down along the Japanese coast. The search is fruitless, and the most insistent word in the poem is "no," which expands from the simple negation of the individual's search for his "little friend" to the universal negation of "the lives' long war, lost war." In "Stalag Luft," whose title indicates its setting, a German prison camp for flyers, the actual details of the prison camp are utterly submerged in the dream or memory of an afternoon long before, when the captured flyer, a boy, dozed and daydreamed in the grass with his pet rabbit. His daydream seems to be about being captured by Indians, "far-raiding captors" who wear quills on their "milky leggings" and ride "dappled mustangs"; they bind his wrists with "numbing laces," but release him with praise after he shows fortitude through "some feverish days." [13] No release comes to the grownup in the poem, just the melancholy remembrance of happier days past.

A more complicated dream is that in "The Child of Courts," called "The Prince" in *Selected Poems*, where it is included with the poems of childhood and books, "Once Upon a Time," rather than with the war poems. It would seem that the protagonist is a child, despite the fact that several images of the last stanza suggest that he might be a grown-up military prisoner comforting himself with fantasy, like the flyer in "Stalag Luft."

The main images of the poem recall Freud's statement that, in dreams, figures of kings or emperors stand for parents, while the prince or princess is the dreamer.[14] So it is in "The Prince," who dreams of his dead father or brother. After his mother, or perhaps his captor, leaves him alone in the dark, he hunches "beneath the covers, in [his] curled/ Red ball of darkness," and feels, as every child has, "someone . . ./ In the other darkness." It is one from the dead who bends over the child's body, while he shrinks "like the rabbit/ They gave me when he—." The next word should be "died," but

13 Perhaps based on a memory of Cooper's *The Prairie*, in which Natty Bumppo is released by his Sioux captors because they admire his stamina.
14 "The Interpretation of Dreams," in Freud, *The Standard Edition of the Complete Psychological Works*, ed. James Strachey (24 vols.; London, 1953–64), V, 353.

in the quasi-dream, that word is unacceptable. The dead presence then seems strangely to be the rabbit, as the "prince" hears "his fingers rasping, like five paws,/ Up through the dirt"; but when he reaches out to touch the other, nothing is there.

The dreamer returns to full consciousness and sits up, where he sees starlight barring a window and hears a sentry call out. Though starlight might bar any window with crossing supports, and though a sentry is appropriate to a king's court, as well as to a prison or an army camp, the last two lines of the poem echo an idea of many of Jarrell's war poems, that soldiers are used up, like commodities, by the states.

> A man dies like a rabbit, for a use.
> What will they pay me, when I die, to die?

The early title, "The Child of Courts," was obviously meant to be ambiguous, and to suggest both royal courts and courts of law, which can condemn people to prison or death. "Divorce courts" are a further possibility; perhaps the child's fears of abandonment and death, and his sense of guilt, arise from his real domestic situation. The later title, "The Prince," stresses the idea of royal courts to the exclusion of law courts, perhaps because Jarrell actually meant the poem to be about a real prince, but more likely, I believe, to stress the dreamwork in which every man can imagine himself a prince. Although his suffering is not lessened thereby, it is given scope and dignity.

The most complicated of the dream poems in *Losses*, "In the Ward: The Sacred Wood," links the dream to Greek mythology and Christian legend. The dream itself is more complex than in any of the poems, perhaps because the dreamer is in a more painful psychic situation. He has been wounded in the war, and like the sick man in "The Christmas Roses" (*Blood for a Stranger*), he expects to die. Consequently, his wish-fulfillment concerns being saved, being resurrected, or simply immortal. "The Sacred Wood" is another of Jarrell's punning titles, for though the phrase is traditionally associated with the Sacred Grove at Nemi, a sanctuary of Diana, Jarrell's primary meaning focuses upon the Cross. Perhaps "wood" should also be read as "would," for the poem records a sacred wish.

Jarrell's note is illuminating, as much for what it omits—all reference to the Grove of Nemi—as for what it includes. "In 'In the Ward: the Sacred Wood,' the wounded man has cut trees from paper, and made for himself a sacred wood; with these, the bed-clothes, the nurse, the doctor, he works his own way through the Garden of Eden, the dove and its olive-leaf, the years in the wilderness, the burning bush, the wars of God and the rebel angels, the birth and death and resurrection of Christ." [15] His construction of trees and birds is therapy, and it expresses his desire for life. His bed is not a deathbed, but a "bed of life," he says; it is also the theater where his whole life is now being played out.

> The trees rise from the darkness of the world.
> The little trees, the paper grove,
> Stand woodenly, a sigh of earth,
> Upon the table by this bed of life
> Where I have lain so long: until at last
> I find a Maker for them, and forget
> Who cut them from their cardboard, brushed
> A bird on each dark, fretted bough.
> But the birds think and are still.

Though he has cut them from cardboard himself, though he is vulnerable and mortal, in imagination he would have them sacred, consecrated to some deity, a divine and immortal creator. The birds, whom he imagines as alive—"thinking"—neither support nor deny his wish. Once he has imagined, or dreamed, a creator that is his projection of himself, his mind begins the progress described in Jarrell's note; Eden, the flood, the forty years in the wilderness. But other materials get in: images almost surely from Eliot's *The Waste Land*, one possible reference to the Actaeon story (also mentioned in Eliot), and one apparent allusion to Shelley's *Prometheus Unbound*.

> The thunder mutters to them from the hills
> My knees make by the rainless Garden.
> If the grove trembles with the fan
> And makes, at last, its little flapping song

---

15 Jarrell, *The Complete Poems*, 6.

That wanders to me over the white flood
On which I float enchanted—shall I fall?
A bat jerks to me from the ragged limb
And hops across my shudder with its leaf
Of curling paper: have the waters gone?
Is the nurse damned who looked on my nakedness?
The sheets stretch like the wilderness
Up which my fingers wander, the sick tribes,
To a match's flare, a rain or bush of fire
Through which the devil trudges, coal by coal,
With all his goods; and I look absently
And am not tempted.

The thunder's muttering from the hills (the mounds his knees make in the bedclothes) and the rainless Garden recall Section V, "What the Thunder Said," of *The Waste Land*, which begins with a passage referring to Christ in Gethsemane. His death is associated with the spiritual death symbolized in the wasteland. The thunder speaks, giving directions for the spiritual renewal that must precede new life, symbolized traditionally as rain. But Jarrell has said that the Garden is not Gethsemane but Eden, paradoxically the beginning place of life, but also the place where death first came into being through man's sin. Eden without rain is a wasteland. On the other hand, God once made a wasteland with forty days and nights of rain, thus *un*making his world, as the speaker in the poem finally does. The dreamer comes to seem Adam and Noah in one. As Adam, he fears the Fall, an image of death. For the moment, however, he is saved from the "flood" that claimed his comrades of war. The image of floating enchanted on a white flood, lulled by a song, calls to mind the song of Asia that concludes Act II of *Prometheus Unbound*, beginning "My soul is an enchanted boat/ Which like a sleeping swan doth float/ Upon the silver waves of thy sweet singing." In her song Asia celebrates the transcendence over evil that will soon reunite her with Prometheus and bring forth a new flourishing of life. Jarrell's image also recalls Ferdinand's "This music crept by me on the waters," in *The Tempest*, which Eliot had also used in *The Waste Land*.

Floating or flying, Freud wrote in *The Interpretation of Dreams*,[16]

[16] Freud, *The ... Complete Psychological Works*, IV, 271–72.

are images of sexual pleasure; to the soldier in the poem, the pleasure may simply be that of continued or renewed life. A bat, traditionally associated with death, but perhaps also with the baby-faced bats of "What the Thunder Said," rather than a dove—life, peace—brings this Noah a sign, not a leaf but a scrap of paper. In line 19, the speaker alludes to Noah's cursing of Ham, who saw his nakedness, but a secondary reference might be to the chaste Diana, enraged at Actaeon who spied her bathing in the Sacred Wood. One of the immortals, Diana is sterile because of her rigid chastity, thus embodying both life and death. Her rites, as Frazer observed in *The Golden Bough*, are associated with fertility and include human sacrifice. (Compare "Orestes at Tauris.") An interesting and relevant facet of Frazer's account is that the priest of the Temple of Diana at Nemi was invariably killed by his successor.[17]

Lines 20 to 22 fleetingly describe the Exodus from Egypt, the journey through the wilderness to a Promised Land of milk and honey: new life. Thus the sickbed is a wilderness, barren and dangerous, through which the man must pass. In his cardboard grove, "a match's flare" is the burning bush, but no God speaks from it. Instead, by its light he sees "the devil" trudging "with all his goods," the temptations of life, which he rejects, as did Christ in the wilderness (Luke 4:1–13).

The last lines of the first verse paragraph form a transition dealing with the war in heaven, as related in the Apocryphal Book of Enoch, and they refer to the soldier's condition; his life, like the third part of the Angels, lies "in doubt." He awaits the outcome passively.

> Death scratches feebly at this husk of life
> In which I lie unchanging, Sin despairs
> Of my dull works; and I am patient . . .
> A third of all the angels, in the wars
> Of God against the Angel, took no part
> And were to God's will neither enemies
> Nor followers, but lay in doubt:
> > but lie in doubt.

---

[17] James George Frazer, *The Golden Bough* (London, 1913), I, 9. See also IV, 205.

In the second verse paragraph the dreamer consistently identifies himself with Christ. Here, as in "Burning the Letters," Christ is an ambivalent symbol. Like man, He died, but His legend insists that He overcame death and that through belief in Him, others can also.

> There is no trade here for my life.
> The lamb naps in the crêche, but will not die.
> The halo strapped upon the head
> Of the doctor who stares down my throat
> And thinks, "Die, then; I shall not die"—
> Is this the glitter of the cruze of oil
> Upon the locks of that Anointed One
> Who gazes, dully, from the leafless tree
> Into the fixed eyes of Elohim?
> I have made the Father call indifferently
> To a body, to the Son of Man:
> "It is finished." And beneath the coverlet
> My limbs are swaddled in their sleep, and shade
> Flows from the cave beyond the olives, falls
> Into the garden where no messenger
> Comes to gesture, "Go"—to whisper, "He is gone."

The first line of the section is difficult. "No trade" means "no occupation," but also "no exchange" or perhaps even "no change." The speaker feels useless, but also fairly secure, because his life cannot be used anymore (as in war), in exchange for anything. In his white bedclothes he is the lamb in the crêche who sleeps but will not die. The doctor with his reflector, a "halo," is one of the immortals, but he abandons his patient to death, or so the worried mortal believes. Christ was anointed, as the traditional symbol of His being chosen by God, but also as a sign of His impending death. (See Mark 14:3–9, Matt. 26:6–13.) The soldier, comparing his situation to Christ's, is afraid.

In the dream, the Father does not pity his son, but abandons him, as Jesus feared His Father had when He cried from "the leafless tree," "My God, my God, why hast thou forsaken me?" God's son turns out to be only a son of man, capable of dying, and the God, not the dying man, says indifferently, "It is finished." In his bed the dreamer is swaddled like a newborn Christ, *not*, he insists, wrapped in burial garments, which are also white. The grave, the sepulcher hewn from rock in the garden, another sacred wood, is called "the cave beyond the olives." No angel is there to comfort the mourners, and even the unspoken message is negative. In the gospels, the angel at the tomb says, "He is not here: he is risen," but the poem's messenger, had he spoken at all, would only have said, "He is gone."

The final section consists of only four lines, in which the dreamer wakes to utter hopelessness:

> The trees rise to me from the world
> That made me, I call to the grove
> That stretches inch on inch without one God:
> "I have unmade you, now; but I must die."

As in a real dream, the images are condensed and multiple in meaning. The literal gesture is the speaker's raising his knees, thus toppling the grove, which he has apparently moved from the table onto the bed. Stretching "inch on inch" the grove is a microcosm of the wilderness of this world. It has no God, neither Diana, the immortal, nor Christ, who died but rose again. If its creator *un*creates, he is no longer a creator of a world, no longer omnipotent and immortal. He himself was made by a world, and his immediate world, the hospital, is a place where he attempts to evade recognition of his expected death by playing at being a God of creation. The hospital world is linked directly to an outside world, a war, that destroys the people, the cultures which produced myths of immortality: the cult of the fierce Diana, whose priests die in her service, and the religion of the gentle sufferer, Christ. The world of the myths is another of the worlds that "made" the speaker, for it is to the myths that he reaches psychologically for comfort and hope. In destroying his sanctuary, the mythic world he made and lives in, immortal through dreams, he acknowledges impending death, perhaps soon, but certainly sometime.

"In the Ward: The Sacred Wood" questions the efficacy of Christian legend to reconcile man to his physical death through the promise of eternal life, if only one "believes." Unfortunately for his peace of mind, the speaker lies "in doubt." His sacred wood is a sterile wilderness not of red rock but of bedclothes and cardboard trees. Like all dreams, his dream of immortality is temporary; on waking his suffering is as acute as ever.

The use of analogous mythic materials, and the emphasis on identifying with an immortal figure as a means of avoiding the thought of death are two important themes of "In the Ward: The Sacred Wood." Both these themes are developed in another poem written at about the same time (late 1945–early 1946), "The Märchen." This poem seems to me the most difficult in all Jarrell's work, not only because it is one of the most allusive but because its form is meditative and associational rather than narrative; it progresses swiftly through a long series of images, and grammar is often jettisoned in the rush. There is a protagonist, Everyman, called "Hansel" and at times presented as the Hansel of the Grimms' tale, but also as Hansel's father, the poor woodcutter (ll. 36–38, 105–108), and as Christ (ll. 26–35). The basic identification is the same as in "In the Ward . . . ," "Eighth Air Force," and "Burning the Letters," because Hansel, like the protagonists of these other poems, is a scapegoat who suffers—futilely—in place of others. Essentially, "The Märchen" is about men's desires to live and to rule over their environment. Because their lives are continually beset with frustration of these desires, they invent stories in which they or their surrogates are successful in combating the evils ranged against them—the wicked stepmother, hunger, darkness, cold, death, the devil, "giants, warlocks, the unburied dead/ Invulnerable to any power."

The fundamental obstacle to fulfillment is the world itself, seen in the first eight lines of the poem as the forest, which is animated by some spirit of its own, ever alien and opposed to men. "Long ago," men attempted to enter the forest, to live there, armed invaders with their axes, making places for themselves. In expressing the living and encroaching qualities of the forest, Jarrell uses images of the sea. Both sea and forest are common traditional symbols of the mind, and it is not impossible that Jarrell means to compare the mysterious "forest" of Nature with the "forest" of the mind. When the men first attempted to penetrate the forest, it was with stone axes held together by the skins of animals (the forest's original "dwellers"), but the final conquest of "islands" in the "tides" of the forest was made with "iron." In the daylight, men could believe that their wish to conquer the wilderness had been successful, could be assured of their potency.

> The sunlight fell to them, according to our wish,
> And we believed, till nightfall, in that wish;
> And we believed, till nightfall, in our lives.

Lines 9 to 20 seem to describe the real forest, by moonlight, in winter. The dead bird, the dead leaf, may come to new life, but somehow it does not seem altogether certain. These images give way to the hunter, perhaps human, perhaps animal, and the skeleton of the "charcoal burner," a familiar figure of the Black Forest. Several charcoal burners appear in the Grimms' tales, usually to be duped by a clever protagonist. This one, dozing among the trees, has been taken in by the forest.

From this multiplicity of images the figure of Hansel emerges. His story undergoes continuous changes in the poem. Instead of casting bread or pebbles to mark the way home, Jarrell's Hansel casts "his bones/ Up clouds to Paradise," in an apparent sacrifice. He gets home, however, not to a cottage but to a cave, where his relatives are "furred in the sooty darkness." It seems that he must be the first avatar of Hansel, a cave man, contemporaneous with "the old gods." When this Hansel falls into an enchanted sleep he dreams away ages and awakes as the crucified Christ,

> ...eternal corpse
> Of the Scapegoat, gay with His blood's watered beads,
> Red wax in the new snow...

The drops of blood in the new snow recall the beginning of the Grimms' tale "The Juniper Tree," whose protagonist's birth is foretold by his mother's pricking her finger and letting fall several drops of red blood upon snow. This little boy, like Hansel, has a wicked stepmother who wants to kill him, and in "The Juniper Tree" she successfully carries out her wish.

In "The Märchen" Hansel feeds on dreams ("airy kine") like those devout and benighted people who for centuries paid for and depended upon Christian relics such as the wood "of the true Cross," which appears in the poem as "Christ's bark." But Hansel, now the father of his own hungry children, sends his little ones out, in the stories he imagines or dreams, not to death or the devil but to glory. Godfather Death (l. 39), in Grimms' tale of that name, finally tricks his overreaching godchild and claims him, but the Hansel-father sends his children out "to a king" as fathers do in other of the Grimms' tales. The children (usually the youngest, the good or stupid ones) perform prodigious tasks, with the threat of death ("the headsman [with] his gnawn block") hanging over their possible failure. But they do not fail; they win the king's daughter and the kingdom, too.

If there are kings in dreams and tales, there are dark powers too, "giants, warlocks, the unburied dead," whom Jarrell sees, in the manner of his early poems, as "the Necessity/ Men spring from, die under"; but he goes beyond this abstraction to a unifying image: "the unbroken wood," or the natural forces that strive to restore the wilderness, obliterating man's islands and wishes both. Jarrell's "Necessity" here is an ominous version of Frost's joking "something" that "doesn't like a wall." In his phrase, "the unbroken wood," Jarrell embodies the sum of man's difficulty and frustration; Dante's *selva obscura* is the same wood as that in which Hansel and Gretel are lost for three days and nights, the same wood through which little Snow White runs in terror after being released by the queen's huntsman. Through the symbol of the forest, which appears in more than a third of the Grimms' tales, Jarrell unites the real world and that of the Märchen, thus defining the value of the stories to men's lives, which is vicarious identification: ultimately the tales' protagonists find a way out of the forest, and their wishes are fulfilled.

The next section of the poem, from line 50 to line 65, develops the sun as a source of insight, that is, light, by which men may better understand the significance of the symbols embodied in the characters and actions of the tales. At first, the light is clear and strong: "Noon, the gold sun of hens and aldermen/ Inked black as India, on the green ground,/ Our patterns . . ." In the bright gold light, our materialistic wishes, "homely, mercenary, magnified," are fulfilled in bold strokes, as in those happy stories about the farmer whose deal in turnips tricked the devil (l. 54); or the tale of the brave little tailor (l. 55) whose expression "Seven at one blow!" he parlayed into a kingdom complete with a royal bride. The next two tales in Jarrell's list are humorous, but have unhappy endings for the animal characters. "The Cat and the Mouse in Partnership" and "The Louse and the Flea" begin with visions of unusual domestic amity, but cat and mouse finally quarrel over the lard which the cat has eaten, and the mouse subsequently follows the lard into the cat's gullet; while both the louse and the flea perish. These tales are amusing only if we laugh at the absurdity of the animals and do not identify with them.

The scene changes at evening, when the sun is a "poor light." "Sun of misers and of mermen, the last foolish gold/ Of soldiers wandering through the country with a crutch . . ." Seen in conjunction with the "horned sooty lantern patched with eyes" (a possible image of the moon) the soldier suggests, as Sister M. Bernetta Quinn has noted, the story of "The Blue Light," but several other of the Grimms' stories, such as "The Nose," also concern poor old soldiers. "The Blue Light," though not golden, is a wishing lamp, and through it the soldier's wishes come true.

Lines 65 to 81 present a vision of "the great world," where "everything is just the same" in men's minds as it is in the fantasy they recognize as fantasy, the world of the tales. Here God is the magical father figure, an "uncomfortable overseer." In this world, not soldiers but palmers wander and "freeze to bliss," a transformation similar to that of being turned to stone in the *Märchen*. The magic implements of their world, "splinters of the Cross, the Ark, the Tree," [18] put out the purgatorial fires. The last line of the section, "As the circles spread, the stone hopes like a child," seems to be commentary on the preceding lines as well as upon those which follow. The idea is that, as we see the interrelations of the various patterns of dream, fairy tale, religion, and the world of things, we hope more and more for fulfillment of our wishes. In "Yorinda and Yoringel," the young men made into stone by the witch of the castle presumably hope for release back into life, a kind of resurrection.

---

[18] This tree seems to be the Tree of Life which God planted in the Garden of Eden; it is associated with other mythic trees, such as that whose bough protected Aeneas in Hades.

A common form our generalized wishes take in the stories is the motif of the weak or simple-minded but good protagonist who is rewarded for his helpfulness or generosity (l. 88). Jarrell found the motif especially appealing, and had used it in "Children Selecting Books . . . ." There are helpful animals (l. 83), also, in several stories, notably "The Two Brothers," in which the animals aid in the rescue of the dead brother. In the poem "the beasts who ruled by their god, Death,/ Bury the son with their enchanted thanks/ For the act outside their possibility" seem more to be transformed humans, burying Christ, and hoping for something beyond animal capacity: resurrection. The reward is always in view: "When had it mattered whom we helped? It always paid." In another version, we know the promise as "Give, and it shall be given unto you" (Luke 6:38).

The two concluding sections of the poem, lines 89 to 102 and 103 to 112, focus directly upon the nature of wishes, at first in general, then with specific reference to Hansel. The primeval wish is simply that the wishes be fulfilled. Thus Jarrell writes of the dead man on whose broken heart was found the motto, "*The wish has made it so./* Or so he wished." Among the wishes most frequently fulfilled in fairy tales is the wish for food; The Magic Pot, The Cloth Be Laid (which appears in several stories), and the Gingerbread House of the Hansel story are all marvelous sources of food and drink. Jarrell emphasizes the artificiality of their fictional fulfillment in his image of the platter "appliquéd with meals for parents, scraps for children, gristle/ For Towser, a poor dog." The wish for a magical means of sustenance is easily understood, but other motifs are less clear. Why would one wish for a "broom that, fretting for a master, swept a world;/ The spear that weeping for a master, killed a child"?[19] Sexual interpretations readily suggest themselves, but the second of the two images also implies a desire for conquest and dominance, one of the wishes that causes the greatest sufferings in the real world, as does the desire for gold, alluded to in line 96. These wishes are to be fulfilled not because of the "wisdom" or "virtue" of the wisher, but through "Grace," a purely free supernatural action, which Jarrell sardonically compares to the remembering of children in their parents' wills: "The son remembered in the will of God." But the "will of God" is as mysterious as wishes and some-

19 Neither of these motifs appears in any of the Grimms' tales.

times as disappointing to the one who depends upon it. Still other fairy tale motifs are hard to interpret as wishes. The ever-truthful magic glass (1. 99) shows a scene of death, with the ruler of the dead a twin (or Shadow) of the speaker. Although we must finally recognize death, we try to avoid seeing our own death; we prefer "somewhere else, someone else."

In the middle of line 102 Jarrell shifts abruptly back to the figure of Hansel, who now becomes the protagonist of "The Fisherman and His Wife," wishing to the flounder—a fish, and as such the traditional symbol of Christ and of eternal life and fertility. His wish is not for anything concrete, as were the wife's wishes in the tale, but the basic wish for fulfillment of wishes. In the story and in dreams, "it was granted." Hansel undergoes another swift metamorphosis, to become, apparently, his own father, "powerless/ To shelter your own children from the cold/ Or quiet their bellies with the thinnest gruel." The passage reminds us that Hansel has already been identified with Christ earlier in the poem. Some of Christ's most impressive miracles have to do with the feeding of multitudes from the simplest, most meager supplies—five loaves and seven fishes, for example—and in the most basic sense these miracles are wish-fulfillments: "the son remembered in the will of God." In the real world "Hansel" is ironically powerless to repeat the miracle of his wishful avatar, Christ, or of the fairy tale Hansel, who finally got home with all the witch's wealth and lived happily ever after.

What, then, should we have learned from our tales, tales which are finally not about "beasts" or faraway "kingdoms," or even "their Lord"—Christ, or whatever miraculous God we please—but of "our own hearts," the source of all the dreams and wishes that satisfy our deepest psychic needs? At the last, because of our mortality, the kingdom we seek is "the realm of death." Jarrell asserts that the tales (both *Märchen* and religious myth) show us what our wishes most truly are: "to change, to change!": that is, to transcend our sufferings through metamorphosis. The tales show this in various ways; some of them simply utilize metamorphosis in their plots. Christ changes his mortality for immortality. The most significant and universal kind of change the tales embody is the change from real life, which has death at the end of the story, to art, in which the protagonists live happily ever after. Though they become kings, they need not rule (l. 112) and they need not die, either. That is the desired state: to exist in comfort and freedom; but to attain this state, one must certainly change.

The poem "The Märchen" is closely related to several earlier Jarrell poems, in particular to the library poems "Children Selecting Books . . ." (December, 1941) and "The Carnegie Library . . ." (Winter, 1944), both of which examine the relevance of myths and folk tales to real life and conclude that it has to do with "change," a transformation that makes possible the fulfillment of men's deep need to feel secure in their own existence. In the earlier poems, the distinction between men's lives and the "lives" in the stories is kept clear, but in "The Märchen" one merges with the other, as in a dream. The Hansel of line 102 may be mostly a storybook character, but Hansel of line 105 is a man, any man "too powerless/ To shelter [his] own children from the cold," who once upon a time told or heard and understood a story about two hungry children lost in a forest.

The lesson of "The Märchen," "to change, to change," is one that people are never able to learn, for change means transcendence, and it is finally only in dreams, stories, and mythology that men can transcend their sufferings, their mortality. Because these imaginative modes are the only means of transcendence, they are necessary to men's inner lives, for through them, men find the fulfillment denied, except sporadically, by the real world.

The quest for transcendence is at the heart of the poetry of *Losses*, and it emerges even more strongly in *The Seven-League Crutches* and *The Woman at the Washington Zoo*. The quest is central in such important war poems as "The Rising Sun" and "Burning the Letters." In "A Camp in the Prussian Forest," and "Jews at Haifa," the failure of men's transcendental myths is cause for bitter irony. "Eighth Air Force" puts the freeing of conscience as prerequisite to transcendence, but innocence and terrible guilt stand in equal poise in that poem, where no rationalization will effect release. "The Dead in Melanesia" and "The Subway from New Britain to the Bronx" admit that the only change is that of life for death; in "The Dead Wingman" and "In the Ward: The Sacred Wood" dreams are attempts at transcendence, but they fail. Several of the civilian poems of *Losses*, beginning with "The Märchen" (1946), develop the theme of change, and "Lady Bates" (1948), one of the latest poems in the volume, expresses it in traditional but ironically used images of Christianity. In the humorous dramatic monologue, "Money," a rascally millionaire of the Muckraker era finds transcendence of a sort in philanthropy!

In general, the poems of *Losses* can be seen to continue and develop the attitudes and subjects of *Little Friend, Little Friend*. There are remnants of the familiar Jarrellian outrage at the senselessness of men's suffering, the insistence that they recognize and accept their own guilt as actors in the drama of "the States" and their Gods. However, the increasing emphasis on the search for transcendence in *Losses* is a logical and necessary response to the enormous frustration embodied in the war poems of *Little Friend* . . . , in which the soldiers are merely "things" used up in the warfare of the States. Even though the quest for transcendence is never successful except for a moment, in dreams or stories, it opens up a little light upon the terribly dark and deterministic world of the earlier volume.

In the later civilian poems of *Losses*, such as "The Breath of Night," with its echoes of Hardy in the last stanza, or "A Country Life," with its subject and idiom of Frost, Jarrell seems to be moving toward readjustment to the peacetime world. But in the poems most characteristic of his own distinctive work, such as "Lady Bates," the psychic war still goes on, proving the truth of Jarrell's own comment, in reviewing some war poetry in *Partisan Review* in 1945, that "the real war poets are always war poets, peace or any time." [20] Lady Bates, like the soldiers, suffers and dies a victim of her society, of her state, and only Death shows pity or tenderness towards her; even he teases a little. It is such lostlings of the great world—whether soldiers or children or prisoners of mind or matter—that Jarrell found and cared for and wrote about. He made their war his, and fought it with such weapons of wit and language as were his finest gifts. Even though in poem after poem he found transcendence beyond his characters' abilities, he never dropped the quest, pursuing his goal patiently, like Hansel following his pebbles home again.

[20] Randall Jarrell, "Poetry in War and Peace," *Partisan Review*, XII (Winter, 1945), 122.

4 · The Seven-League Crutches

WHERE THE POEMS of *Losses* may be generally classified as elegiac, those of *The Seven-League Crutches* are meditative, although they do not belong to any formal school of disciplined meditation, such as that of seventeenth century English devotional poetry. They are meditative in the way they fix upon their subjects, methodically examining one aspect after another in an attempt to reach some new understanding. In tone and attitude, too, the poems of *The Seven-League Crutches* are meditative; many are hesitant, even slow as they explore the situations and characters. There is scarcely a trace of the stridency of the war poems, and if some of the poems develop comic aspects of their subjects, they are still basically serious. In some poems, especially the longest, "The Night Before the Night Before Christmas," it is as if Jarrell had come back to unfinished business, left pending when the war broke out, and returned to in a less imperative time.

The interest in German folk tales, so pronounced in *Losses*, continued to occupy Jarrell in the late forties and early fifties; approximately a quarter of the poems in *The Seven-League Crutches* use folk or fairy-tale elements, including one of Andersen's tales, "The Little Sea Maid" (in "A Soul") as well as the familiar Grimms' tales, "Hansel and Gretel" (in "A Quilt Pattern" and "The Night Before the Night Before Christmas"), and the "Hawthorn Blossom" (in "Sleeping Beauty: Variation of the Prince" and "La Belle au Bois Dormant"), and snatches of other tales and lore, as in the vampire poem, "Hohensalzburg: Fantastic Variations on a Theme of Romantic Character." Other literary sources are prominent as subjects: *Robinson Crusoe* in "The Island," the Book of Jonah in "Jonah" various literary and operatic sources in "An English Garden in Austria," *Eugene Onegin* and others in "A Girl in a Library," Goethe's *Faust* in "A Conversation with the Devil," and *The Odyssey* in "A Rhapsody on Irish Themes." "Nollekens" is a poem constructed almost entirely of biographical details from an eighteenth century source, while "The Knight, Death, and the Devil" is a poetic recreation and commentary on Dürer's famous engraving. More than half the poems in the volume, in fact, have literary or other artistic sources used not incidentally but as essential to the subject of the poem. I would stress the point that literature was not a new subject for Jarrell. His earliest poems were full of literary references, and several treat literary sources directly, as in the two early library poems and "The Memoirs of Glückel of Hameln." For such a copious and thoughtful reader as Jarrell, it must have been only natural to explore the relations of art to life. Musical sources, too, appeared in some of the early poems. However, the strong interest in opera and the visual arts seems to coincide with Jarrell's first trip to Europe, in the summer of 1948, when he taught at the Salzburg Seminar in American Civilization. Like so many other Americans, before and since, Randall Jarrell was fascinated by the cultural feast provided by Europe for the eyes, ears, and mind of the visitor. The impact of subsequent European tours is recorded in *The Woman at the Washington Zoo*, *The Lost World*, and in the "Last Poems" section of the *Complete Poems*. It may be, too, that Jarrell's sensibility, so exacerbated by the war and its aftermath, and perhaps personal problems as well, sought its own escape into the safer, more satisfying world of art. As in the use of *Märchen* and myth in several of the *Losses* poems, Jarrell's reliance on literary sources springs from a compulsion to understand the meaning and value of art to human existence. His choice of sources tends to focus on common themes, and the resultant poems are fundamentally critical and philosophical responses to the themes and imagery of the source works. The responses come through the process of meditation.

There are several types of poetic meditation represented in *The Seven-League Crutches*, ranging from the very simple recreation and reshaping of the subject, as in "Jonah" or "The Knight, Death, and the Devil," to those which make substantial changes in the original story, as in "Sleeping Beauty: Variation of the Prince" or "The Island." Still others bring together many disparate elements and seek to perceive relationships, as in "An English Garden in Austria" and "The Night Before the Night Before Christmas." In the poems without literary sources, an individual meditates on his personal experience and attempts to come to terms with it, as in "Terms" and "Seele im Raum." In discussing Jarrell's accomplishment in *The Seven-League Crutches*, I will examine several poems of each type.

One of the simplest reshapings of a literary source, but a subtle poem, is "Jonah"; all but seven of its forty lines are quoted or very slightly altered from the four brief chapters of the Old Testament Book of Jonah. All Jarrell did was to edit and unify the already poetic material of the King James translation by having the whole take place in the mind of the recalcitrant Jonah. From his vantage point outside Nineveh, Jarrell's Jonah remembers his descent into the ocean. The second and third stanzas are a collation of phrases mainly from chapter 2 of the Book of Jonah, and the material of the remaining stanzas comes from the last two chapters. Only line 35, "And I wept, to hear its dead leaves rattle," is wholly Jarrell's addition, while lines 34 and 36 to 40 are almost exact quotations from the last two verses of Jonah 4. The poem does two things to the original biblical story: it emphasizes the poetic (psalmic) qualities of Jonah's symbolic death (stanza two, Jonah 2:3,5,6) by putting his prayer into verse lines and condensing it; and it brings into clearer focus Jonah's moral struggle. Jonah is a prophet against his own will from beginning to end. He is angry, in the Bible and in the poem, because of God's mercy in saving Nineveh, notwithstanding his own rescue from the whale. When the king of Nineveh announces his intention to repent, Jonah knows that the Lord will be merciful and will not carry out the punishment He had Jonah foretell. Jonah's response is such intense disgust that he wishes to die. In the poem, as in the Bible, Jonah's relation to the gourd that God "prepared" is ambivalent. He is glad for the shade of the gourd's leaves, which seem to soothe the anger in his heart, but when God destroys the gourd, Jonah's pity—partly self-pity—again is expressed as anger: "I do well to be angry even unto death," he tells God. Neither the Bible nor the poem attempts to give Jonah's response when God shows Jonah the discrepancy between his pity for the gourd, with which he does identify, and his lack of pity for the six-score thousand persons of Nineveh, with whom he should identify. So far, the story tells what we might expect of God's way with a reluctant servant. But the last, curiously abrupt phrases of the Book of Jonah throw strange light back over the whole. Jarrell renders the sentence,

> "And should I not spare Nineveh, that city
> Wherein are more than six-score thousand persons
> Who cannot tell their left hand from their right;
> And also much cattle?"

The sentence is grammatically peculiar in the King James Bible, as in Jarrell, because there is no modifying clause describing the cattle (livestock, generally) to parallel the one that modifies persons; moreover, the persons are grammatically equated with the cattle. God points out Jonah's lack of compassion in the analogy with the gourd, but He also implies that He wishes to save the livestock, apparently appealing to Jonah's sense of husbandry or, more crudely, economy! Because the poem, like its source, ends without further comment, the reader is left to moralize or not, as he wishes.

"Nollekens" takes a larger range of material, a biography or memoir of the English sculptor Nollekens, written by his contemporary, "the little Smith," [1] and picks out amusing and telling details, exactly the sort of thing the average reader remembers from such a book. Like "The Memoirs of Glückel of Hameln," "Nollekens" is about a self-centered but curiously representative man of his age. Jarrell brings together the random details into a kind of essential picture of Nollekens, which pieces itself together until the reader—the poet—recognizes the distinctive and disreputable little figure in his mind's eye: "I nod acquiescingly: 'Why, it is Nollekens, the Sculptor.' "

In "The Knight, Death, and the Devil," Jarrell develops the method of "Jonah" and "Nollekens" in a significant way. Although he had used a work of art as a starting point for a poem previously, in "The Head of Wisdom" (*Blood for a Stranger*), there it was merely the subject, the head of Beethoven, and not the treatment of the original that interested him. Here, and in the superb "The Bronze David of Donatello" in *The Woman at the Washington Zoo*, it is the artist's vision in the creation that Jarrell meditates upon. In the note in

---

[1] Jarrell's note, Jarrell, *The Complete Poems*, 34.

Selected Poems, Jarrell calls the poem simply "a description" of Dürer's engraving.

As a description of the figures in the 1513 engraving, the poem is exceptionally perceptive, but if that description were the whole of the poem, we should consider it merely an exercise. The poem does not substitute for the picture, of course; it does not even attempt to place the figures in Dürer's striking symbolic setting, but simply moves from one figure to the next, as a kind of guide to understanding Dürer's allegory. Instead of beginning, as the eye does, with the classically idealized equestrian figure that takes up the great center of the design, Jarrell sees the grotesque subsidiary figures first, leading up climactically to the mounted knight.

As he enumerates the details, Jarrell infers the allegory: "Cowhorn-/ crowned, shockheaded, cornshuck-bearded,/ Death is a scarecrow . . ." The "boar-snouted" devil is "a scapegoat aged into a steer. . . ./ His eye a ring inside a ring inside a ring/ That leers up joyless, vile, in meek obscenity." Dürer's conception of the devil as the knight's pikeman, with an absurd conglomeration of monstrous animal characteristics—a traditional concept brilliantly organized and realized—is recognized by the poet as morally appropriate: "Flesh to flesh, he bleats/ The herd back to the pit of being."

The portrait of the knight is a succession of simple details: the armor, the lance decked out with "the bush of that old fox"—the devil; the dog, symbol of faithfulness; the horse, "pacing . . . in ceremonious magnificence." He is a prototypal knight: but with such attendants?

> So, companioned so, the knight moves through this world.
> The fiend moos in amity, Death mouths, reminding . . .

In Dürer's picture, Death looks at the Knight, and the Devil looks out toward the viewer, but the Knight's eyes, mostly hidden by his helmet, appear to be directed ahead and somewhat downward, toward the lower left corner of the sheet. What he looks at, if anything, is not in the picture. It is this look which catches Jarrell's fancy; the knight "has no glance/ To spare for them but looks past steadily/ At—at—/ a man's look completes itself." The unfinished phrase, the repeated preposition without its object, are typical Jarrell techniques. The reader, frustrated in his expectation of being told just what the knight looks at, is thrown forcibly upon the explanation, "a man's look completes itself," which suggests that the look is actually directed inward, that the knight may be seeing something other than what his eyes appear to rest upon. This possibility is a modern response to the Renaissance work, one justified but not demanded by Dürer; it further implies that the knight's studied indifference to his companions may be evidence of his profound awareness of them.

The last verse paragraph of Jarrell's poem comments upon Dürer's allegorical method, then interprets the figure of the knight. The subsidiary figures (and the setting, Jarrell might have added) are

> The death of his own flesh, set up outside him;
> The flesh of his own soul, set up outside him—

Although he is aware of these things which belong to him, like an existential hero he perseveres in his course; "his face is firm/ In resolution, in absolute persistence." Dürer seems to be saying, through the face of his knight, "*A man does what he must.*" But, as Jarrell "reads" the picture, "The body underneath it says, 'I am.'" The human body in mail, but also the splendid body of the horse, full of its muscular vitality, assert their being, imposing themselves over the puny, decrepit nag and figure of Death, and the grotesque ineptitude of the Devil. It is interesting that Jarrell chose to end on this note of relative triumph, for a Renaissance interpretation of the picture would more likely have been an application of the medieval concept that the strength and vitality of the man are mocked and undercut by the ridiculous monsters. The logic of the poem convinces us, however, that Dürer's vision must have been what Jarrell articulates.

Another type of simple meditative poem which, like "The Knight, Death, and the Devil," takes its cue from a work of art is "The Face." There, an episode from *Der Rosenkavalier* inspires Jarrell's poem, an episode which is itself a meditation. Near the end of Act I, after the hairdresser and the other attendants have gone, leaving the Marschallin alone, she reflects upon the glimpse of herself she has caught in the mirror, an old woman. She sadly looks forward to the time when people will call her "die alte Frau, die alte Marschallin." Jarrell uses this phrase as epigraph to the poem. In a sense we may take the poem as a free variation of the Marschallin's meditation in von Hofmannsthal's libretto; but it is completely generalized and universalized. Not the Marschallin, but Everywoman says the poem. As he has understood the allegorical meaning of Dürer's engraving, Jarrell also fixes the broader significance of the Marschallin's reverie. The poem goes beyond the Marschallin's rueful recognition, which for her is intimately bound up in her love affair with Octavian. Jarrell's speaker is not concerned with the possible ending of love, but with the change which overtakes and alters the outward appearance while inside one is still the same, or so one would like to think.

The poem uses the flat, colloquial statement characteristic of Jarrell's later style. One of its striking qualities is the complete absence of imagery.[2] Its poetic impact resides in the repetition of words and the shifting of tenses, both of which bring a new perspective; not a little of the poem's effect comes from its silences:

> You are, and you say: I am—
> And you were . . . I've been too long.
> . . . .
> I thought: If nothing happens . . .
> And nothing happened.
> Here I am.
> But it's not *right*.

"The Face" prefigures the theme of several of the poems of *The Lost World*, notably "Next Day" and "The One Who Was Different." "The Face," because of its exaggerated simplicity, is even more striking than these later poems.

The four poems, "Jonah," "Nollekens," "The Knight, Death, and the Devil" and "The Face," represent four different, but very simple approaches to meditative poetry. All are relatively short, for the simplicity of approach, a deliberate strategy, works partly through

---

2 John Crowe Ransom, who has always insisted on imagery as the *sine qua non* of poetry, curiously enough admires "The Face" very much. See Ransom, "The Rugged Way of Genius," in Lowell, Taylor, *et al., Randall Jarrell, 1914–1965*, 173.

surprise and concentration. All four of the poems have subjects from other works of art, and in a sense are critical responses to these subjects. Another kind of response to a literary subject is that which changes the dénouement, or even the entire plot, or the nature of the characters. Jarrell had experimented with this response before in the narrative poem "Orestes at Tauris," in which he gave a "truer" ending than Euripides had to Orestes' troubled life.

Just such a poem is "The Sleeping Beauty: Variation of the Prince," in which Jarrell proposes a different ending to the Grimms' tale "Hawthorn Blossom," also known as "Briar Rose," or, in Perrault's elegant version, "La Belle au Bois Dormant." In the story, the princess along with all the castle is awakened by the prince at the end of the hundred years' sleep. In Jarrell's "variation" the prince does not awaken the princess with his kiss, but falls asleep beside her, chastely, with Death's sword between them. In the last two stanzas the prince looks forward to the end of time, which he rejects even as he considers it. "When the world ends—it will never end—"; and "When they come for us—no one will ever come—." When, or if, Death does come to claim her, he too will fall asleep like a child listening to a bedtime story, and the story will have no end.

> I shall whisper, "Wait, wait! . . . She is asleep."
> I shall whisper, gazing, up to the gaze of the hunter,
> Death, and close with the tips of the dust of my hand
> The lids of the steady—
>   Look, He is fast asleep!

Where the original story clearly embodies a wish to transcend death, Jarrell's poem is a curious, ambivalent combination of the Freudian death wish—for a return to a permanently undisturbed state—with the wish for transcendence of death. The prince rejects sexual satisfaction with the princess by laying between them Death's sword, and he regards the long, dusty sleep as "the last long world/ That you had found; that I have kept." In the poem the deathlike nature of the sleep is characterized by images of dust, rust, and cobwebs, and by the gentle, lulling rhythms. The "Variation of the Prince" is at once a recognition that the princess will not awake and a wish for the peace of Death without its horrors.

"La Belle au Bois Dormant" is another poem that uses the Sleeping Beauty story, but in a grotesque way, for the beauty is a woman who has been murdered and dismembered by her lover. The "wood" is a trunk left at a railway station. The poem is ingenious in working out the basic metaphor, linking the sordid crime with the haunting beauty of the tale, but it finally comes to seem *only* clever, rather than a meaningful vision of a lonely death without transcendence.

Still another kind of variation of a source is the very striking short poem "A Soul." This poem was first published six months after "The Sleeping Beauty . . ." and just before "Hohensalzburg . . ." in the spring of 1949, and it has thematic concerns in common with both. Sister M. Bernetta Quinn, in *The Metamorphic Tradition in Modern Poetry*, regards the poem as a simple "happy ending" for Andersen's poignant and beautiful tale, "The Little Sea Maid," [3] but I believe there is more involved in Jarrell's meditation of this theme. In Andersen's story, the little mermaid trades her beautiful voice to the sea witch in return for the legs that hurt her with knifelike pains, in order to be with the mortal prince whom she loves. In "A Soul," the mermaid retains her fishy tail; the "I" of the poem strokes "the scales of [her] breast" as he speaks with her, and she is not voiceless, but quite able to speak to him. The implied story behind "A Soul" is in many ways more like that of several of the Child ballads, in which sea people's earthly lovers abandon them and return to the land. Jarrell does use the conception of the soul from the Andersen story, however. There, the sea maid attempts to win an immortal soul by winning the love of a prince. When he marries a real woman, she expects to dissolve in sea foam; but because of her great devotion, she is given another chance to win a soul through a three-hundred-year period of service to men, in the form of a spirit of the air. In Jarrell's poem, the sea maid refers to the man as her soul, and apparently desires to be united with him.

The poem consists mainly of a brief conversation which implies a reunion between the mermaid and her mortal lover. He has returned to the water's edge after an absence, during which she has been wait-

---

[3] Quinn, *The Metamorphic Tradition*, 172. Jarrell returned to the idea of a mermaid with an earthly lover in his beautiful and amusing children's book, *The Animal Family* (New York, 1965).

ing, for she begins, "Thou art here once more." She is delighted by his being "warm and dry as the sun" and by his legs: "Yes, here is one,/ Here is the other . . . *Legs* . . ./And they move so?" One recalls Andersen's little sea maid and her fascination with the sun and with legs. (She is told that men regard the fish tail as ugly; it represents to man the limitations of the "lower" orders of nature, hence, of death.)

The man's response hardly matches the mermaid's joy: "I stroke the scales of your breast, and answer:/'Yes, as you know.'" Since he has come back, the reader assumes that he has come voluntarily, or out of need for her, but he does not seem happy about it. In the last two quatrains the mermaid reproaches him gently for having stayed away so long. "Many times I had thought thee lost . . . forever," she says in each of the stanzas, first to her "poor love," then to her "poor soul." Although we might be content to accept this as a happy ending to the story of the little mermaid, I believe we should first consider further the symbolism of the original story and of the ballads.

The little sea maid is a creature of nature; like all of the Order of Nature in the medieval-Renaissance tradition, she has only a mortal soul; in Andersen, only if she gets the love of a man can she share in his immortal soul. The sea maid wants his love, and the transcendence that comes with love; otherwise she would presumably rather become sea foam at once than live out the three hundred years of service once her lover has married another. Though she does not get the human love she needs, because of her own devotion she is promised eventual transcendence.

In Jarrell's poem, however, it is the soul, embodied in the man, which seems compelled to return to the water, to the mermaid, to the Order of Nature, to find fulfillment. The mermaid, in this instance, seems the agent of Grace or transcendence through joy, while the soul, the "poor love," is "lost" without her, and seeks her out. The man's return to the water and to the sea maid must recall, to anyone who has read the opening passages of Jung's "Archetypes of the Collective Unconscious," Jung's parable of the nixie.

All those who have had an experience [of searching in the unconscious] will know that the treasure lies in the depths of the water [the "commonest" symbolic representation of the unconscious, according to Jung] and will try to salvage it. Whoever looks into the water sees his own image, but behind it living creatures soon loom up; fishes, presumably, harmless dwellers of the deep—harmless, if only the lake were not haunted. They are water beings of a peculiar sort. Sometimes a nixie gets into the fisherman's net, a female half-human fish. . . . The nixie is an even more instinctive version of a magical being whom I call the *anima*. . . . An alluring nixie from the dim bygone is today called an "erotic fantasy," and she may complicate our psychic life in a most painful way.[4]

Jung's name for the archetypal image symbolized in the nixie is *anima*, the Latin word for *soul*, but he means by the image, basically, the urge to life, sexual and natural, which attracts the civilized, self-controlled persona. In Freudian terms, the nixie might represent the id, while the man symbolizes the ego, which must come to terms with the primal urges of the id. In Jarrell's poem, it is the mermaid who embodies life and joy, while the "poor soul" seems listless and empty without her. Andersen's story uses, and implicitly criticizes, the Christian tradition of the soul, for in his story, too, the mermaid's love is stronger and wiser than that of the prince. Jarrell's poem uses the more congenial tradition of modern psychology, and his "story" ends with the union of the lovers, who seem to represent prudent, intellectual nature in the landsman and sensation and feeling in the mermaid. "A Soul" is superficially a simple poem; its structure is lucid and brief, its choice of detail restrained but effective. Nonetheless, it suggests a great deal about an important human concern, the need for joyousness in love.

The ambivalence with which civilized man accepts the instinctual forces of his nature is again treated in "Hohensalzburg: Fantastic Variations on a Theme of Romantic Character." Here, in contrast to "A Soul," but like "The Sleeping Beauty . . . ," the man's choice of love is a kind of living death, for his lover is not a gentle sea maid, but a vampire. The "Briar Rose" story plays an important role in "Hohensalzburg . . . ," for the girl-ghost is explicitly identified with the Sleeping Beauty in lines 65 to 76, and as in the poem "The Sleeping Beauty

---

4 *The Basic Writings of C. G. Jung,* trans. and ed. by Violet S. de Laszlo (New York: Modern Library, 1958), 308–309.

. . ." the man comes to sleep with her forever. "Hohensalzburg . . ." is much longer and more complicated than the earlier poem. While the former addresses itself exclusively to a peculiar kind of death wish in a reinterpretation of a single story, "Hohensalzburg . . ." uses a multiplicity of folk materials in a poem that shifts its narrative ground as abruptly as a dream. The death wish again unites with the wish for transcendence; what the speaker and his ghost-lover both want is something, a word, that will do "forever," but the man also desires and accepts death from the ghost, a vampire who sucks away his blood, so that they may be united in death as spirits of the earth.

As Sister M. Bernetta Quinn has noted, the ghost is actually one with the man: "She is really his life; somberly, she adds to his voicing of this truth that she is also his death." [5] As in "A Soul," the super-natural female is part of the man's own personality, but she now lures him to death, not life.

Along with several others, the poem was inspired by Jarrell's stay in Austria, at the Salzburg Seminar in American Civilization, in the summer of 1948, very near the supposedly haunted castle of Hohen-salzburg. The speaker of the poem, apparently a young man, begins by introducing his awareness of certain unknown spirits of the wood, and his frustration that he cannot understand "a final word:/ Pure, yearning, unappeasable—" which the wood repeats perpetually.

The girl is introduced as a "dweller of the Earth," and her past is briefly recounted; she may not have always been a spirit. As a girl she had "run, all evening, by the shore/ Naked, searching for [her] dress upon the sand," and visited each evening an old woman who told her "What you do will do,/ But not forever . . ." The girl thinks that a husband and children "*will do, but not forever.*" Her wish is not for beauty, but invisibility (l. 30), which seems to be a wish to escape the appearance, and hence the reality, of aging and death.

The man, waking at night in the shadow of the castle, feels her presence but cannot see her, since she has become, as she wished, invisible. He believes at first that she is "only a ghost," but unlike other German ghosts, which are "harsh clumsy things . . . [that] change/ Men into things, things into things." Lines 56 to 61 recount

[5] Quinn, *The Metamorphic Tradition*, 177.

a series of metamorphoses which at first recalls the Grimms' tale, "Fundevogel," as Sister Bernetta has pointed out, but also "Lover Roland." In these tales, the metamorphoses save the two pairs of lovers from witches who seek their lives. Metamorphosis to stone, perhaps a symbol of art, has already been mentioned in "Hohensalzburg . . . ," and metamorphosis is actually a central thematic concern. The last image in the series of metamorphoses, in which stars "set in the antlers of an iron deer" are seen as former sleepers "wandering through the wood," comes not from a story, but, according to Sister Bernetta, from an actual iron deer having gilded stars in its antlers, "which stood at the entrance to the park of Leopoldschloss where Jarrell stayed during the time that he taught at the Salzburg Institute." [6]

Vampirism is introduced as a theme in the same passage: "A ghost wants blood;/ And it will do—but not forever." At this point the speaker sees the girl as the Sleeping Beauty and promises to stay with her forever. The details are similar enough to suggest that perhaps "Hohensalzburg . . ." grew out of "The Sleeping Beauty: Variation of the Prince." The ghost's response to his fantasy is that he must be asleep when he speaks so, but she cannot help going on to reveal her dark intentions:

> *I shall come to you there asleep,*
> *I shall take you and . . .*
> > Tell me.
> *No, no, I shall never.*
> > Tell me.
> *You must not know.*
> > Tell me.
> *I—I shall kiss your throat.*
>
> My throat?
>
> *There, it is only a dream.*
> *I shall not so—I shall never so.*

But in fact she does suck away his blood, and he awakes at the moment of death to express not horror but desire: "I said: 'I want

[6] *Ibid.*, 175.

you.' " Moreover, as in "The Sleeping Beauty . . . ," sexual union is rejected, this time by the ghost, who says she is too young: "*You must not so./ I am only a girl.*" In the *Poetry* version of "Hohensalzburg . . ." (April, 1949), there is explicit identification of the girl with the man's own past, now dead, sucking away his "blood"—his life—into the earth.

The following section of the poem (ll. 119–39) relates the ritual search for and capture of the vampire through the utterance of the greeting, "*Grüss Gott.*" The ghost is killed anew, boiled to death and served up in a forbidden "black-pudding." The final section of the poem (ll. 139–62) describes the transformations the pair will undergo: stars in the antlers of the iron deer, "but not forever." The girl-ghost insists, "In the end we wake from everything," but the man still needs and wants the "one word" he has not understood; it is "the one spell [that] turns above us like the stars." He concludes that, "at the last, all these are one,/ We also are forever one:/ A dweller of the Earth, invisible."

Although, considering its full title, the poem may to some extent be thought of as an elaborate, fantastical joke, like "The Sleeping Beauty . . ." and "A Soul" it also demands serious attention as a meditation on a psychological truth. To grasp its full import, we need to see it in the context of those earlier poems about death in *Losses*: "Burning the Letters," "The Dead in Melanesia," "The Subway from New Britain to the Bronx." In those poems death is confronted naturalistically; the sea and the earth, take back into their elements the bodies of the dead. Unless one mythologizes, as the wife in "Burning the Letters" does, there is no separable spirit. The islands in "The Dead in Melanesia" are technically personified, but they are limited to a single human trait: indifferent acceptance; and their action, the dissolution of the bodies left there, is the essence of impersonality. The dead in these earlier poems neither desire nor fear death, they are simply annihilated, victims of war, of "the great Necessity."

In "The Sleeping Beauty . . ." and "Hohensalzburg . . . ," a living person contemplates his death. In both poems death is envisioned as transformed life. In the first it is an eternal sleep; in the second it takes a multiplicity of forms: a stone maiden, china roses in a chandelier, a swan, gilt stars in the antlers of an iron deer, ghosts, a vampire, dwellers of the Earth. There is no dissolution, but there is also no real transcendence. The dead remain on earth, taking forms other than human or becoming invisible. Death in each case is associated with a young woman, and love seems an important force, but sexual union is overtly rejected. As in "A Soul," the female "spirits" seem part of the male speaker, not separate individuals.

While the sleeping princess merely lies passive beside the prince, the ghost-child sucks away the lifeblood from her lover, a rather interesting substitute for sexual consummation. As "The Sleeping Beauty . . ." treats a kind of sublimated death wish, "Hohensalzburg . . ." does also, exploring simultaneously the folklore of transformation and ghosts in the search for something "that will do . . . forever." The poem also involves a need to come to terms with the earth, with the forest, the world of things: "the others." Like "The Märchen," "Hohensalzburg . . ." inquires into the relevance of traditional tales in human psychology.

"The Black Swan" is another *Seven-League Crutches* poem that investigates the death wish, this time in the context of a child's desire to join her dead sister, who has in her dream been transformed into a black swan. Sister Bernetta has dealt admirably with the different transformations that appear in the poem and has pointed out its relation to the ballet *Swan Lake*.[7] Although there seems to be no specific folk story from which Jarrell has drawn the plot of "The Black Swan," it is nonetheless a reworking of folk materials: the swan, often an image of transformation, often associated with death (as in the Swan of Tuonela); and the litttle sister who seeks to aid a sibling in distress. The poem is exceptionally beautiful in the images Jarrell creates to convey the shifting sensations of the dreaming girl, who feels that she, too, is transformed into a swan: "My legs were all hard and webbed, and the silky/ Hairs of my wings sank away like stars/ In the ripples that ran in and out of the reeds . . ." Lying in her bed, she dreams that she reaches "to the lap and hiss of the floor." Liquid and sibilant consonants enhance the predominantly long vowel sounds, an effect that underlines the soothing content of the dream, in which

---

7 *Ibid.*, 187–88. Sister Bernetta does not deal with the apparent paradox that in the ballet *Swan Lake*, Odile, the "Black Swan," is the evil double of Odette, the "Swan-princess."

there is no jarring death, only transformation into the beautiful, floating bird.

In *Selected Poems*, "The Black Swan" is included in the section called "Dream-Work"; of the five other poems in the group, four are also from *The Seven-League Crutches*. Two of these have very interesting variations on familiar stories: "The Island," which except for the last three lines is the monologue of a figure named Robinson Crusoe; and "A Quilt Pattern," in which a boy dreams the Hansel and Gretel story so that it reveals some of its latent meaning.

In "The Island," Robinson dreams of Northern Europe, of trolls and industry and a "white mistress," and perhaps war ("He is Mars," the "Snowshoefooted hare" whispers to Robinson's mistress). The dream occupies only eight of the forty-five lines, but, in a sense, the poem as a whole is a dream-worked version of the Robinson Crusoe story. Jarrell's Robinson is a dreamer, not a man of action, and his monologue deals not with his ingenuities, but with his dreams, his introspection. His island does not yield a black Friday; in fact, Robinson himself turns black, even as his beard whitens. In lieu of human company, Robinson has only a parrot and some goats: his "half-human loves." The symbolism of the island is quite interesting. It is first of all a haven, saving Robinson from death in the sea, but it is also a place of meditation, of finding oneself. As the years pass, Robinson projects himself back into Europe: the past, his active, commercial life. In his dream he speaks to his followers, dwarfs mainly—in a significant parody of Mark Anthony's funeral oration—"Friends! subjects! customers!"

Waking, he must relinquish his wish-fulfillment, which is like various fairy tales. Apparently he has at times imagined his herd as humans or half-humans, comforting his "absent life." At the end he rejects not his dreams so much as the world they represent; he says finally, "There is no Europe." In the last three lines a neutral narrative voice pictures Robinson waiting for death with his parrots and goats. They are answered by the sea "in its last thundering spray," no symbol of life, but of annihilation. Jarrell has interpreted Defoe's archetypal story not as the myth of self-reliant, ingenious man imposing himself upon alien nature with success, but as the myth of the outcast and introvert who dreams his life away. The island is a warmer, brighter version of the Sleeping Beauty's castle, and the turning away from life is accomplished less easily by Robinson than by the torpid prince.

An equally transformed story is embodied in "A Quilt Pattern," despite the fact that much of the original plot of "Hansel and Gretel" remains in the dream that forms the narrative line of the poem. As Jarrell had linked Hansel to Christ in "The Märchen" (1946), he now identifies him with Adam, tasting the forbidden fruit, the gingerbread house that represents the protagonist's mother.

The poem begins with a sick child lying in bed under a quilt made in the so-called "Tree of Life" pattern. The quilt and its pattern are not mentioned again in the poem, and the only other explicit references to the Eden story come some two-thirds of the way through the eighty-four-line poem, when the gingerbread house asks Hansel to hold out his finger, but instead of judging his flesh says "No, you don't know./ Eat a little longer." The boy thinks, "I don't know . . . No, I don't know." The food that brings knowledge is not from the Tree of Life, but the Tree of Knowledge, which is quite another matter. In the Genesis story, it is to prevent Adam and Eve from also eating of the Tree of Life after they have fallen through eating of the Tree of Knowledge that God decides to put them out of Eden. The Tree of Life may be associated with other supernatural, life-preserving plants such as holly and mistletoe or the "sacred wood" of the tree from which came the Golden Bough. The Tree of Knowledge, on the other hand, is identified with repression and death. What place have these trees, or a quilt with a stylized tree on it, in a poem about a boy who dreams he is Hansel? There are other oppositions in the poem which may be related to the ideas of life (freedom, satisfaction) and death (suppression, frustration) embodied in the emblem of the trees. The boy sees himself as having two aspects, "Good me" and "Bad me." There is a "Good mother," but also the unidentified "Other" who at the end perishes in the oven; there are health and illness; the quilt keeps one warm and also carries a talisman against evil in the soft mosaic of its pattern, but it too is stifling after a time.

In the first section the boy is seen as having spent a "long day" in his bed, and though his mother has read or told him "many tales," we can assume from his dream that he feels imprisoned by her solicitousness. As soon as he falls asleep, he begins to dream of himself as Hansel, living in the forest, his good mother dead. She is identified with a house from the first; her face is square and "scaling in the steam of a yard/ Where the cages are warmed all night for the rabbits." There are no rabbits in the Hansel story, though Jarrell elsewhere seems particularly partial to rabbits as pets ("Stalag Luft," "The Child of Courts," "The Lost World," the children's book, *The Gingerbread Rabbit*). The detail in the boy's almost classically Freudian dream may come from the nursery song, "Bye, Baby Bunting," which is alluded to more specifically later in the poem. In real life, rabbits, not boys, are kept in cages and grow fat, and they may eventually be "skinned" to wrap a baby bunting in. The boy rejects their deaths, however (l. 18). He identifies with the rabbits and dreams of eating blackberries, gathered through the wire loops of his cage.

In the following section (ll. 24–43), Hansel seems to be in the forest, far from home, but the house keeps insisting "We are home." "Good me" and "Bad me" in one feels trapped: "Sits wrapped in his coat of rabbit skin/ And looks for some little living thing/ To be kind to, for then it will help him." His identification with rabbits is part of his fear of being eaten; indeed, he sees "Bad me" as being basted, not washed, in the bathtub.

He begins eating the house (ll. 44–60), and the familiar question and response of the tale are invoked, somewhat rearranged:

> "Who is nibbling at me?" says the house.
> The dream says, "The wind,
> The heaven-born wind";
> The boy says, "It is a mouse."

A familiar English version, the one used in Humperdinck's opera, gives the witch's question as "Nibble, nibble mousekin,/ Who's nibbling at my housekin?" and the children's answer as "The wind, the wind, the heavenborn wind." Jarrell, of course, has the house-mother speak, and the boy, who cannot identify with the free wind, thinks of himself instead as a "small furry thing." When he is asked to hold out his finger, he holds out the "bone" of the house's "finger" he ate (ll.

44–45), and whether the house recognizes it in reproaching him for lack of knowledge is not clear. The association of the house with the Tree of Knowledge is not the least curious of the poem's connections. The boy is "eating" his mother, the house; that is to say, he depends on her for sustenance and pleasure, yet, as in the fairy tale, he feels that her bounty has some hidden threat or danger. Similarly, Adam wishes to enjoy the fruit of the Tree, though he is aware of its danger. Both Hansel and Adam, like "Bad me" are aggressively disobedient and deceitful in their repast, and both expect punishment: death. What Adam learns, according to Milton, is that he has sinned; he learns good by evil. What the boy might learn, if he could interpret his dream, is that he has "sinned" against his mother by secretly resenting her.

Lines 61 to 70 parallel the Hansel and Gretel story closely, though with dreamlike freedom of progression, as "Good me" or "Bad me" stands by the oven and at the proper moment pushes "something" inside, where it "scream[s] itself to death."

> . . . it is not the mouse
> Nor anything of the mouse's. Bad me, good me
> Stare into each other's eyes, and timidly
> Smile at each other: it was the Other.

In the last section of the poem, the boy half wakes to hear his mother outside the door, but does not answer her, perhaps because his rejection of her is still very close to his consciousness, perhaps even because he feels guilty about what he has just done in the dream.

That Jarrell's poem is psychologically valid gets rather surprising independent confirmation in a 1963 book, *A Psychiatric Study of Fairy Tales*, by Julius Heuscher, M.D. In his analysis of "Hansel and Gretel," Dr. Heuscher describes precisely the sort of experience which must be attributed to the child in the poem. "To the child the frightening frustrations of everyday life become so intolerable that (especially at night, namely in the less conscious realms of their personality) they long for a return towards an earlier existence, when food was unlimited, nay when to the children the house was almost equal to food and to mother, when their existence consisted of eating and of sleeping in nice little beds." [8] In the poem, the ordinary frustrations of the child's life are intensified by his enforced stay in the hot bedroom, under the quilt, and the enforced companionship of his mother, whose attentions, though kind, are associated with the oppressive illness.

Heuscher's analysis of the gingerbread house and its veiled threat is also relevant to Jarrell's interpretation of the story in the child's dream.

> But the witch had built the gingerbread house only in order to catch the children. In other words, "there is a catch" in this regression to the earliest, heavenly, childhood stage. The catch is that this regression carries with it the loss of whatever experience of physical and psychologic independence the children had acquired through their previous frustrations. This threat to their independent existence is well expressed in their gradual realization that the witch's aim was: to eat them up.
>
> Psychodynamically this realization implies a process of *projection*, since the mother does not *really* have a desire to destroy the child's identity, and since the child's fear of being gobbled up by the mother-witch is a direct result of his own wish to return to an early existence when he and the mother were still one.[9]

Jarrell's substitution of "Good me, Bad me" for the two children in the fairy tale seems psychologically true, even though neither corresponds exactly to either of the children in the tale. Both "Good me" and "Bad me" imply the child's application of his mother's standards to himself. "Good me" is the child who conforms to his mother's wishes, while "Bad me" satisfies his own impulses. Dr. Heuscher's discussion of the Hansel-Gretel dichotomy, while not precisely analogous to the poem, nonetheless helps to explain both the division of the one persona into two elements and the projection of hostility against the mother in the destruction of the witch.

> Representing the more conscious, intellectual aspect of the soul (animus), [Hansel] leads the development of the individual; but he is equally the one most immediately threatened (though the witch is planning to also eat Gretel), when the path towards individuation demands an active

[8] Julius Heuscher, *A Psychiatric Study of Fairy Tales* (Springfield, Ill., 1963), 65.
    [9] *Ibid.*

Randall Jarrell at fourteen

With Reddy Rabbit

"A shape in tennis shoes and khaki riding-pants . . ."

Under the eucalyptus with Mama

Tucson, Arizona, 1945, with "Kitten"

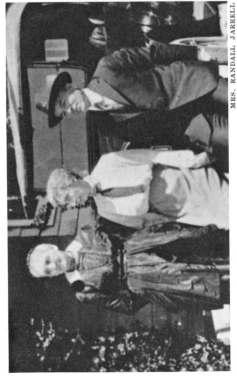

Dandeen, Mama, and Pop, Jarrell's paternal great-grandmother and grandparents

The ~~[crossed out]~~ Death of the Ball Turret Gunner

(~~Escaped from my mother~~)
From my mother's sleep I fell into the State
And I hunched in its belly till my wet fur froze;

Dream gasped   being nightmare
Dreamed   gasped for air   dreaming
we air gasped among   faster   fighters
   I   black flack, and the nightmare fighters
   woke to
              my hery—
I gasped a dream of warmth and air. of life,
I gasped for my life, and made a dream of air,
gasping for life,   made a dream of warmth —flack
And   made a dream of warmth and
to woke to black flac and the night man air fight—
When I died they washed me out of the
      turret with a hose.

From my mother's sleep I fell into the State
And I hunched in its belly till my wet fur froze;
30,000 ft from the earth, I lost the dream of life
              (gasped out) my the dream of life
And woke to black flac and the nightman's
Seven miles from earth, I —— its dream of fighters.
  or Six
When I died they washed me out of the
      turret with a hose.

I gasped through   unlearned their dream
                 learned better than of up

UNIVERSITY OF NORTH CAROLINA, GREENSBORO, LIBRARY

Manuscript page, "The Death of the Ball Turret Gunner"

Randall Jarrell, Robert Lowell, and Peter Taylor,
Greensboro, about 1948

Robert Penn Warren in Jarrell's office, University of North Carolina,
Greensboro, about 1961

The Washington Zoo, 1957

Mary and Randall Jarrell, Rock Creek Park,
Washington, D.C., 1957

With "Elfi"

Greensboro, 1964

Randall Jarrell in the Phillips Gallery, Washington, D.C., 1957

reappraisal of the earliest mother-child period. Less directly threatened, the feeling aspect of the soul (Gretel, anima) is that which can prevent the destruction of the barely emancipated individual (Hänsel-Gretel).[10]

In Jarrell's poem, it is (probably) "Bad me" who gives "the Other" a push into the oven, but even so, the child does not want to identify the thing screaming there with himself or his mother—"It was not the mouse nor anything of the mouse's"—because he cannot overtly turn upon the mother he knows consciously to be "good." His feelings are too strong, however, to allow him to accept her approach outside his door at the end of the poem.

Jarrell's analysis, or meditation, on the Hansel and Gretel story captures its psychological truth as well as any prose analysis, but it has the added power of emotional experience to move as well as to convince us. The elements of the Genesis story of the Fall enrich the experience presented in the poem by viewing the idea of growing up and separating oneself from the parent as a coming into knowledge or understanding of one's own impulses. All the elements are subsumed under the meaning of the title, "A Quilt Pattern." The "pattern" is traditional and passes through the experience of succeeding generations. It is made of scraps and pieces of the inner world. That the pattern is called the "Tree of Life" and represents a tree is significant not only in relation to the Eden story, but as a general symbol of life and growth.

The poems of *The Seven-League Crutches* in which Jarrell modifies substantially an already existing story are, like "Orestes at Tauris," fundamentally narrative in structure rather than meditative; they are the result, not the act, of meditation. However, there are several poems in the volume which do utilize a meditative structure. These include "A Rhapsody on Irish Themes," "A Game at Salzburg," "An English Garden in Austria," and "A Girl in a Library"; another, which is predominantly meditative in strategy even though it has a dialogue structure, is "A Conversation with the Devil." The long poem "The Night Before the Night Before Christmas" combines

---

[10] *Ibid.*, 68–69. Dr. Heuscher does not use the terms "animus" and "anima" in precisely Jungian senses. In Jung's formulation "Good me" and "Bad me" might represent the "self" and what Jung calls the "Shadow," or "dark side" of the persona.

narrative and meditative elements. These poems have in common a peculiarly modern aspect of meditation, in that they bring together many diverse elements and attempt to find relationships among them.

The simplest of these poems is "A Game at Salzburg." In it there are actually several games, not just one, going on. In the tennis game, the speaker has as a partner a former German war prisoner who was held in Colorado, and liked it there. The second game is a singing game which, as Jarrell relates in his note, "Germans and Austrians play with very young children." [11] In it the child, here a little girl, says, "Hier bin i'," with a rising inflection, and the speaker answers "Da bist du," with a falling inflection. The third game, which is a variation of the singing game, begins in the final lines of the poem after a description of the garden of the Salzburg Institute, fallen into a semi-ruined state: the statutes of nymphs are "pocked, moled with moss," and a stone horse "has sunk in marsh to his shoulders." But when the sun emerges after a rainstorm "and the sky/ Is for an instant the first rainwashed blue/ Of becoming," the speaker feels that the world, like the child, "whispers: Hier bin i'." In his note to the poem, Jarrell explains his notion about the game; "It seemed to me that if there could be a conversation between the world and God, this would be it." All the disparate elements of the poem, the war-prisoner, the child with her sherbet, the sleigh of Maria Theresa, the stone nymphs, and the withered grass, are the world, and they speak to anyone who will listen—God, the poet—"in anguish, in expectant acceptance," listening for confirmation of their existence in the response, "Da bist du."

Far more complicated in its range of reference, "An English Garden in Austria" is a meditation on the transition from the Enlightenment to Romanticism and the relation of this historical movement to the world of the present. The 104-line poem is a mélange of references to eighteenth century Europe, with chief emphasis on the relationships of musicians and men of letters to political figures and movements: Farinelli to King Philip V of Spain; Voltaire and Goethe to Frederick the Great; the Mozart of *Le Nozze de Figaro* to the French Revolution; Goethe to Napoleon. Jarrell's long note in the

[11] Jarrell, *The Complete Poems*, 6.

Introduction to *Selected Poems* tacitly recognizes that some readers will not be familiar with many of the allusions, and supplies a concise but useful summary of the main narrative line, identifying the personalities and various quotations from Frederick, Napoleon, Marx, and Lincoln Steffens.

The setting of the poem is an English garden of the "Gothic" style, but it is not only the garden which stimulates the poet's reflections on the beginnings of modern Europe. A note in parentheses beneath the title informs us that the garden was seen after a performance of *Der Rosenkavalier*, and it is Strauss's Mozartean opera, first performed in 1911, that catalyses and brings to a conclusion the poem's reflections on an earlier time. That *Der Rosenkavalier* was Jarrell's favorite opera is amply evident from many references in his poems, in *Pictures from an Institution*, and in essays. The attractiveness of the opera, in which Strauss avowedly imitated the idiom of Mozart, and its continued popularity—unrivalled by any opera of its time except the even more archaic and sentimental operas of Puccini—have an essential meaning in the poem. The opera is itself a meditation on the past: von Hofmannsthal's plot and many of his characters are brilliant recreations of stock situations and figures from eighteenth century Italian *opera buffa*, including the female singer who plays a male role, a spoof of the *castrati*, male sopranos who dominated *opera seria* in the early part of that century. Strauss's music, too, looks to the past, to the waltz music of the other Strauss, and to the era in Austrian history that music reflects. Jarrell uses Strauss's boorish Baron Ochs von Lerchenau as a foil to the historical figures. This "rustic beau of thirty-five," as he is described in the libretto, belongs to the aristocracy and has all its vices with none of its virtues of grace, beauty, and wit. Even his music, as Jarrell notes, is not the sophisticated Viennese waltz, but the peasant *Ländler*. In an early part of the poem, Ochs, overhearing a public appearance by Rousseau, supposes that he is the famous librettist of *opera seria*, Metastasio. He is rushed away, "grumbling about the 'luck of all us Lerchenaus.'" In *Der Rosenkavalier*, the phrase becomes a joke, for in spite of the baron's notion that he is lucky, especially with women, all his plans come to nothing and he retreats, in the last act, in disgrace. His disappointment is the low comic counterpart to the disappointment of the Marschallin, whose "Heut' oder morgen kommt der Tag," is used in the resolution of Jarrell's poem.

One basic metaphor for the conflict between the Enlightenment and Romanticism is the shift to the neo-Gothic from neoclassical pastoralism, which embraces the musical milieu of Metastasio, Farinelli, Faustina and Adolf Hasse, and extends—through his membership in the Arcadian Academy—to Goethe. Thus the pure, rather frigid beauty of *bel canto* and the fixed forms of recitative and aria in *opera seria* correspond to the highly conventionalized pastoralism of the seventeenth and eighteenth centuries, and to the frigid humanism of such enlightened monarchs as Frederick. The rise of the Gothic, with its artificially picturesque ruins, foreshadowed the rise of Romanticism. Jarrell comments,

> You went for this pleasing terror to the past
> And built it here, an image of the Possible:
> Well ruined, Ruin! ...
> > But I come late.

The second-last phrase parodies the comments of the onstage audience to the Athenian craftsmen's performance of "The Most Lamentable Comedy of Pyramus and Thisbe" in *A Midsummer Night's Dream* (V, i, 270–74). In Shakespeare's play, the on-stage critics respond with jeering praise to the craftsmen's ludicrous inability to cope with the double demands of verisimilitude and the artifice of dramatic illusion; Jarrell facetiously applauds the same failure in the perpetrators of the neo-Gothic.

The social shift from Classic to Romantic Jarrell depicts by invoking *The Marriage of Figaro*. This first of Mozart's *opera buffa*, written after he had composed several *opera seria* (including one with a libretto by Metastasio), though it is eminently Classical music, is based on a comedy by Beaumarchais that is incipiently Romantic. In the opera, da Ponte adapts Beaumarchais' theme, which is essentially the triumph of personal dignity, irrespective of social class, to the conventions of New Comedy, but the result merely shows forth an eighteenth century version of the traditional New Comic plot in which the clever servant outwits his master. In Jarrell's version, the opera and the *Masonic Funeral Music*, a more "Romantic" work, are both adjuncts of the French Revolution. But the ideals both of the French Revolution and of the French *Encyclopédie*—a monument to the Enlightenment—fail. Napoleon emerges, and although he was able to appreciate Goethe as Frederick the Great could not, his respect for individuals was generally as slight as that of the Prussian emperor. Like the Walrus and the Carpenter, whose poem Jarrell echoes in line 84, he did away with "the others." To Jarrell, Napoleon's Romanticism foreshadows that of Hitler and Stalin. Their motto might be that of the Beethoven quartet, *"Es muss sein."* [12]

This phrase is followed by several others the reader must relate to it: one from Marx—"Others have understood the world; we change it"; a second, pragmatic, "Truth is what works"; and Lincoln Steffens' remark about Soviet Russia, "I have seen the Future and it works." All three corroborate the underlying concept of "Es muss sein!" the old Spinozan Necessity emerging once again in Jarrell's thought.

The final nine lines of the poem return to a contemplation of *Der Rosenkavalier*. Jarrell had called Stalin a *Spielverderber*, a spoilsport, in line 92, and the term is now related to Baron Ochs who, when he is vanquished by Octavian and the Marschallin at the end of *Der Rosenkavalier*, leaves insisting that "No Lerchenau was e'er a spoilsport." For all his boorishness, the baron has a human appeal, a naïve zest for life that makes him infinitely superior to a Stalin, but his age is past. He is a "ghost." An involved masquerade is staged by Octavian to expose Ochs as a cad to Sophie's father, and when it is successful and the Marschallin has arrived to restore order and relinquish Octavian to Sophie, there is a moment at which all three sing, with different meanings, the phrase, "Ist halt vorbei"—"It is all over"—and in a sense that is true. The masquerade is over, though Octavian is still not clearly Sophie's; the Marschallin's affair with Octavian is over; *Der Rosenkavalier* is over, almost. And then the Marschallin recalls her presentiment, so recent, that "Today or tomorrow comes the day ..." when Octavian's love should fade, when she herself should grow

---

[12] Jarrell had already used the phrase as epigraph to *Blood for a Stranger*.

old. She had resolved to bear it "lightly, lightly," and although the day has come much sooner than she anticipated, she is equal to the occasion; a cousin of Baron Ochs, she is no spoilsport, either.

Der Rosenkavalier, which contains so many "Classical" elements in its emphasis on true aristocracy and in many of its dramatic conventions, is nonetheless primarily Romantic in its idealized treatment of characters and of love, but the idealism fades almost before our eyes. In a different way than the politics of power, it accepts the Necessity that "Today or tomorrow comes the day," the day that love dies, the day that a man dies. *Der Rosenkavalier* originally appeared almost on the eve of the first modern war. In spite of the attractiveness of the Marschallin's determination to bear whatever comes "lightly, lightly," history keeps proposing men and events that cannot be taken lightly. The English garden, and *Der Rosenkavalier* itself, are adjuncts of historical and social movements, innocent and beautiful in themselves. Indeed they help us to bear all the rest "lightly." But to the speaker of the poem they have suggested much else, and to him they are for a moment images of death:

> The stars go down into the West; a ghostly air
> Troubles the dead city of the earth.
> ... It is as one imagined it: an English garden.

Like almost every Jarrell poem, no matter how playful, "An English Garden in Austria" takes the world seriously, and beneath the sparkling surface lies a realm of profound feeling. In this case, even though it is extremely brilliant in its manipulation of sources, the poem seems too much merely a tour de force, a whirlwind trip through European cultural history from the eighteenth century to the mid-twentieth, a poem more strictly for intellectuals than even *The Waste Land*.

Some of the same techniques of allusion and historical perspective are used in "A Girl in a Library," but the poem has a much broader potential audience, and a deeper human appeal, perhaps because it focuses on a "real" protagonist. The poem, which stands first in *Selected Poems*, might be termed the quintessential Jarrell poem, for it brings together his major themes and his most characteristic methods. In some ways, it is an "easy" poem; as its title indicates, it is a portrait of a girl in a library. Despite the fact that she sits, as she would say, "studying," she is no intellectual. Her subjects are home economics and physical education. Her dreams are simple, like those of a kitten. Of any uses to which she might put the library, other than studying these subjects or napping, she is blissfully unaware. She is observed by a mature male speaker who is intellectual, who does know what dreams and lives the library holds. He sees the girl as she is, and also in her potential, mythic self.

> (Yet for all I know, the Egyptian Helen spoke so.)
> . . . .
> I see Brünnhilde had brown braids and glasses
> She used for studying; Salome straight brown bangs,
> A calf's brown eyes, and sturdy light-brown limbs
> Dusted with cinnamon, an apple-dumpling's . . .

He thinks of how this girl might be regarded by Pushkin's Tatyana Larina, a figure embodying the essences of female mystique. As a girl, Tatyana Larina was passionate and idealistic; after being rejected by Eugene Onegin, she became a woman of great beauty, sophistication, and moral courage, irresistibly fascinating to the man who had refused her love before. To her, the girl in the library would be as incomprehensible as she to the girl, if, incomprehensibly, the girl should ever read of her. Tatyana Larina

> Asks, smiling: "But what is she dreaming of, fat thing?"
> I answer: She's not fat. She isn't dreaming.
> She purrs or laps or runs, all in her sleep;
> Believes, awake, that she is beautiful;
> She never dreams.

The two key words of the poem are "dream" and "waste." The girl is "an object among dreams" in the first line, but the dreams on the library shelves do not trouble her "sleep of life." Although the narrator tells Tatyana that the girl does not dream, in Tatyana's sense, she does "dream" of her commencement, her "bachelor's degree/ In Home Ec, [her] doctorate of philosophy/ In Phys. Ed." In the closing lines of the poem, a "long, blind, dreaming story" is implied in her sleepy smile. Dreams are a waste of time, in one sense, yet they are all that makes life worth living. The girl wastes her time in the library because she is sleeping, but also because she is studying such things as recipes and *The Official Rulebook of Basketball;* but, as the narrator says, "The soul has no assignments, neither cooks/ Nor referees: it wastes its time." Ultimately, she wastes her life, "the blind date that has stood [her] up." Jarrell explains, parenthetically:

> (For all this, if it isn't, perhaps, life,
> Has yet, at least, a language of its own
> Different from the books'; worse than the books'.)
> And yet, the ways we miss our lives are life.
> Yet...yet...
>   to have one's life add up to *yet!*

The "yet"—Jarrell's favorite qualification in the last three volumes of poems and in *Pictures* . . .—is important. The narrator and Tatyana are condescending to the girl much of the time, and yet—the narrator recognizes that she is like himself, like all mankind.

> ...One sees in your blurred eyes
> The "uneasy half-soul" Kipling saw in dogs'.
> One sees it, in the glass, in one's own eyes.
> In rooms alone, in galleries, in libraries,
> In tears, in searchings of the heart, in staggering joys
> We memorize once more our old creation,
> Humanity: with what yawns the unwilling
> Flesh puts on its spirit, O my sister!

He also recognizes her relationship to the characters in the books: in spite of her lack of self-awareness and awareness to the romantic potential of life, she dreams—like a kitten, to be sure—her simplified version of any woman's dream of love and fulfillment, precarious and ending in tragedy: as Jarrell puts it, "I have seen/ Firm, fixed forever in your closing eyes,/ The Corn King beckoning to his Spring Queen." The balance achieved between the narrator's impulse to ridicule the girl and to love her is exactly right. His mind, which goes out "in tenderness,/ Shrinks from its object with a thoughtful sigh." Intellectually, he must judge her, as the reader also must. Yet he sees in her a "divine spark," almost, which identifies her in part with Cleopatra, with Brünnhilde and Salome, with the Spring Queen, and even with Tatyana Larina. Finally, inescapably, she reflects a part of himself.

Jarrell displays in "A Girl in a Library" the same astonishing wit in description that dazzles so in his essays and in *Pictures from an Institution*. His wildly metaphorical impression of southern speech, for example, probably renders superfluous any further attempt to describe it: "that strange speech/ In which each sound sets out to seek each other,/ Murders its own father, marries its own mother,/ And ends as one grand transcendental vowel." Or the girl's world view: "For nineteen years she's faced reality:/ They look alike already." Like "An English Garden . . . ," "A Girl in a Library" is full of allusions, but unlike the other poem, the sources of the allusions are often not essential to one's understanding and enjoyment of the poem, though of course that is part of the fun. One does need to know who Tatyana Larina is, and Jarrell has provided a note about her. Here, as often in Jarrell's work, one suspects that the poet has used the allusions and written the notes in order to direct the reader's attention to Pushkin or some other of his favorite writers. Like several of his essays, "Poets, Critics, and Readers," for example, his poems are often exhortations to "Read!" [13] And while it is not, perhaps, necessary to know that Schiller wrote "Against stupidity the Gods themselves struggle in vain," one must recognize the phrase itself in Jarrell's version: "The gods themselves, against you, struggle in vain."

The primary center of interest in the poem is the speaker's response to the girl, in the specific context of the library, and it is useful to see the poem as a development of Jarrell's two earlier library poems, "Children Selecting Books in a Library" and "The Carnegie Library, Juvenile Division." Both of the earlier poems portray the children, generalized protagonists, as seeking some undefinable satisfaction from the books, mainly myths and fairy tales, in the library. In both poems, too, the need that remains unfulfilled is a need to change. The earlier of the two poems ends with the lines, "And we see bending to us, dewy-eyed, the great/ CHANGE, dear to all

---

[13] Randall Jarrell, *A Sad Heart at the Supermarket* (New York, 1962), 113.

things not to themselves endeared." And the later, less hopeful, ends, "We learn from you to understand, but not to change." Change is not even broached in "A Girl in a Library," and indeed it is clear that the library will never change *her*: she is completed already, and of her type she is perfect, as the narrator perceives. In the two earlier poems, the narrator is primarily an observer, coming to his conclusions by projecting himself into the children's search for "one cure for Everychild's diseases/ Beginning: *Once upon a time there was . . .*" In "A Girl in a Library," the narrator is still an observer, but in the sense that he suffers from what he observes, he is the protagonist, and the sleeping girl, like the slumbering Furies of Jarrell's "Orestes," is an antagonist. The narrator, not the girl, has searched the library's shelves, it is plain from his allusive speech and from his analysis of her "studying." Because she goes to college and takes a degree, or several, she will think of herself and others will think of her as educated, but educated to what? Not to life, surely, the narrator thinks. And yet, to fall back with him, she *is* very human.

A phrase from Santayana that Jarrell avoids springs to mind as an explanation of the poem's conclusion: "Those who cannot remember the past are condemned to repeat it." Thus, the girl, who cannot learn from the books among which she catnaps, is seen as the Spring Queen in the last line of the poem. Although she will not live in the same way that the narrator does, or tries to, her life will enact the timeless human ritual of love and suffering represented by the myths of the Corn King and the Spring Queen. The narrator's feelings are ultimately a blending of love, contempt, pity, and identity with the girl he observes.

"A Girl in a Library," a very literary poem, curiously enough tends to discount any essential value of literature for a great many lives. Another poem, almost exactly contemporaneous with it, "A Conversation with the Devil," also seems to take the position that literature may not really be necessary. It, too, is full of allusions, many of them to Goethe, but to other sources as well. The "Conversation" is also closely linked with Jarrell's essay "The Obscurity of the Poet";[14] both the essay and the poem begin with a general plaint

14 In Randall Jarrell, *Poetry and the Age* (New York, 1953), 3–27.

about the meagerness of the poet's public. In "A Conversation . . ."
the poet invokes and inverts Father Time's sad explanation, "We was
too many," from Hardy's *Jude*; the poet hopes his readers will whis-
per, when he dies, "We was too few." The Devil, a parody of
Goethe's (l. 81), in the past tempted the poet with great popular
success, but they could never come to terms, partly because the poet,
unlike Faust, was *not* bored, and would only offer his Shadow
(Jung's archetype of the dark side of man's personality) at the hour
when he would *not* say, "Stay, thou art so fair." The devil, who is
identified at the beginning of the poem as "some poor empty part"
of the poet's ego, ridicules the poet's self-congratulating, self-pitying
sacrifice:

> Renounce, renounce,
> *You sing in your pure clear grave ardent tones*
> *And then give up—whatever you're afraid to take,*
> *Which is everything; and after that take credit*
> *For dreaming something else to take its place.*
> *Isn't what is already enough for you?*
> *Must you always be* making *something?*
> *Must each fool cook a lie up all his own?*
> *You beings, won't even being disgust you*
> *With causing something else to be?* Make, make—
> *You squeak like mice; and yet it's all hypocrisy—*
> *How often each of you, in his own heart,*
> *Has wiped the world out, and thought afterwards:*
> *No need to question,* now: *"If others are, am I?"*

The Faust of Thomas Mann's *Doctor Faustus*, the composer Lever-
kühn, sells his soul (his life), or imagines that he does, in order to com-
pose great works of music, and the novel, like several of James's stories,
implies that any artist must renounce much of his human fulfillment
in order to create. Jarrell's devil ridicules this notion because of his
judgment that what is created ("lies") is valueless. To him, as to
Wittgenstein, the poet says, "the world divides . . . into facts." [15]
But the devil's place, in this world, is as useless almost as the poet's;

---

[15] See the *Tractatus Logico-Philosophicus*. The phrase is a translation of Wittgenstein's proposition numbered 1.2.

he is, he says, obsolescent because as "a specialist in personal relations" he is no longer needed.

> *I disliked each life, I assure you, for its own sake.*
> *—But to deal indifferently in life and death;*
> *To sell, wholesale, piecemeal, annihilation;*
> *To—I will not go into particulars—*
> *This beats me.*

The poet, summing up his impression of the conversation, accepts the devil's indictment of modern man, using the traditional terminology of Free Will:

> ... How often he has said,
> "I like you for always doing as you please"—
> He couldn't. Free will appealed so much to him;
> He thought, I think: *If they've the choice* ...
>
> He was right. And now, to have no choice!

Neither the poet nor the devil has much use in such a world, yet neither willingly gives up his vocation. The poem is a more sweeping rejection of mankind than "A Girl in a Library," which finds some grounds for affection as well as judgment, but "A Conversation" is at the same time much more jocular in tone. The extravagant wittiness of the poem keeps its dreadful message at a comfortable distance from the reader, "indulgent, candid, or uncommon" as he may be.

The disguise of a scathing denunciation in wild hilarity is also the strategy of "A Rhapsody on Irish Themes." The poem apparently grew out of a brief visit to Ireland, the original home of Jarrell's maternal ancestors. As its title suggests, its form is free and its mood ecstatic, but the tone is purest sarcasm. Jarrell points out in the notes that "a certain amount of 'A Rhapsody on Irish Themes' is a sort of parody of the *Odyssey*," but Jarrell's Ulysses, unlike Joyce's, flees in mock terror from his Irish home, which is to him Circe's Island or the Land of the Lotos-eaters.

His chief impressions of the Irish, embodied in a made-up "Great-grandmother," are avarice and sham. When he first sees her, she is trying to sell him a souvenir:

At six in the morning you scratched at my porthole,
Great-grandmother, and looked into my eyes with the eyes
Of a potato, and held out to me—only a dollar—
A handkerchief manufactured with their own hands
By the Little People . . .

After a series of visual and aural images, many evoking the Irish religious, the speaker explains his antipathy to Ireland:

> Well, I hold nothing
> Against you but what you are. One can almost bear
> The truth in that soft shameless speech
> That everything is a joke—from your Sublime
> To your Ridiculous is one false step—
> . . . .
> But one settles at birth on that step of the stair
> And dislikes being shown that there's nothing there.

The country itself is "A sleepwalker fallen from the edge of Europe/ A goosegirl great among publicans and censors," but proud and disdainful of everyone else, especially Americans. The poem ends with an epigram attributed to Goethe, "a lover of Ireland,"

> *In peace*
> *Keep tidy*
> *Your little coops.*
> *In war*
> *Get along*
> *With quartered troops.*

Written in a style that combines Jarrell's usual conversational idiom with Irish rhythms and clichés ("Faith, I'm raving entirely"), "A Rhapsody on Irish Themes" seems more an occasional poem than anything else; and the "occasion" is getting certain unpleasant impressions off one's chest.

A far more serious poem, and a more important one, is the longest in the volume, the longest of all Jarrell's poems (375 lines), "The Night Before the Night Before Christmas," first published in the winter of 1949. This poem brings together a number of important elements for meditation, but it is the protagonist of the poem, a motherless adolescent girl, who meditates, rather than the poet. The point of view is James's "central intelligence": the girl's thoughts are reported in the third person rather than as dramatic monologue, giving the illusion that no conscious manipulation of the thoughts comes between them and the reader. The poem bears the marks of a long period of composition; it has thematic elements and poetic techniques of many of the poems of the middle forties, including the problem of Christian faith in an apparently unjust world, and a very simple use of the Hansel and Gretel story. "The Night Before . . . Christmas" is also linked to some of Jarrell's last poems, in particular, "The Lost World," as it recreates the interests and the properties of American life of an earlier time. The time of the poem is 1934, a note beneath the title indicates, but by the time of the *Selected Poems* it was already necessary for Jarrell to supply notes about allusions to some of the most widely known works of the early thirties: Jack London's *The Iron Heel*, John Strachey's *The Coming Struggle for Power*, Brecht's "In Praise of Learning."

The difficulties which the girl has to resolve in her meditation are of three sorts: personal, social, and religious. Her personal problems center about the death of her young and beautiful mother, two years earlier; the illness of her brother, who may also be dying; the death, a winter before, of a squirrel she had befriended; and the usual problems of lonely adolescent girls, mainly preoccupation with her looks, a crush on a new teacher, hope for future fulfillment, as yet undefined. Socially, she is caught up in communistic dreams of a better world; she suffers inwardly for all the poor of the world, of whom she is not one. Because of her sense of social injustice and of the injustice of Nature in the deaths of her mother and the helpless squirrel, and the ambiguous illness of her brother, she has concluded that there is no God, but bits and pieces of Christianity keep intruding on her consciousness: the story of Mary and Martha; Christ's words, "The poor ye have with you always"; Christmas and the Star of Bethelehem.

The search for what is "real" and true is the dominating impetus for the poem, and the discrepancy between the real world and the ideal world is the source of all the girl's suffering. She lives in the Arden Apartments, but she does not "fleet the time carelessly, as they

did in the Golden World" of Shakespeare's *As You Like It*. Her
world is far from golden.

The girl's dreams are an important part of her experience and her
quest. In the opening passage she dreams of her dead mother, beautiful and young, who "disappears in fur," leaving for a ball with the
girl's new teacher; later in the poem (ll. 69–80), while awake, she
shows dissatisfaction with her own looks, as well as inability to see
herself as she appears to others. "She thinks: What do I *really* look
like?/ I don't know./ Not really./ *Really*."

Just after she has fallen asleep, having read to her brother, wrapped
her "improving and delightful" Christmas gifts for her family and
friends, and read to herself several chapters of *Das Kapital*, which
has a strong reality for her, she dreams of the pet squirrel. In the
dream the squirrel is alive, and with his fellows he is attempting to
transcend his natural limitations through the Communist panacea of
education, a concept which keeps running through the girl's waking
life in Brecht's song "In Praise of Learning." The squirrel would not
have died, the girl wishes, "if he were educated . . ." But her dream
does not fulfill the wish quite as she would like it to.

> She sees six squirrels in a row
> Thinking in chorus, in slow, low,
> Hissing, radiator-steam-valve voices:
> "Wherefore Art Thou, Romeo?"
> The big squirrel says, "No.
> No, that is not *just* it.
> Try it again."
> Their skein-silk lashes
> Tremble, and they look sidelong up at her—
> And cry, softly, in their sly,
> Dumb, scared, malicious pain . . .
> And try it again.

The education of the squirrels represents, in a dream, all the girl's
waking wishes for a better world through education (or edification).
She wants to read to her brother from London's *The Iron Heel*, as
Jarrell notes, a novel about "the worker's struggle against the Fascist
state of the future," but to the boy, "It's not real." He wants *Stalky
& Co.*, Kipling's stories of strictly un-Marxian education at an English

Public School. Unfortunately for the girl's sense of social responsibility, her brother perceives that Kipling's illusion of reality is truer than Jack London's, regardless of the girl's knowledge of the "facts" of Hitler's recent rise to power in Germany (l. 59).

That Jarrell chose the story "Regulus" to have the girl read may be significant. "Regulus" is not one of the stories of *Stalky & Co.* (1899) but a later story (1917) about the same characters. Like so many of Kipling's later stories, it is extremely complicated formally, but its main theme seems clearly to be the relation between liberal education and real life. The story begins with the Fifth Form boys' classroom translation of Horace's Regulus Ode; in the rest of the story the boys apply the principles implied in the Ode to their own relationships. In the story, too, the vain and occasionally tyrannical Latin Master, King, argues with the science teacher Hartopp about the value of learning Latin, which to King represents all the values of literature, "Balance, proportion, perspective—life." [16]

In addition to her brother, the girl is trying to educate a friend by giving her *The Coming Struggle for Power*, and herself by reading *Das Kapital*. She would like also to educate her father, whose life seems to her dominated by meaningless clichés, immortalized on the signs decorating his office: "Do It Now," and Stevenson's "To Travel Hopefully Is A Better Thing Than To Arrive."

What she herself has learned from her world, and from the books she reads, is that the world is unjust and that, therefore, there is no God.

> She thinks, as she has thought,
> Her worn old thought,
> By now one word:
> "But how could this world be
> If he's all-powerful, all-good?
> *No*—there's no God."

As she drifts off to sleep, however, the images in which she sees herself and the working world about her—a passing train, the radiator—are those of Mary and Martha; she is Mary, "in her bedsocks, listening guiltily/ To the hollow answers of her Lord." Her Lord, at this point,

[16] Rudyard Kipling, *A Diversity of Creatures* (New York, 1917), 264.

is her idealism, and Engels is one of its angels (ll. 330–31). With his white beard, seen in a picture, he also resembles Santa Claus, with whom he merges in the girl's dream.

Her third dream occupies the last quarter of the poem, lines 282 to 375. Underlying the significance of this dream is the promise of Christmas: transcendence through love. In the snow outside her room, the bushes look like the shepherds watching in the fields; beside them, in the dream, stand Hansel and Gretel, children from outside the Christmas story, lost children who need a star's guidance or an angel's message.

> Staring, staring
> At the gray squirrel dead in the snow,
> She and her brother float up from the snow—
> The last crumbs of their tears
> Are caught by the birds that are falling
> To strew their leaves on the snow
> That is covering, that has covered
> The play-mound under the snow. . . .
> The leaves are the snow, the birds are the snow,
> The boy and girl in the leaves of their grave
> Are the wings of the bird of the snow.
> But her wings are mixed in her head with the Way
> That streams from their shoulders, stars like snow:
> They spread, at last, their great starry wings
> And her brother sings, "I am dying."

The series of transformations is quite breathtaking. The snow seems leaves, then birds, confused, in a kind of metonymy, with their feathers; it covers the burial mound of the dead squirrel, and the children rise above it into the sky—an obvious symbol of transcendence. They become birds and then angels, as their snowy wings blend with the stars of the Milky Way, and the brother sings a swan song: not "I am flying," like the children in *Peter Pan*, but "I am dying." Whether he is really dying, the girl is unable to determine: even the dream cannot quite overcome her doubt, her secret fear. "And she cries: 'I don't know, I don't know, I don't know!'" The children continue to fly, homeward as it seems, and on the earth beneath them "there are words on the graves of the snow./ She whispers, "When I was alive,/ I read them all the time.' " The social burden the girl has carried is thrown off, along with her fear of death, which turns out to be not horrible, but pleasant and free in the dream. Her father's motto is also mysteriously changed and blended with the words of Sydney Carton's self-sacrifice in *A Tale of Two Cities*: "To End Hopefully/ Is a Better Thing—A Far, Far Better Thing." But the dream, with its veiled wish for death and transcendence causes her to wake in tears. Although it reveals the depths of the girl's trouble and her need, the dream cannot provide any real help.

"The Night Before the Night Before Christmas" embodies Randall Jarrell's most extensive character development outside his novel, *Pictures from an Institution*, and that is combined, almost as in fiction, with a detailed setting that is important to the characterization. The poem might almost have been developed as a short story, though it has no plot, in the normal sense, as a formal base. Rather, it resembles the kind of story Joyce developed in *Dubliners*, in which often disparate elements coalesce in a moment of illumination or "epiphany." In Jarrell's poem the epiphany is not a sudden movement, but the gradual revelation, through the girl's dreams, of the inner relationship of the various concerns of her life. The wish-fulfilling transcendence she so fleetingly achieves in the bird-star dream shows the reader what is too painful for the girl to bring to her consciousness. Her inability to believe in a God in this wicked, uncertain world leaves her, like the widow of "Burning the Letters," hopelessly hoping for a new life, a better world. Along with the lonely, mind-tortured woman of "Seele im Raum," the woman at the Washington Zoo, Su-su's mistress in "The End of the Rainbow," and the woman in "Next Day," the widow and the girl bear as best they can intolerable burdens of grief and loneliness.

The sharp focus on the meditation of a single individual without the obvious intervention of the poet's voice and without reference to other literary treatments is developed in several poems of *The Seven-League Crutches*. One of these, "Seele im Raum," must be numbered among Jarrell's most perfect works. All of the nonliterary meditations deal with mental anguish, from the simple loneliness and dissatisfaction of the boy in "A Sick Child," who wishes, like Gottfried Rosenbaum in *Pictures from an Institution*, that beings would come from another planet and make him their pet, to the despair of the woman in "Seele im Raum," whose anxieties have already sent her once to a mental hospital. "Terms" is the earliest written of this group of poems; in some ways it seems to belong more to *Losses* than to *The Seven-League Crutches*. It was a poem Jarrell liked to read, and there are several recordings of it. The protagonist of "Terms" is a veteran, "one-armed, one-legged, and one-headed." Because of his amputations, he is a pensioner and his life is, essentially, a long wait for death, a kind of living death in which the arrival of his pension checks and the fall of leaves in autumn are analogous; they measure out the empty time. The man has changed, as so many Jarrell protagonists wish to, but he is not happy with the change. In Part II of "Terms" he recalls his dream, in which

> ... "My arm and leg—
> My wooden arm, my wooden leg—
> Wrestled with each other all last night
> The way you whet a carving-knife
> Till they stood crisscross against dawn
> Over what seemed to me a tomb.
> I felt for the dog tags on the cross.
>
> "I could find one number on the leg
> And a different number on the arm.
> The grave was empty.
>
> "I thought first, 'I have arisen ...' "

His dream is a wish for transcendence; he would rise, like Christ, like the sun, if only he could. Awaking to the real world, in which, every morning, toast "pops up, all brown, from its—" (from its grave, one instinctively completes the phrase) he concludes that he is "a grave dreaming/ That it is a living man." The poem ends on a hesitating but positive note as the man, staring at his own and his artificial hands together, reflects that, after all, he is a man, is alive, is real. In a word, he comes to terms, accepts a new definition. In arranging his poems in *Selected Poems*, Jarrell placed "Terms" last, presumably so that the recognition of humanity—whole as well as broken—implicit in the final lines should reflect back through the entire volume. It was not an infelicitous choice.

Another poem of the same type is "The Venetian Blind"; like "Terms" it concerns a man's attempt to identify himself by relating to the external world. It is also, perhaps, akin to "The Face." This character's situation is complicated by the peculiar patterns into which his world is broken when he unwillingly awakes beneath the bright shadows of a venetian blind. The blind provides a kind of vision to his half-dreaming self, an Angel who says, "in mocking tenderness:/ 'Poor stateless one, wert thou the world?' " In spite of the fact that he is aware that his body lies beneath the bars of sunlight, part of him keeps asking, "But where am *I?*" Where, he wonders, is the real man, the man he was, not the sick, dull, old man who lies beneath the blind. His question goes unanswered.

One of the most distinctive and distinguished of all Jarrell's poems belongs to this group in which individuals contemplate their inner distress: "Seele im Raum." It is a monologue, like the Rilke poem from which its title is taken, but there the relationship ends—almost. Rilke's poem is spoken by a disembodied soul, which wonders if it will ever again dare to enter the clumsy, oppressive embrace of flesh. Jarrell's poem is about a woman who, for much of her life, saw an eland at her dining room table, but has now been "cured." The situation, thus described, seems almost comic, but the poem is among Jarrell's most painful. The eland is a projection of the woman's entrapped soul, the feeling part of her being, and although she is "cured" of her hallucination, her loneliness and her anxiety remain.

The image of the eland is developed in the first thirty lines of the seventy-five-line poem. It is seen only in relation to the dinner table, where it eats with the woman and her family; it is here, of course, that it seems most incongruous, obviously an imagined animal, but apparently accepted by the family out of love and hope for the wife and mother.

At first only a plate of greens was set for it, but later, "we put silver/ At its place at meals, fed it the same food/ We ourselves ate and said nothing—." It is when the eland tries to speak, unsuccessfully, when it whispers to the woman "so that [her] eyes turned backward

in their sockets/ And they [the family] said nothing" that she understands that the eland is real only to herself. At this acute stage of her
illness "the others came/ And took it from me—it was ill, they told
me—and cured it . . ."

The situation in which the eland is seen—a place left for it—and its
imaginary existence strongly recall another of Rilke's poems, the
fourth in the second set of *Sonnets to Orpheus*, quoted here in M.
Herter Norton's translation,[17] which is more literal than Jarrell's later
"adaptation" of the sonnet.

> O this is the creature that does not exist.
> They did not know that and in any case
> —its motion, and its bearing, and its neck,
> Even to the light of its still gaze—they loved it.
>
> Indeed it never was. Yet because they loved it,
> A pure creature happened. They always allowed room
> And in that room, clear and left open,
> It easily raised its head and scarcely needed
>
> To be. They fed it with no grain, but ever
> With the possibility that it might be.
> And this gave the creature such strength,
>
> It grew a horn out of its brow. One horn
> To a virgin it came hither white—
> And was in the silver-mirror and in her.

Up to the middle of the sestet, the images and situations are strikingly
like those of Jarrell's poem, though the tone of Rilke's sonnet, and the
movement, in English as well as German, are of joy and peace rather
than of suffering. Nevertheless, Rilke's is not a poem about an ante-
lope, but the unicorn, an imaginary beast that many sane men believed in for many centuries. "Doch weil sie's liebten, ward/ ein
reines Tier. Sie liessen immer Raum": "Because they *loved it* . . ."
Rilke commented on the meaning of his unicorn in a letter: "In the
Unicorn no accompanying parallel with Christ is meant; only all love
for the not-proved, the not-tangible, all belief in the worth and reality

---

17 Rainer Maria Rilke, *Sonnets to Orpheus*, trans. M. Herter Norton (New
York: W. W. Norton Co., 1942), 77. Jarrell's interest in the sonnet is confirmed in
his "adaptation" of it, which appears in the "Unpublished Poems" section of Jarrell, *The Complete Poems*, 482, dated 1960.

of that which our spirit has through the centuries created and exalted for itself, may be praised in it." [18]

In Jarrell's poem the eland seems almost to invert the significance of Rilke's unicorn, even as the ungainly figure of the animal contrasts with the idealized form of the mythic beast. Perhaps to the woman the eland represents *doubt* "in the worth . . . of that which our spirit has . . . created . . ." She describes it as a "different size/ And order of being, like the live hard side/ Of a horse's neck when you pat the horse—." It has "great melting tearless eyes/ Fringed with a few coarse wire-like lashes."

Why the woman is considered mentally ill for believing in an imaginary animal, when the generations who believed in the unicorn were not, is on the surface clear: the unicorn was usually conceived of in a mysterious symbolic context, general and universal rather than personal and realistic. But the psychological principle of projecting feelings into an imaginary beast is the same: the unicorn and the eland fulfill a human need not otherwise met. The eland is not wild and free, but captive, like the woman and unlike the gentle unicorn in the tapestry to which Rilke refers, the first of the series "La Dame à la Licorne," in which the lady shows the unicorn his likeness in a silver mirror.[19]

That the eland is a projection of the woman's own struggle to bridge the space between her inward life—her soul—and her husband and children is borne out in her discovery that the German word *elend*, a near homonym, means wretched. She identifies with the eland so closely that, when she goes away to be cured, she thinks of it as the eland's departure and cure. Her separation from the eland becomes its death.

In the last half of the poem, the woman looks back to the time when she saw the eland, and attempts to understand it. She recognizes the psychological nexus between the name of the animal and the German word for wretched; her mind, in its need, had translated the word into an image, as in a dream. Even now, the woman's life is not happily integrated. The inner self, which was once projected as the

---

[18] Rilke, *Sonnets to Orpheus*, 155.
[19] This wonderful series of medieval tapestries is on display at the Musée de Cluny in Paris.

eland, is still lonely, still wretched. The woman cannot identify herself with either her outward being or that inner self:

> ... Is my voice the voice
> Of that skin of being—of what owns, is owned
> In honor or dishonor, that is borne and bears—
> Or of that raw thing, the being inside it
> That has neither a wife, a husband, nor a child
> But goes at last as naked from this world
> As it was born into it—

And the eland comes and grazes on its grave.

Though these images do not "make sense," they express a truth
about existence not otherwise perceivable, as dreams and poetry often
do. It finally seems to the woman that there is no link between the
outer world and the inner; that any attempt to explain or understand is impossible because the outer world inevitably falsifies the
inner world. "To be at all is to be wrong." All that one can do is to
come to terms with the impossible, to say,

> ... across a table
> From—
>   from what I don't know—
>   in a voice
> Rich with a kind of longing satisfaction:
> "To own an eland! That's what I call life!"

One might really own an eland, an animal quite distinct from oneself
and belonging to the world of "the others," and be considered merely
eccentric, extravagant, or exotic. But to have her kind of eland, an
imagined one, is unacceptable even though her eland expresses a
truth that the phenomenal eland never can. Jarrell's point is pro-
foundly disturbing: our sickness is more truthful than our health;
our dreams and imaginings more real than our substance. To live
happily in this world, one must compromise one's awareness of it.
Better, in some way, to be, or love, the girl in the library, who,
though she is doomed to suffer all the ills flesh is heir to, enjoys her
life and believes that she truly lives it, simply because she does not
perceive any discrepancy between *her* life and *ideal* life.

"Seele im Raum" provides an interesting comparison to other poems discussed in this chapter, those like "The Sleeping Beauty . . ." or "A Soul," in which Jarrell varies a well-known story in order to arrive at a new understanding of the psychological elements that constituted the original work. Rilke's sonnet is used quite differently; Jarrell takes Rilke's understanding of the unicorn, and the basic qualification for its origin—a place left for it—and develops an entirely different situation, in which the imagined "space" is filled by anxiety rather than love. In a truer, more tragic sense James Thurber's "Unicorn in the Garden," Jarrell's poem is a "Fable for Our Time."

The poems of *The Seven-League Crutches* range through a wide variety of subjects, sources, and settings, but thematically they present a closely unified collection, aptly described by the volume's title. After the outrage of *Little Friend*, after the resignation of *Losses*, Jarrell began to search for a remedy to man's suffering, restless soul. But before the cure comes the understanding, and in the meantime, the invalid must get along with whatever help he can find, in his dreams, in his imaginings, in stories and legends. These crutches are magic, of course, like the seven-league boots of "Hop-O'-My-Thumb" or the Grimms' tale, "Fundevogel," and they cover the ground in great strides, so that as he uses the crutches the sufferer draws nearer and nearer his goal. It is not surprising, given such a thematic center and such means of moving toward it, that the primary mode of these poems is meditation, a mental exploration of the tales, of the folklore, of history, of the individual lives.

Illness, physical and mental, is often in the poems a metaphor for the general condition of mankind, as it is in the Christian scriptures. In several poems, the death wish is treated as a desire for release from the distresses of loneliness and pain in life. But the wish for death is always a wish for transcendence, from the simplest desire to escape dissolution by an eternal sleep in "The Sleeping Beauty . . . ," to the wish for metamorphosis into angelic freedom in "The Night Before the Night Before Christmas."

The Seven-League Crutches is not a happy book, but it is not a morbid one, either, in spite of the subject matter of some of the poems. In poems such as "The Sleeping Beauty . . . ," "A Soul," "The Black Swan," and "Hohensalzburg . . . ," Jarrell invests death and loneliness with ethereal, at times ecstatic, beauty of visual and aural imagery. In other poems, such as "A Conversation with the Devil" and "An English Garden in Austria," he distances his seriousness with brilliant, witty allusiveness, the *sprezzatura* of a born comedian. He seems determined to bear the burdens of life, and age, and eventual death with the fortitude of Strauss's beautiful Marschallin: "Lightly, lightly."

5 · The Woman at the Washington Zoo

W H E N *The Woman at the Washington Zoo* appeared late in 1960, it was Randall Jarrell's first new volume of poetry in nine years, and it contained only nineteen previously uncollected Jarrell poems, along with a dozen exceptionally fine translations, mostly from Rilke, with one each from Radauskas, Goethe, and Möricke. Even so, two of the nineteen original poems were revised from much earlier ones: "The Elementary Scene," one of Jarrell's earliest (*Southern Review*, 1935), and "A Ghost, a Real Ghost" (*Kenyon Review*, 1945). Several others had been published in periodicals well before the appearance of *The Seven-League Crutches*: "The Traveller," "Charles Dodgson's Song," and "Deutsch Durch Freud" in 1950, and "The Girl Dreams That She Is Giselle" in June, 1949. "In Those Days" and "The Sphinx's Riddle to Oedipus," both of which have some characteristics of Jarrell's early work, were published in 1953, but not included in *Selected Poems*, which did, however, include two poems not in any previous volume, the epigram "A War" and "The Survivor among Graves." There were, then, only eleven wholly new poems collected from approximately seven years work,[1] a very striking contrast to the prolific decade preceding. Five or six of the eleven, however, are among Jarrell's best, where of the earlier poems in the volume only "The Girl Dreams That She Is Giselle" might be so considered. The translations, particularly those of Rilke, are extremely sensitive and beautiful; one sees in them an enormous creative effort, comparable to that of writing original poems. The work of translation does not, of course, explain the very great difference in the number of poems Jarrell wrote in the forties compared with the fifties. Another factor was the fullness of Jarrell's extra-poetic life: in 1952 he married Mary von Schrader, who brought with her into the family two half-grown daughters; on leave from Women's College, he taught at Princeton,

---

[1] From the same period, *The Complete Poems* includes three uncollected poems and ten unpublished poems, five of which are translations or adaptations from Rilke.

then at Indiana and Illinois universities, and later at the University
of Cincinnati. From 1956 to 1958 he was poetry consultant at the Library of Congress. He wrote his one novel, *Pictures from an Institution*, many essays and reviews, and had a busy career as a lecturer.
All these factors are external; the real reasons for Jarrell's decreased
flow of poems lie mainly within the poetry itself; two significant
causes are apparent. First, though Jarrell had always been a painstaking writer, who made many, many drafts of his poems, he seems to
have labored unusually long over almost all of the new poems of *The
Woman at the Washington Zoo*. The library of the University of
North Carolina at Greensboro has a fairly full collection of work
sheets from this period, fuller than for any other, so that it is not entirely safe to deduce that Jarrell substantially increased his work
time, but it seems likely from the *types* of work sheets that he did.
There are well over fifty sheets of "Jerome," a thirty-eight-line poem.
"The Bronze David of Donatello," a poem twice as long, has more
than twice as many work sheets, some of them entitled simply "David's Face," "David's Stone," "David's Grace," "Goliath's Sword,"
and scribbled all over with images and descriptive phrases. The jewel-
ing of lines, perhaps stimulated by the translations, is plain in the
work sheets and apparent in the finished poems. In no other book is
Jarrell's line, the familiar, conversational, unrhymed irregular pentameter line, so musical, so perfectly controlled. A second reason behind the falling off in the number of poems seems to be the lapsing
of certain areas of interest, certain subjects, without new ones to take
their place.

Like some other writers of a fixed world view—particularly Americans, for some reason—Jarrell seems to have had his say about what
interested him, then kept relatively quiet. In his first two books, and
in some of the poems of *Losses*, Jarrell had expressed a particular view
of society, common enough in the thirties and early forties: that it
victimizes people through avarice and mindless lust for power. That
view, though it had not changed much in the fifties, at least went
underground. Never politically inclined, and interested in "the State"
only in its role as monolithic consumer of citizens, Jarrell moved beyond his early, simplistic analysis or abandoned it in the later poems
of *Losses* and succeeding volumes.

Since undergraduate days at Vanderbilt, Jarrell had been deeply interested in Freudian psychology, particularly in the idea of wish-fulfillment through dreams and stories. In *Losses* and *The Seven-League Crutches* he had explored very fully the mechanisms of dreams (the "dream-work") and folk literature in compensating for the frustrations of every day and especially of wartime. "The Girl Dreams That She Is Giselle," though it appears in *The Woman at the Washington Zoo*, clearly belongs with such poems as "Sleeping Beauty: Variation of the Prince," "Jonah," or "A Soul" in epitomizing the crucial experience of its protagonist, here the heroine of Adolphe Adam's famous ballet. In the ballet, no direct insight into Giselle's response to Myrtha, Queen of the Wilis, is possible; Jarrell provides one in the *dream* of a girl who imagines herself as Giselle.

> The gray veilings of the grave
> Crumple, my limbs lock, reverse,
>
> And work me, jointed, to the glance
> That licks out to me in white fire
> And, piercing, whirs *Remember*
> Till my limbs catch. Life, life! I dance.

Content in her "cold cave," like Lady Bates, until the whirring summons to "Remember," Giselle must dance as a mechanical ghost, remembering not her lover, but "Life." This particular aspect of ghostly memory is developed in the earlier poem, also collected in *The Woman at the Washington Zoo*, "A Ghost, a Real Ghost," which ends, "What is he [a ghost] except/ A being without access to the universe/ That he has not yet managed to forget." These lines may also be seen to explain the ghost's behavior in "Hohensalzburg...." (See chapter 4 above, pp. 121–25.)

"Cinderella" (1954) is the only one of the later poems in *The Woman at the Washington Zoo* to have a fairy tale as its central motif, though "The Frog Prince" is a prominent element in "The End of the Rainbow," and several other tales are briefly alluded to in other poems. Daydreams remain important, but sleeping dreams disappear except in "The Girl Dreams That She Is Giselle" and "Jerome," where the dream is much more rigorously structured than the earlier "realistic" dreams of "The Black Swan," "A Quilt Pattern," or "The Dream of Waking." "Deutsch Durch Freud" is a light-hearted spoof of matters—literature in particular—that Jarrell had taken seriously in earlier poems; and like "The Girl Dreams That She Is Giselle," it seems more akin to the poems of *The Seven-League Crutches* or the prose of *Pictures* than to the later poems.

The poems written between late 1953 and 1960 fall into two general groups; the first and largest group is composed of poems dealing with loneliness and aging, mostly dramatic monologues or central-intelligence point of view poems with a quasi-narrative supporting meditation. Except for the very brief poem "Aging," and the long poem "The End of the Rainbow," these are between thirty and forty lines long. The second group is smaller, three poems, and the poems do not have a common theme so much as a common method. Like some of the poems of *The Seven-League Crutches*, they are concerned with exploring the psychological content of their central images: a painting of Pocahontas saving John Smith in "Jamestown"; Donatello's statue in "The Bronze David of Donatello"; a newsboy with a magical name in "Nestus Gurley." These are somewhat longer poems, "Jamestown" having just over fifty lines, the others about seventy-five. All three were written between 1955 and 1957.

The poems of loneliness and aging are foreshadowed in several poems of *The Seven-League Crutches*, but the two themes are brought forcefully together in *The Woman at the Washington Zoo*. In one delightfully ironic poem the loneliness is voluntary: "Cinderella." Jarrell's version of the Cinderella story, like his "Sleeping Beauty" or his "Hansel and Gretel" (in "A Quilt Pattern"), probes behind the fairy tale to a psychological condition. In Jarrell's "Cinderella," it is the ash girl who rejects the world in favor of an "imaginary playmate," the godmother, and not the world which treats Cinderella badly. Jarrell, prefacing a 1962 reading of the poem, said it was about "the underside of Cinderella." [2] The fairy tale we know was her wish-fantasy; and her habit of fantasy, when she grew up, made her "a bad wife and worse mother, but a pretty good grandmother and an ideal inhabitant of Hell." Jarrell also identified his Cinderella

[2] At the National Poetry Festival, October 24, 1962. Tape recorded and available from the Library of Congress (LWO 3870, reel 1).

as "a lady writer (not a lady-poet)" perhaps linking her with his other lady writer, Gertrude Johnson of *Pictures*, who displays some of the same traits as his Cinderella. As in "Orestes" and "Sleeping Beauty: Variation of the Prince," Jarrell tells the "truth" about a story whose original presents a wish rather than reality.

The unifying image of the poem is the fire on the hearth, in whose ashes the fairy-tale Cinderella was forced to sit. In the poem, Cinderella loves to sit by the fire, there to imagine her playmate, the wish-fulfilling godmother, who wears "sea-coal satin," has "flame-blue glances," and "wings gauzy as the membrane that the ashes/ Draw over an old ember." With her Cinderella gossips about men, alien creatures. When she grows up, she imagines a gown of gauze, a shy prince who finds her bewitching; but when she marries in reality, under the "ashy gauze" of a bridal veil, "She wished it all a widow's coal-black weeds."

Drawn unwilling from her satisfying, comfortable fantasy world, "A sullen wife and a reluctant mother,/ She sat all day in silence by the fire." As a grandmother, she is a good storyteller, sitting by the fire, though indifferent to the grandchildren who believe she tells the stories to them, not just to herself. But last of all, in Hell, by the eternal fireside, she is happy once again. To her the flames show forth

> The Heaven to whose gold-gauzed door there comes
> A little dark old woman, the God's Mother,
> And cries, "Come in, come in! My son's out now,
> Out now, will be back soon, may be back never,
> Who knows, eh? *We* know what they are—men, men!
> But come, come in till then! Come in till then!"

The situation of this marvelous stanza is drawn from the Grimms' tale, not of Cinderella, but of "The Devil with the Three Golden Hairs," in which a young man, a luck child, goes to Hell for the Devil's three gold hairs, the "price" of a royal bride. There he gets help from the devil's grandmother, who hides him and plucks out the hairs for him. In the poem, the Devil's grandmother is only Cinderella's godmother, found again in Hell. Since Hell is Heaven to

Cinderella, the Devil's mother, or grandmother—the tale's distinction is not kept up—is to her "the God's Mother," ready for tea and gossip by the fire.

As a symbolic statement about a woman whose fantasy life centers exclusively upon herself—for the godmother is her mirror image —and who rejects men, beginning with the authoritative "Father" who perhaps interfered with her childhood fantasy, the poem is brilliant in its insights. Its poetic organization is equally impressive, as it makes the transition from the fireside of childhood comfort to the fires of damnation, in which Cinderella can contemplate her own image eternally, a Narcissus of flame, not water.

Most of Jarrell's isolated characters, unlike Cinderella, are unhappy in their loneliness. The speaker of "Windows," the most Rilkean of all the Jarrell poems in the volume, longs to enter the lives of other people that he sees through windows, his own and theirs. These others are like actors seen in a movie: they "have nothing of today/ That time of troubles and of me." He imagines a time when he might enter one of the houses, one of the worlds different from his own, and be accepted by the inhabitants, fed and comforted by them, given a place to rest on their sofa, soothed by a hand that "moves so slowly that it does not move.[3]" In his desire that the man he sees reading through the window will read him "what I have never heard," that the woman will show him "what I have never seen," the speaker of "Windows" is like the sick child of the poem in *The Seven-League Crutches* who cries, "All that I've never thought of— think of me!" The man's daydream of acceptance and love also recalls the dream of the lonely soldier in "Absent with Official Leave" who was welcomed by the loving women of the cottages.

The speaker in "The Lonely Man" might be another aspect of the man in "Windows." He no longer hopes for human responses, but contents himself with the friendly (though sometimes suspicious) attentions of the domestic animals who live along his street. A collie "bounds into [his] arms" and one cat, a "soft half-Persian sidles to [him]." Another dog, a "fat spaniel" defensive about his domain,

---

[3] An echo of "The Snow-Leopard": "They move so slowly they are motionless..."

merely comes out to watch the man go by. Of these animals, the man says, "I know them, just as they know me." The people who "feed these, keep the houses," are a different matter:

> ... I don't know them, they don't know me.
> Are we friends or enemies? Why, who can say?
> We nod to each other sometimes, in humanity,
> Or search one another's faces with a yearning
> Remnant of faith that's almost animal. ...

The word "humanity" has an ironic force here, for it is the animals, not the people, who display recognition and responsiveness to the man. The "remnant" of animal faith he senses suggests to the man that all men were perhaps animals once, that the gray cat introduced in the first stanza, which sits "all day, every day" on the sidewalk and allows itself to be touched "then slides away," is probably practicing to be a person, indifferent and lonely, too.

Neither "Windows" nor "The Lonely Man" has the verbal intensity of Jarrell working at his highest level; they are interesting but minor poems. "The End of the Rainbow," Jarrell's third longest poem (315 lines) is another poem that does not quite achieve full aesthetic success, but it has a great deal of emotional strength in places and presents a major poetic statement of Jarrell's vision of the individual in isolation.[4]

The protagonist of the poem, ironically named Content ("A name in the family for more/ Than seven generations"), has something in common with Jarrell's Cinderella, for it is through her own self-centeredness and her suspicion of men that she lives out her life alone; unlike Cinderella, she is not "content" with her self-contemplation. At times she must feel, as Jarrell had threatened the girl in the library, that her life has been a "blind date that has stood [her] up."

The "end of the rainbow" is California, specifically, one of the beach communities of Southern California to which moderately wealthy people retire. Mrs. Randall Jarrell had come from the Los

---

[4] Compare Sister M. Bernetta Quinn, "Jarrell's Desert of the Heart," *Analects,* I (Spring, 1961), 24–28. The essay fixes upon isolation as the central theme of the poems and translations of *The Woman at the Washington Zoo*. Though the conclusions are somewhat different, several of the analyses agree closely with mine.

Angeles area, and the Jarrells spent the summer of 1953 in Laguna Beach, just south of Los Angeles. It was there that the poem was conceived. Much of the color imagery of the poem is inextricably related to this setting; both setting and imagery are symbolic.

The woman protagonist has come to Southern California from Ipswich, Massachusetts, where she lived in a "marsh-o'erlooking, silver-grey, unpainted salt-box." In California, by way of contrast, she has "five sheets of plate-glass, tinted green." Her house is also a store, a gift shop, where she sells, infrequently and among other things, her own paintings, "land- and seascapes." In her painting, the bright, often harsh colors of the Pacific coast translate into the undiluted pigments of her paint:

> Beyond the mahlstick a last wave
> Breaks in Cobalt, Vert Emeraude, and Prussian Blue
> Upon a Permanent White shore.

These intense colors have a sinister implication, further developed in the false blue color with which the hairdresser has rinsed her "silver" hair, "finer and redder once/ Than the finest red sable brushes." The word "color" can refer not only to pigment but also to rhetorical "color," the manipulation of language which ornaments or disguises, and can make reality seem different, more—or less—appealing than plain speech. Content's great *dis*content springs from her longing to color the unpleasant reality of her loneliness and of her aging. Like many others she has come to California seeking some nameless satisfaction, the gold at the end of the rainbow, but fulfillment eludes and deceives her.

> The sun of Southern California streams
> Unlovingly, but as though lovingly,
> Upon the spare, paint-spotted and age-spotted hand's
> Accustomed gesture.

There is even the suggestion that she may have arrived in Hell, for although the lawns grow ice-plant and geraniums (the two most common, most brilliantly colored ground covers of the region), the meadows are "eternal asphodel," the flower of the Classical underworld.

The source of Content's trouble is her rejection, in youth, of a man who now appears in her reveries as "The Frog-Prince, Marsh King." There is some evidence in the work sheets that the Frog Prince was to have had his own poem, but that his story complemented Content's and merged with it after a few early drafts.

The image of the Frog Prince is central to the poem, and it is related to the image of the merman, who, as a female friend tells Content, was really a seal (silkie).[5] The Frog Prince comes from a famous Grimms' tale; he requires a princess' love to regain his human form. The seal-lover of the ballad, "The Great Silkie of Sule Skerry," has a child by a human being; later rejected by her he takes his son and returns to the sea, predicting that when the woman takes a husband, the husband will kill him and his child. In some versions the ballad continues to this sad end. Matthew Arnold's poem, "The Forsaken Merman," based on a Scandinavian ballad, is also alluded to in "The End of the Rainbow." In Arnold's poem the merman is simply abandoned by his human wife, who had borne him several children under the sea. Content's former suitor appears as the Frog-Prince, goggling at her "from the bottom of the mail slot" with brandy on his breath, near the beginning of the poem. Later, she sees him as "The Great Silkie, his muzzle wide in love," holding out "maimed flippers." Still later, she dreams of "a friend" whom she meets in the water:

> He has shaved now, and smells of peppermint.
> He holds out to her
> With hands like hip-boots, like her father's waders,
> A corsage of watercress: the white bridal-veil-lace flowers
> Are shining with water-drops. In their clear depths
> She sees, like so many cupids, water babies:
> Little women, little men.
> He pulls his feet with a slow sucking sound
> From the floor where he is stuck, like a horse in concrete,
> And, reaching to her, whispers patiently
> —Whispers, or the wind whispers, water whispers: "Say.
> Say. Say now. Say again."

---

[5] Sister M. Bernetta Quinn has suggested that seal here may also be "a pun on the German noun for soul (*Seele*)." Quinn, "Randall Jarrell: Landscapes of Life and LIFE," *Shenandoah*, XX (Winter, 1969), 59.

                                    A slow
             Delicious shudder runs along her spine:
             She takes off her straw sailor.
             Red again, and long enough to sit on,
             Her hair floats out to him—and, slowly, she holds out to him
             In their white, new-washed gloves, her dry
             Brown leather hands, and whispers: "Father,
             If you come any closer I'll call Father."

Her rejection of him in the dream is part of a general pattern of
rejection that has shaped her life. She is unable to trust other people.
Early in the poem she hears the voices of seals (actually California
sea lions) from the seal rocks just off the coast at Laguna Beach.
They seem to repeat "Proverbs of the night": "*Go slow. Go slow.
You owe it to yourself./ Neither a borrower nor a lender be./ Better
to be safe than sorry.*" The crux of the matter is money: "*Is it my
money they're asking or me?/ It must have been the money.*" Her
inability to trust people is ironically contrasted to her capital, mone-
tary as well as emotional; part of both are still in Massachusetts "in
trust to the end of time."

             But life, though, is not left in trust?
             Life is not lived, in trust?

Because she could not trust, her life has been as guarded and cold as a
trust fund, and Death is to be her executor, "presenting/ To the
trustees of the estate, a varied/ Portfolio . . ." The Frog Prince, however, married another "frog" and "has little frogs" in Massachusetts,
while Content moves through life like a Buddhist nun, not Untouch-
able, but certainly "Untouched." In one of the most fearful passages
in all Jarrell's poetry, she

             Goes through the suburbs with a begging-bowl
             Of teak, a Wedgewood cowbell, ringing, ringing,
             Calling: *Untouched! Untouched!*
                                    The doors shut themselves
             Not helped by any human hand, mail-boxes
             Pull down their flags, the finest feelers
             Of the television sets withdraw.

Although Content rejected her suitor from a concern for material goods, she needs spiritual "compensation," a word that, like trust, can have both spiritual and material meanings which in certain circumstances conflict. She reads, along with her "Scriptures/ With a Key by Mrs. Eddy" a book called *Compensation.*[6] She keeps, as compensation for her loss of the Frog Prince, a dwarf black Pekingese, Su-su, fourth of that name. Her primary compensation is her work, painting.

> She says: "Look at my life. Should I go on with it?
> It seems to you I have . . . a real gift?
> I shouldn't like to keep on if I only. . . .
> It seems to you my life is a success?"

> Death answers, *Yes. Well, yes.*

Her paintings give the necessary color to her world; they are the "rainbow" which leads to a final compensation; they reproduce the "local color" of Southern California. Near the end of the poem Content is almost forced to see the world "in black and white"—the plain truth of death—but she is still able to turn "with an accustomed gesture/ To the easel, saying:/ Without my paintings I would be— why, whatever would I be?" Her compensations are sufficient to lull her asleep, to dream of "unpeopled landscapes" that "run down to the seal-less, merman-less seas." Her dream is juxtaposed to Su-su's, "that he is sleeping/ In the doorway of the little turquoise store," but any comparison is left to the reader, for the poem ends with this account of Su-su's dream.

"The End of the Rainbow," in spite of all the skillful manipulation of its elements, and in spite of some striking moments, does not seem to me a fully successful poem. It loses rather than develops intensity through its form, in which dreamlike flashbacks alternate with de-

---

[6] Probably a separately bound copy of Ralph Waldo Emerson's essay, "Compensation," which relies heavily upon a rhetoric of money metaphors to describe spiritual values, and which suggests, among other things, that suffering may "assume the aspect of a guide or genius" to help men change their lives. See R. L. Cook (ed.), *Ralph Waldo Emerson: Selected Prose and Poetry* (New York, 1950), 124–25.

tails of Content's California life. Sometimes, as in the passage beginning, "Little Women, Little Men" and ending "with one down pillow on an uninhabited/ Hair mattress" (ll. 86–107), a passage apparently related to Content's childhood, materials are introduced that never become integrated with the main movement of the poem, even though their phrases and images—"little women, little men," "water babies," and a mysterious "red agate" marble that represents, perhaps, life— are reintroduced elsewhere. The poem seems too long and diffuse, and at the same time it leaves the central characters undeveloped; they are more caricature than character. Jarrell's unerring and copious choice of detail in the description of Content's way of life so accurately depicts a very numerous Southern California "type" that his detachment and judgment of her seems almost cruel: a criticism of hundreds of lonely women, because it is judgment of Content's rejection, not compassion for her circumstances, that characterizes the tone.

The themes of loneliness and aging culminate poetically in "The Woman at the Washington Zoo" and "Jerome," both of which were written during Jarrell's tenure as poetry consultant at the Library of Congress (1956–58). Both poems are set, at least in part, at the large national zoo in Rock Creek Park, and some lines of "Jerome" begin to appear on worksheets with the later parts of "The Woman at the Washington Zoo." Consequently it is not a great surprise to find Jarrell calling "Jerome" a kind of "counter-poem" to "The Woman at the Washington Zoo," in the introduction to his essay on the composition of the latter.[7]

Originally written as an appendix ("How a Poem is Made") to Brooks and Warren's revised edition of *Understanding Poetry,*[8] this essay is the best possible gloss on the poem, for it not only recalls the backgrounds, including selected passages from the work sheets, but it explicates as well. In the essay, Jarrell lists the women of "The End of the Rainbow," "Cinderella," and "Seele im Raum" as "distant relatives" of his Woman at the Zoo; he might have added others. For most readers of Jarrell's poetry, this poem consummates the theme

---

7 In Jarrell, *A Sad Heart at the Supermarket*, 161.
8 Cleanth Brooks and Robert Penn Warren (eds.), *Understanding Poetry* (3rd ed.; New York, 1960), 531–38.

and the character of a great many poems. For all its richness of imagery, the poem is stark in its meaning, and the distancing of the third person narration which softens the pathos of "The End of the Rainbow" and "Cinderella" disappears in the anguished voice of the dramatic monologue. It is one of the most visual of Jarrell's poems in the frequency and kind of its images. By relying primarily on visual imagery—color, shapes, places, visions of the animals and people of the zoo—Jarrell was able to concentrate into a splendid dramatic economy the same kind of loneliness that haunts Content in the sprawling narrative of "The End of the Rainbow."

A girl in an earlier poem of Jarrell's, "Hohensalzburg . . . ," had wished to be invisible; amid all the vivid visual imagery of "The Woman at the Washington Zoo," its protagonist *is* invisible, and she does not find the effect pleasant. Realizing that people—men, any man—do not see her and have not seen her for a long time, in her "dull null navy" print dress, she goes to the zoo, because in her loneliness she feels akin to the caged animals, who are at least not invisible: people look at them. She can see herself there: "small, far-off, shining/ In the eyes of animals, these beings trapped/ As I am trapped but not, themselves, the trap . . ."

All the woman's frustrations find outlet in her vision of the caged animals "visited" by the free, wild animals which come into the cages to scavenge on the leftover food:

> . . . sparrows pecking the llamas' grain,
> Pigeons settling on the bears' bread, buzzards
> Tearing the meat the flies have clouded. . . .

She wants something "wild" and free to come to her, to devour her, in a metaphor that is obviously and horribly sexual. As Jarrell puts it, "the stale flesh that no one would have is taken at last by the turkey-buzzard with his naked red neck and head." [9]

Literally she does not desire the vulture, of course; she wants to be changed to a new form of life through the agency of love. If she is now "the white rat that the foxes left," cannot the buzzard be a

---

[9] Jarrell, *A Sad Heart at the Supermarket*, 171.

metamorphosed man, ready to resume his human form and change her back to hers? Jarrell wrote of the "red helmet" of the vulture's head that "the bestiality, the obscene sexuality of the flesh-eating death-bird is really—she hopes or pretends or desperately is sure— merely external, *clothes*, an intentionally frightening war-garment like a Greek or Roman helmet." [10] It can be compared to the various skins of enchantment in such tales as "The Seven Ravens," "The Six Swans," "The Frog Prince," or "Johnny-Hedgehog," in which the animal pelts are shed and the victims at last step forth as men.

As a man, the vulture will show himself lord over the animals, like Mowgli in Kipling's *Jungle Books*.[11] Instead of devouring her, then, she asks that he change her, and though she does not specify into what form, it is clear that she wants to return to some form in which love can come to her.

The final cry of the poem, "Change me, change me!" recalls those less desperate but not less serious appeals of earlier Jarrell poems: the poet's demand that the child of "For an Emigrant" (1940) change so as to be unlike the hypocrites and murderers of her world; the wish for change to indefinably better lives embodied in the tales and legends of "The Carnegie Library, Juvenile Division" (1944), or "Children Selecting Books in a Library" (1941), or "The Märchen" (1946); the myriad changes, for better and worse, desired and feared in the war poems. The irony which underlies the appeal is apparent to readers of other Jarrell poems; changes in human lives are apt to be for the worse. The Woman at the Zoo will change indeed. It is inevitable that she should. She will get old and die.

"The Woman at the Washington Zoo" is unquestionably the most powerful of the poems about aging and loneliness in the volume, because the intensity of feeling is so effectively supported by the intensity of the imagery. It is a poem in which nothing is wasted, in which all the ideas are fully formed into sensed experience. The woman's loneliness is at first merely pitiful, but as she identifies first with the animals, then with their rejected food, it becomes intolerable.

10 *Ibid.*
11 Jarrell mentions that he had in mind the story "In the Rukh," in which Mowgli appears as a grownup. It does not appear in the *Jungle Books*, but in *Many Inventions* (1893).

The only possible end is a cry of pain and despair: "Change me, change me!"

It is not difficult to imagine why Randall Jarrell began a "counter-poem" to "The Woman at the Washington Zoo." Although in that poem Jarrell speaks for and through the woman in the dramatic monologue form, as a poet and a man he necessarily stands aside, considering with the reader the woman's dreadful predicament. The vulture will not help her or her kind; who can?

"Jerome" is a poem about a psychiatrist and a saint, who are and are not the same. The original title, as the work sheets show, was "The Fools," and in the first drafts references to St. Jerome are absent. One sheet even indicates that St. Anthony was briefly considered as an alter ego for the psychiatrist-protagonist. It is interesting to speculate on the direction the poem might have taken had St. Anthony remained; his preaching to the fishes, with its disheartening aftermath, forms a peculiar, reversed mirror image of the psychiatrist's relation with his patients, in which *they* talk and he listens. Although Jarrell was a great admirer of Freud and took pleasure in the fact that his birthday and Freud's were the same,[12] the psychiatrist of the poem is not idealized as a savior of men's minds. He is troubled by his inability to help his patients, and to some extent "affrighted" by their dreams. In the early work sheets the patients are "the fools" of the title, because they have utter faith in the doctor's wisdom.

St. Jerome, as he appears in the poem, is the St. Jerome of the wilderness, the meditative, penitent Jerome, with his companion the lion. A very detailed picture of this Jerome is given in the fourth and fifth stanzas; it appears to the psychiatrist, himself an old man, as a vision in which he assumes the role of the lion, listening for the angel to speak to Jerome.

> *...I see*
> *—There is an old man, naked, in a desert, by a cliff.*
> *He has set out his books, his hat, his ink, his shears*
> *Among scorpions, toads, the wild beasts of the desert.*
> *I lie beside him—I am a lion.*
> *He kneels listening. He holds in his left hand*

---

12 Mrs. Jarrell notes this in a letter to the author, dated October 28, 1968.

The stone with which he beats his breast, and holds
In his right hand, the pen with which he puts
Into his book, the words of the angel:
The angel up into whose face he looks.
But the angel does not speak.

This picture, which corresponds more or less closely to a number of Renaissance paintings of the saint, develops some of the central concerns of Jarrell's poem. Although the historical St. Jerome spent his years in the wilderness as a fairly young man, the man in the pictures, like the psychiatrist, is old. Although Jarrell's Jerome does not beat his breast with a stone, he suffers inwardly for his incapacity to help his patients; as the saint looks to the angel for guidance, the psychiatrist looks to the night; like the angel, the night is silent.

The night is imagined as a dragon with "great armored paws . . . put together in reflection." Although it is not developed until the third stanza, the dragon image is introduced in the first line of the poem: "Each day brings its toad, each night its dragon." The "toads" are the patients' problems, perhaps transformed by their dreams into unrecognizable but ugly shapes, as they relate their dreams to the analyst. At night, in his dreams, the "toads" become monstrous creatures, "dragons" threatening more pointedly than any toad, magnified by the empty spaces and silences of the darkness. In the work sheets Jarrell toyed with the even more explicit line, "The others' toads, at midnight, are his dragon."

In the second line the protagonist is identified with Jerome, *"der heilige Hieronymus,"* although "his lion is at the zoo." His profession is listening through "the long, soft, summer day." The tone of line 4 is somewhat comic, as the patients' dreams are said to "affright his couch," and their unconscious—"the deep"—"boils like a pot." As if he were a priest or even truly *der heilige Hieronymus*, the patients call him or think of him as "Father." The modern Jerome, or perhaps the narrator, recalls that the saint had spoken to his lion as "Son," but by the time he decides what to say to his patient, "the man is gone." The psychiatrist's life, like Jerome's in the wilderness, is monastic. On the wall of his "cell" he keeps not a crucifix but "a plaque of Gradiva," the bright-stepping heroine of Wilhelm Jensen's novel, *Gradiva*, which Freud had analyzed.[13] Freud and his followers, according to Ernest Jones,[14] liked to keep on their walls replicas of the original Pompeiian basrelief, now in the Vatican museum, which had inspired Jensen. Abstemious, "Jerome" eats for dinner only an egg, which he boils for himself. Through the evening, he hears again, in memory, the patients' stories. Finally, "he lies down where his patients lay."

In some fairly developed drafts of the poem, Jarrell included at this point an allusion to the psychiatrist's own analysis many years before, the traditional analysis all classical Freudian analysts undergo to prepare themselves for practice. The passage reads, in part, "The old man long ago/ Has healed himself, and yet . . . He lies uncomforted." This particular idea disappears in the last versions, but the protagonist is still seen as a "patient" telling his dreams, or retelling those he has heard, to the night, the great dragon. Like a true psychiatrist, the dragon thinks in Freudian terms of the freedom of libido: "Where Ego was, there Id shall be." The statement seems to carry a secondary punning meaning: "Where I, the confessor, the night, was, there *it*, the other, the unknown, shall be." The triumph of Id over Ego prophesied by the dragon would seem antithetical to the values espoused by the historical St. Jerome, whose sojourn in the wilderness was at least partly in penance for his too great interest in Classical studies in his youth. He became a stern legalist and, among other positions, supported the doctrines of predestination and original sin against the Pelagian heretics. Instead of disputing with the dragon—in Christian iconography an emblem of the devil—the poem's Jerome remains a passive spectator observing the struggle between the dragon and "the world."

The concluding lines of this third stanza develop the theme of change, so common in Jarrell's poetry, and foreshadowed in the opening lines of "Jerome." After the dragon's pronouncement, "The world wrestles with it [either the dragon or its statement] and is changed into it/ And after a long time changes it." The conscious

---

[13] "Delusions and Dreams in Jensen's *Gradiva*" (1907), in Freud, *The Standard Edition of the Complete Psychological Works,* ed. James Strachey (24 vols.; London, 1953–64), IX, 7–95.

[14] Ernest Jones, *The Life and Work of Sigmund Freud* (New York, 1955), II, 342. Mrs. Jarrell called this passage to my attention.

waking world becomes the dark night of the unconscious, the id, which the dragon in a peculiar way represents. But the world imparts some of its form to the night, and changes it, too, after a long struggle. Just before waking, the old man has his dream vision of St. Jerome, who appears as if in a painting or etching. In the picture the doctor is not Jerome, but only the lion, in dumb attendance on his master. The saint listens, hopefully, to an angel, but the angel, like the dragon of the night, does not speak out. As the old man slips back toward consciousness in waking, he still awaits some word, but the night slides away before it can answer, just as the patient had vanished before the doctor could answer.

On waking, it is almost as if the old man has been born again; his "flesh is young," his soul "thankful for it knows not what." The alchemy of the night, though it has not told him anything, has neutralized the dreams of the previous day. Where "The deep boil[ed] like a pot" now the air "smells of boiling coffee." In the light, cool air of morning, the old man makes his journey to the wilderness of the zoo.

> The man holds out a lump of liver to the lion,
> And the lion licks the man's hand with his tongue.

Like the speaker of "The Lonely Man" the psychiatrist takes comfort from his loneliness and helplessness in the affection of animals. The lion of St. Jerome, Jarrell implies, must have served the saint in a similar way, giving its silent love as the wilderness saint attempted to penetrate the mysteries of man's relation with the unknown.

Jerome finds comfort instead of horror at the zoo because he does not ask so much of the animals as the woman in the earlier poem. Later in the day, one assumes, he will return to his place beside his couch and listen again in silent torment to the expressed torment of the patients, but at least he has this time of freedom, after "the world" has wrestled with "the dragon" until they achieve a kind of equilibrium, if not a resolution of their conflict. The man accepts the compromise, the balancing of pain with love, and is in his way happy.

The title that accompanied the early drafts of the poem, "The Fools," suggests that quite a different direction and emphasis were originally contemplated. Whether or not the doctor himself was to have thought of the patients as "fools" for their baseless faith in him is not clear. Certainly the Jerome of the finished poem does not see them so, even though he recognizes that, in himself, he cannot truly help them, any more than he can truly help himself in his struggle with the night, a struggle that is curiously depicted as the old man's recounting dreams to an impassive, sphinx-like dragon. Only those who are troubled speak: the patients to the doctor, the doctor to the night; the comforters, those who perhaps have the solutions, remain silent. The dragon, whose formula is in itself a kind of riddle—"Where Ego was, there Id shall be"—does not speak but only *thinks*. The shift in emphasis from the patients' troubles to the doctor's implies that the poet, like his character, came in the course of writing the poem to accept the impasse reached by the world and the dragon, in which both are changed but not sufficiently to make either fully acceptable to men. There is no bitterness in the concluding passages of the poem, only a sense of liberation and lucidity, which is reflected in the diction and the movement of the verse. That the animals are trapped and caged is not an issue in "Jerome" as it is in "The Woman at the Washington Zoo," because the man is able to transcend, if only briefly, in the morning, his own sensation of confinement, his saintly cell. His lion is caged but presumably happy as it "licks the man's hand with his tongue," and the man can take comfort from the lion for his own state. Even if the angel never speaks, even if he himself is never able to speak to the others, he has his moments of peace. In the same way that Jarrell's Siegfried is ironically reduced from his namesake, Jerome is reduced both from St. Jerome and from his professional "godfather," Freud. Like the girl in the library, he is very human.

The qualified hopefulness of "Jerome," the latest written poem in *The Woman at the Washington Zoo*, may be seen as prefiguring the prevailing attitudes of *The Lost World*; in it Jarrell moves beyond the despair of the lonely and the aging, if not to bear these things "lightly, lightly," at least to equanimity.

The three poems, "Jamestown," "Nestus Gurley," and "The Bronze David of Donatello" are meditative poems, and their techniques are closely related to those poems of *The Seven-League Crutches* which explore the possibilities of a human situation, particularly one already embodied in another work of art. Thus "Jamestown," which is a lighthearted meditation on American history via American "myth," unfolds from a picture showing Pocahontas' rescue of John Smith, supposedly remembered from a schoolroom wall. The incident is elevated to the status of a myth of creation and presented as a parody of the Genesis account of God's creation of man. The representation of the incident in the picture, an engraving made by "some true Christian," interprets the main characters as "Man" and "the most voluptuous of newts," condensing both woman and serpent into the figure of Pocahontas.

In the opening line of the poem, the speaker sets up the structure of meditation by addressing himself to look at "what I was, before I die." The picture of John Smith and Pocahontas is his past, what he was, what America was, and Jarrell's droll image sees the picture as "one's photograph in kindergarten." The childish conception of the engraver and of the historians who for generations romanticized the relationship of the "real" Pocahontas and the "real" John Smith is foolish and factually in error, but it expresses a fundamental American need for the romance of civilized man wedded to Nature (ll. 17–18). Quite inappropriately, to the speaker's mind, the picture shows "a captain in a ruff and a Venusian," a European and a pagan; indeed nothing in the picture is "American" except the underlying psychological concept.

Pocahontas is not only "the most voluptuous of newts, met in a wood and lain with" but a "red demon." Though she is called "the mother of us all" she seems more akin to the apocryphal Lilith than to Mother Eve. Together Smith and Pocahontas are "the First Family of Jamestown," a punning blend of creation myth and the American democrat's version of high society. In an imagined sequel to the picture,

> . . . Powhatan, smiling, gives the pair his blessing
> And nymphs and satyrs foot it at their wedding.
> The continents, like country children, peep in awe
> As Power, golden as a Veronese,
> Showers her riches on the lovers: Nature,
> Nature at last is married to a man.

The incongruous union of European and pagan cultures is moralized in the last line of the opening stanza: "Nature at last is married to a man."

The second stanza probes the further "history" of the union: what came after "the two lived happily forever after." The speaker, posing now as Melville's Ishmael, or perhaps as that one of Job's servants from whom Ishmael got the words "I only am escaped alone to tell the story," attempts to trace aspects of the American ethos in the garbled history from which his myth is constructed.

> The settlers died? All settlers die. The colony
> Was a Lost Colony? All colonies are lost.
> John Smith and Pocahontas, carving on a tree
> *We Have Gone Back For More People*, crossed the sea
> And were put to death, for treason, in the Tower
> Of London? Ah, but they needed no one!

Historically, Roanoke was the "Lost Colony," while Jamestown prospered from the first. Smith returned to London well before Pocahontas, not for more people but for support for other explorations.[15] The historical Pocahontas was kidnaped by one Englishman and finally married by another. She went to London, and died there, not in the Tower, but on shipboard as she was embarking on her return journey to Virginia. But the historical facts are not satisfactory myth materials. The mythic John Smith and Pocahontas, says the speaker, "needed no one!" The poem's Powhatan, giving his blessing to his son-in-law, pronounces the central tenet of American self-reliance, represented well enough by the former European, John Smith: "American,/ To thyself be enough!" This parody of Polonius' advice to Laertes raises a problem also raised in *Hamlet*: whether one *can* be true or sufficient to one's self unless he is assured of his own identity, of his own reality. Like the first stanza, the second ends with a generalization: "The True Historie/ of the Colony of Jamestown is a wish." This statement is not, as it seems at first glance, a critical judgment of John Smith's accounts of the settling of Jamestown. Smith's works dealing with Jamestown were called "A True Rela-

[15] Information from Philip L. Barbour, *The Three Worlds of Captain John Smith* (Boston, 1964), *passim.*

tion of Such Occurences and Accidents of Note as hath Happened in Virginia" and "The General Historie of Virginia, New England, and the Summer Isles." In them, particularly the latter, there is no doubt a great deal of wish-fulfilling ego building on Smith's part. The point of Jarrell's formulation is that the psychologically "True" history of Jamestown is an elaborate wish for the union of man and nature that makes a man "enough" to himself.

The third stanza (ll. 35–48) dramatizes the essential symbolic action shadowed forth by the "myth" of Jamestown and developed in the two preceding stanzas. A man, meeting a witch in a wood, is given three wishes, and each time he wishes, "Make me what I am"; one might paraphrase, "Find and reveal my identity; unite my being with my meaning, my archetype." The witch grants the man's wish by turning everything into him. "The world has become you," she says. Even though he encompasses all the rest of his world in his own self-centered sufficiency, he still cannot say who he is, and the witch still offers to tell him, if only he will "Ask, while the time to ask remains to [him]."

The three lines of the last stanza indicate that the man did not ask in time. Back in the present, the speaker of the poem is again confronted by a witch, no longer a red wood demon, but a witch who speaks as if she were a tourist guide to the historical settlement of Jamestown. She says,

> "This is Jamestown.
> From Jamestown, Virginia, to Washington, D.C.,
> Is, as the rocket flies, eleven minutes."

Her relation of Jamestown to Washington condenses the three hundred years of American history, of American wishes, to the eleven minutes it takes a rocket to fly from one to the other. If we wish to see what we were, Jarrell seems to say, we need to look quickly before we are whisked away.

Where "Jamestown" is a kind of fantasia upon the past, "Nestus Gurley" is a fantasia upon the present and future, specifically, the Day of Judgment. In this poem a newsboy with a magical name and a derby hat is wishfully metamorphosed first into the morning star

and then the angel who heralds the Apocalypse. The seven stanzas
of the poem alternate between the present with the "real" Nestus,
and the latter day with its mythic Nestus.

Although the basic identification of the newsboy with the angel
seems incongruous to the point of absurdity, it is presented so simply
and naturally in the speaker's stream of associations that the reader
accepts it, and in doing so comes to understand the speaker's implicit
wish to be awakened on the last day, not by fearsome trumpets, but,
as in life, by the "snatch" of Nestus Gurley's whistled melody. The
musical imagery of the poem is supported by a peculiarly musical
rhythm: like Nestus Gurley's music, the poem presents "a note or
two/ That with a note or two would be a tune."

> Sometimes waking, sometimes sleeping,
> Late in the afternoon, or early
> In the morning, I hear on the lawn,
> On the walk, on the lawn, the soft quick step,
> The sound half song, half breath: a note or two
> That with a note or two would be a tune.
> It is Nestus Gurley.

In the first two and a half lines the rhythms rock gently between the
parallel phrases, then a series of shorter phrases, each echoing part of
the one before, builds a slight rhythmic tension that prepares the
reader for the slow measure of the last line of the stanza, with its
simple announcement: "It is Nestus Gurley."

Even in ordinary circumstances, the boy's advent is somewhat
mysterious; he never comes at midday, but only "late . . . or early,"
and his presence is known by "a soft quick step" already on the lawn
or the walk, and the "sound half song, half breath"—part art, part
merely life. His name is a melody in itself. What sort of boy would
bear such a name? As Randall Jarrell's neighbors in Greensboro knew
when they read this poem, there was a newsboy named Nestus Gurley,[16] about fifteen years old at the time the poem was written, and
he sometimes wore a derby as he walked his route, as the poem says.

---

[16] Nestus is a name passed down through his family. See Anne White, "Nestus
Gurley of 'Nestus Gurley,' " *Greensboro Daily News* (Greensboro, N.C.), April
27, 1956, Sec. 3, p. 1.

The boy in the poem, though he resembles the real boy in particular ways, is much more the response of the poet's imagination to a part of his own life than an attempt at a portrait of the "real" Nestus Gurley.

In the second stanza, the poet begins by identifying Nestus' melody as "an old/ Catch or snatch or tune/ In the Dorian mode," the mode of majesty and dominance, according to the ancient Greek symbolism. To the poet, it is

> ...the mode of the horses
> That stand all night in the fields asleep
> Or awake, the mode of the cold
> Hunter, Orion, wheeling upside-down,
> All space and stars, in cater-cornered Heaven.

Already the speaker's mind has begun to project the little melody into a cosmic dance, in preparation for the other associations he will make later in the poem. The notion of Orion's moving across the sky to music in the Dorian mode evokes the images of the sun's "progress" as a triumphal march; and when "dawn rides over the houses" it is time for another entrance here on earth: "Nestus Gurley/ Delivers to me my lot." The conception of the newspaper as the poet's "lot" or fate is a little strained. It is true that the paper contains his horoscope —perhaps an extension of the cosmic imagery, in which case "houses" might also refer to the "houses" of the Zodiac. In another sense, the newspaper is the man's "share" or "lot" of the world of all mankind for that particular day.

The third stanza descends abruptly from the almost selfconsciously "poetic" mode of the second to describe the real Nestus:

> As the sun sets, I hear my daughter say:
> "He has four routes and makes a hundred dollars."
> Sometimes he comes with dogs, sometimes with children,
> Sometimes with dogs and children.
> He collects, today.
> I hear my daughter say:
> "Today Nestus has got on his derby."
> And he says, after a little: "It's two-eighty."
> "How could it be two-eighty?"
> "Because this month there're five Sundays: it's two-eighty."

This Nestus "collects, delivers," but what he delivers depends on the inner eye, the imagination of the beholder, as the fourth stanza makes clear. Like the second stanza, it poeticizes the subject. The evening is "the soft, side-lit, gold-leafed day," and, personified, it "lingers to see the stars." In this context, Nestus seems to bring the stars themselves: "the Morning Star, the Evening Star/ —Ah no, only the Morning *News*, the Evening *Record*." The *Record*, literally a newspaper, is figuratively the record of men's good and evil deeds kept by the recording angel in what is usually called the Book of Life[17] but which in the poem becomes the Book of Death, because it is used after one's death to determine what judgment is to be rendered. Perhaps the change in the title also implies the kind of judgment likely on such deeds as are recorded there. The Book of Death, in the form of a newspaper, both registers deaths and is itself victim to time and decay, yellowing in one morning's or one evening's sun (l. 39).

The fifth stanza brings together the worlds of waking and sleep suggested earlier. When the poet dreams of Nestus Gurley, the boy brings "News of a different morning, a judgment not of men./ The bombers have turned back over the Pole,/ Having met a star. . . ." The latent fear of atomic holocaust is assuaged in the dream by the coming of the Apocalypse, and on that morning, as on others, Nestus brings the news. The star which meets the bombers is the "Morning Star" of the Last Day, whose birth on earth was also heralded by a new star. The association of the star with the second coming of Christ provides the speaker with the images for a waking meditation. The time of year in the poem is now Advent, and the family's preparations for Christmas come from Moravian customs.[18] The Moravian Star, a many-faceted lamp, and the beeswax candle have not yet been lighted, though they are ready for the proper time. A bun has been saved from the Moravian "love-feast," one of the dozen or so held during the year, at which the congregation shares a simple meal of bread or cakes with coffee as a symbol of their love for one another. The most famous of all Moravian hymns is probably F. F. Hagen's nineteenth century setting of the traditional German hymn "O Mor-

---

[17] Compare "Lady Bates," l. 60.
[18] There is a large community of the "plain people," both Moravians and Quakers, in northern North Carolina.

genstern auf finster Nacht ("O Morning Star . . .") which is sung antiphonally by a soloist and a children's choir. In the hymn, Jesus is the Morning Star who brings light into the souls of the faithful. We have seen in earlier poems in which Jarrell deals with Christianity that religion is more a matter of hopeful idealism of Christ's love and sacrifice than a firm belief that man will be "saved." So the rituals and images of Advent and Christmas enter the poet's meditations as symbols of hope in a world where the realities include bombers that may not be turned back over the pole.

Stanza six, like stanza two, returns to present reality, with only a hint of the supernatural associations—"The dew-hushed drums/ Of the morning," the "gold-leaf" eyes of the cat.[19] But soon the reality becomes fanciful once more as the speaker picks up his newspaper, folded into a hat by Nestus Gurley. Both by content and shape, it seems a "tricorne fit for a Napoleon/ Of our days and institutions," and from the following images it is clear that a modern Napoleon is a madman, as perhaps the first also was. Tempted to put it on, the speaker unfolds it instead, but he does not find the news inside: only the dawn.

The final stanza moves wholly away from the present and the real Nestus, to the reality of death and the hope of transcendent life. In the darkness of the tomb there will be no Moravian Star, no beeswax candle, only "hope," the "hope/ That is not proofed against any-thing" (compare the fireproofed paper pompom of the candle in stanza five). This hope is represented symbolically by "the first, least star/ That is lost in the east on the morning of Judgment." Into this scene the speaker projects a herald for the Morning Star, whose "step/ Or tune or breath" he will know: "recognizing the breath,/ May I say, 'It is Nestus Gurley.'" No dreadful angel, no *tuba mirum*, but the snatch or tune in the Dorian mode and the step that had wakened him so many times before would be a sufficient answer to his hope.

Both "Jamestown" and "Nestus Gurley" are rather free medita-tions on their respective subjects. "The Bronze David of Donatello," like "The Knight, Death, and the Devil" in *The Seven-League*

---

19 "Elfie," the cat, is named after the cow of Miss Batterson's anecdote in *Pic-tures*. The Jarrells also had a cat named "Elfie," who replaced the long-lived "Kitten" (*q.v.* "The Dream of Waking").

Crutches, is a rigorous examination of a single work of art. In a reading given in October, 1961, Jarrell called the poem "a straight description" of Donatello's famous statue, but like all verbal attempts to recreate a visual imitation, "The Bronze David . . ." analyzes its subject in terms of meanings that go far beyond the visual impression.

This particular sculpture, unlike Dürer's conventionalized engraving of "The Knight . . . ," causes difficulty of interpretation even to art critics and historians,[20] for Donatello's emphasis on the sensuous qualities of the boy David's physique is unique in the art of the early Renaissance. Probably the most striking feature of Donatello's conception is having David appear with sandals and greaves covering his feet and shins, and a light, vine-bedecked helmet or hat (somewhat in the manner of a Classical Mercury) upon his head, while he is for the rest totally naked; the figure is clearly Donatello's version of a Classical nude statue, but it is hardly an imitation of the Classical conventions. In the opening third of the poem Jarrell concerns himself with the curious impropriety and suggestiveness of David's appearance. He notes the beribboned, tasselled "bonnet . . . crisped into the folds of frills,/ Trills, graces . . ." and the "curls that lie in separation/ Upon the shoulders." David's essential prettiness encompasses the stone "moulded somehow by the fingers" easily enough, but Goliath's appropriated sword is "alien, somehow, to the hand." Jarrell even misappropriates David's remark about the sword, "There is none like *that*," (I Sam. 21:9) to indicate the weapon's incongruity rather than the superiority suggested in the original context.

Lines 12 through 29 further develop the impression of sexually indifferent sensuousness conveyed by the stance and facial expression of the statue. The body is "still unhandled,/ And thrusts its belly out a little in exact/ Shamelessness." Jarrell notes the way the navel, ribcase, and nipples of the statue seem to form a face, "that holds us like the whore Medusa's," but is finally "sexless . . . like the genitals." The disproportionately tiny genitalia Jarrell characterizes farther along as "green/ Fruit now forever green," queerly recalling Keats's "Ode on a Grecian Urn." The sexlessness coupled with "offending/ And efficient elegance" seems to insulate the figure from the living world. It is totally self-centered—and therefore could not give itself through

[20] See, for example, H. W. Janson, *History of Art* (Englewood Cliffs, 1962), 312.

sexuality—and self-reflecting: "The body mirrors itself." Jarrell has already announced, in line 20, the meaning he attributes to David's perverse attractiveness: victory, which David represents, is sexless, indifferent, finally inhuman.

In a curious appendage to this physical description of David, Jarrell notices "a great crow's foot . . . slashed" where David's arm joins his trunk. He asks, "Who would gash/ The sleek flesh so?" suggesting that perhaps the sculptor shared with the observer frustration at David's imperviousness, and took his own revenge upon his creation. But the gash is finally interpreted as "folds of flesh/ That closes upon itself as a knife closes," thus supporting the earlier statements of David's self-centeredness and self-sufficiency.

David's relation to his victim (ll. 35–47), is expressed in the way he stands upon the fallen head and in the way the feathers of the helmet "clothe" his right leg, reaching lovingly, so it seems, toward "the rounded/ Small childish buttocks. The dead wing warms the leg,/ The dead wing, crushed beneath the foot, is swan's-down." The most interesting aspect of Jarrell's interpretation of Donatello's work is his response to Goliath. Unlike the braggart giant of scripture, Jarrell's Goliath is the image of fallen man; he, and not David, is sympathetic and appealing. The head, in death, is seen at rest. "The head dreams what has destroyed it/ And is untouched by its destruction." There is not even a mark from the stone upon this Goliath's forehead; the head seems merely sleeping, even snoring "a little in satisfaction." Death has come "like a girl . . . like a bird," and Jarrell repeats these similes for emphasis. "The boy is like a girl, is like a bird/ Standing on something it has pecked to death."

The penultimate stanza draws back to consider the ensemble:

> The boy stands at ease, his hand upon his hip:
> The truth of victory. A Victory
> Angelic, almost, in indifference,
> An angel sent with no message but this triumph
> And alone, now, in his triumph,
> He looks down at the head and does not see it.

Were the poem to end here, it would seem almost what Jarrell had said, a straight description, if not of Donatello's own intentions, at least a plausible extrapolation of the appearances, the posture, and glance of David in relation to the head which is not gigantic in proportion to his own, but merely mature, lived-in, as it were. But the final four lines introduce two new elements.

> Upon this head
> As upon a spire, the boy David dances,
> Dances, and is exalted.
>   Blessed are those brought low,
> Blessed is defeat, sleep blessed, blessed death.

First of all, from the indolence of David's pose, we could not presume his dancing. The dance is a projection of David's inward triumph, his total indifference to his victim. He exists only in himself; everything external is merely matter, real to him only as he controls it. The last line and a half are even more curious. Who makes these comments, with their Sermon on the Mount rhetoric, their complete rapport with the fallen man? Does the poet mean to say that Donatello's attitude should be expressed in this way? That "Blessed are those brought low" is somehow the real meaning of the statue? There are suggestions for such a reading in the sculpture, but it takes the essential Jarrell, with his infinite compassion for men defeated by life itself, to explicate that meaning. As his Marschallin says in "The Face," "If just living can do this,/ Living is more dangerous than anything." Goliath has not been defeated by violence but merely by life; his death is not disaster but a sleep, a dream in which he reaches back affectionately, through the plumes of his helmet, to the impervious, immutable grace that has killed him.

"The Bronze David of Donatello" stands last in *The Woman at the Washington Zoo*, just after "Jerome." Although it was written earlier than "Jerome," both poems express a kind of hopeful resignation to the ultimate defeat of human aspirations. Jerome is unable to give his patients the help and assurance they need because he has recognized that no man has assurance of anything except his own being, and that is tenuous and temporary. Still, he can take pleasure in feeding his lion at the zoo. Goliath seems to have been spared even the recognition of his own defeat; in death he is blessed.

In arranging his poems in *The Woman at the Washington Zoo*, Jarrell seems to have intended a movement from the open despair of the title poem, which stands first, and the rejection of life in such poems as "Cinderella" and "The End of the Rainbow," to a qualified affirmation in "Jerome" and "The Bronze David . . . ." The struggle to achieve this truce with the forces opposed to human hopes and needs began in Jarrell's earliest poems, and was always his central concern. His David is one more manifestation of the old Necessity. The specific battlegrounds changed from the political and military arenas to the loneliness of the closed or aging heart, but the issues remained essentially similar: how could a man become fully human, love and be loved, know and be known, give and be given? In part, the painful, ironic resolution arrived at in *The Woman at the Washington Zoo* was influenced by similar attitudes he found and responded to in the poetry of Rilke. The basic likeness of Jarrell's concern for men's psychic suffering to Rilke's helped make Jarrell the best of Rilke's translators, and, it seems clear, also helped him to find his own reconciliation with the hostile, beautiful world.

Stylistically, the poems of *The Woman at the Washington Zoo* continue in the vein of the quasi-narrative poems of *The Seven-League Crutches*: rhythmic, conversational, with a great deal of repetition of phrases and individual words, meter that is essentially iambic but subtly varied, as in the opening passages of "Nestus Gurley" and "The Bronze David . . . ." Jarrell seems to have determined his lines here by their "feeling" right, rather than by counting the feet, for in these mature poems his earlier leaning toward fairly regular blank verse is supplanted by a more varied line length determined by content and emotional quality. In the best poems, his musical sense seems infallible, but in others—"The Lonely Man," "A Ghost, a Real Ghost," parts of "The End of the Rainbow"—the style falls into monotonous flatness. The themes of these lesser poems are the same as those of the best, but their situations or characters (or both) do not resonate in the mind with the same intensity as the outstanding poems.

Unlike Jarrell's previous volumes, *The Woman at the Washington Zoo* does not present any really new subjects or techniques, does not evince any new interests, except for the translations. Instead, it develops fully the themes and style of some of the last-written poems of *The Seven-League Crutches*, for example, "Seele im Raum" and

"A Girl in a Library," refining them and finding new images for their expression. In the process, Jarrell wrote some of his finest, most moving poems, poems which evoke, more exactly than those of any other poet of his time, the quality of *normal* American life in the fifties: "Nestus Gurley," "The Woman at the Washington Zoo," "Jerome." Each shows with remarkable verisimilitude and beauty a particular facet of American hopefulness, American loneliness. It was a theme Jarrell never finished exploring.

6 · The Lost World

The Lost World turned out to be a final volume of poetry for Randall Jarrell, yet nearly all its poems, like those of *The Seven-League Crutches* or *Blood for a Stranger*, give evidence that its author was in transit, moving to open new areas of subject matter and technique. Nearly a third of its twenty-two poems continue to explore the major themes of *The Woman at the Washington Zoo*—loneliness and aging—but in new ways. There are two poems about art and life, but here, too, the treatment and ultimately the meanings are different from Jarrell's earlier poems dealing with works of art. Two poems concern the child's fantasy world, the *Märchen* recreated in dreams, but one of these is an extension of previous development of that subject and the other, which does resemble earlier treatments, is actually a revision of a poem first published in 1948.

The distinctively new poems of *The Lost World* include a panegyric on women that successfully unites homely, often humorous American images with the exalted tone of Rilke's *Duino Elegies*; a beautiful dramatic monologue, "The Lost Children," based on a real dream of Mary Jarrell's; and two wonderful poems about Jarrell's own boyhood, "The Lost World" and "Thinking of the Lost World." Besides these, there are some very small, perfect poems about a mockingbird, an owl, and some bats taken from Jarrell's children's book, *The Bat Poet*, and one called, simply, "Well Water."

The poems as a whole are easier, less obscure than those of any of the earlier volumes, and though the range of allusions in a few poems is far-reaching, knowledge of the sources seems almost irrelevant; the allusions are used for their intrinsic beauty and appropriateness to the subject, not for the esoteric fun of pointing to their contexts. Most of the poems are written in the subtle, flexible free verse of Jarrell's maturity, but one, "The Lost World," is in terza rima; paradoxically, it seems most free.

The most predictable of the poems of *The Lost World* are those which develop Jarrell's old themes of loneliness and aging. "Next

Day," the poem that begins the volume, is a reworking of the themes, and some of the images, of "The Face" and "The Woman at the Washington Zoo." Like Jarrell's Marschallin, the woman who narrates "Next Day" looks at herself in a mirror and discovers that, without her consent or will, she has changed—become old—and she finds the change terrible.

> I am afraid, this morning, of my face.
> It looks at me
> From the rear-view mirror, with the eyes I hate,
> The smile I hate. Its plain, lined look
> Of gray discovery
> Repeats to me: "You're old." That's all, I'm old.

Like the woman at the zoo, she wishes to be seen by others, especially men, of course. Unlike the woman at the zoo, she has been looked at in the past, when she was pretty and desirable; now it "bewilders" her that she is apparently invisible. But the differences between the woman of "Next Day" and the aging women of the earlier poems are important ones. This woman is not a Marschallin, not a woman of wealth and aristocratic birth, and neither is she neurotically hysterical in her fantasies of sexual fulfillment, as is the woman at the zoo. She is a daughter of modern, middle-class America. She shops at a well-stocked supermarket; drives home in her own car; has a successful husband, a lovely daughter and sons "away at school"; a housemaid; and, outliving her friends, she goes to their funerals. The irony of her life is that she has everything thought necessary to human happiness by modern American mythmakers (advertising agencies), yet she is not happy. Though even her laundry detergents have fabulous names—Cheer, Joy, All—to express the satisfaction supposedly experienced by those lucky housewives who use them, she is left at the end of the poem "confused with [her] life, that is commonplace and solitary."

The title of the poem seems to refer to the time it takes place, a day after the speaker has gone to a friend's funeral and has recognized in the corpse her own end.

My friend's cold made-up face, granite among its flowers,
Her undressed, operated-on, dressed body
Were my face and body.
As I think of her I hear her telling me

How young I seem; I *am* exceptional;
I think of all I have.
But really no one is exceptional,
No one has anything, I'm anybody,
I stand beside my grave . . .

Her newly found knowledge serves only to make her increasingly self-conscious. Though she resents her invisibility to the supermarket bag boy, she herself "overlooks" the other "selves" who are "slacked or shorted, basketed, identical food-gathering" selves in the super-market. She even justifies her "wisdom" in overlooking them by recalling a phrase from William James. It seems possible that Jarrell is suggesting that her invisibility is related to her lack of insight. None-theless, like Eliot, he is moved by "the notion of some . . . infinitely suffering thing," even in the guise of a suburban homemaker.

"In Montecito" and "The One Who Was Different" relate the ultimate end of such a woman. "In Montecito" is one of the shorter poems of *The Lost World*; it is a horrific fantasy on the death of a woman, wealthy but lonely, who lived in comfort in "a fashionable suburb of Santa Barbara." The violent deaths of the children and the young soldiers of Jarrell's war poems were dreadful enough, but never so personal as the death of Greenie Taliaferro.[1] The dead woman appears to the poet in a dream as "a scream with breasts."

. . . As it hung there in the sweet air
That was always the right temperature, the contractors
Who had undertaken to dismantle it, stripped off
The lips, let the air out of the breasts.

The image is both horrid and ludicrous, combining the surrealism of nightmare with the image of the dead woman as a house[2] or auto-

---

[1] Taliaferro is pronounced "Tolliver" in the South. Mrs. Jarrell informs me that her husband, amused by this displacement, intended the name to be read as Tolliver in the poem.

[2] Compare the Freudian dream image of the mother in "A Quilt Pattern."

mobile, vacated or abandoned and being demolished so that another, later model can take its place. The conversion of a person to a thing in death is absurdly real, and the poem ends in a grotesque parody of transcendence: "Greenie has gone into the Greater Montecito/ That surrounds Montecito like the echo of a scream." [3]

The image of demolition is used again in "The One Who Was Different," a longer poem that is a peculiar, irascible elegy for a woman Jarrell calls "Miss L____." It is a dramatic monologue spoken at the funeral, so that the spectacle of Miss L____ in her casket—a "great lead-lined cloak/ Of ferns and flowers,/ Of maidenhair, carnations, white chrysanthemums"—portions of the burial service, and a glimpse of a young "survivor" interweave with the speaker's memories and reflections. In this poem, "the world" is seen as "disassembling" the woman's features because her life, which from this perspective is only "a way things look for a while,/ A temporary arrangement of the matter," has ended. The woman has been an eccentric in life, and the speaker urges her to try to be different in death, as well.

As he hears the words of St. Paul (I Cor. 15) read over her body, he is moved by their majesty and promise, but somehow they do not seem to apply to the woman that he remembers, and he is unable to reconcile St. Paul's notion of the corruptible's putting on incorruption, the mortal's putting on immortality with "this former woman,/ This nice dead thing that used to smile/ Like a woodchuck." The playfulness of this image, which strikes the reader as condescending and disrespectful to the dead, is meant to heighten the incongruity of the elevated rhetoric of Christian rites of burial in the context of a particular woman's death. The speaker is baffled: "I feel like the first men who read Wordsworth./ It's so simple I can't understand it."

His sight of a little girl seated with Miss L____'s family, looking into the coffin "eagerly,/ For this secret that the grownups have, the secret/ That, shared, makes one a grownup," precipitates his plan for Miss L____'s unusual transcendence.

[3] Not, apparently, an allusion to Siqueiros' well-known painting, *The Echo of a Scream.*

> If a man made up his mind
> About death, he could do without it.
>
> . . . .
>   Oh, Miss L——,
> If only I could have made you see it!
> If only I could have got you to make up your mind
> In time, in time! Instead of someone's standing here
> Telling you that you have put on incorruption,
> You would have lain here—I can see it—
> Encased in crystal, continually mortal,
> While the years rolled over you . . .

The image of Snow White entranced in her crystal tomb was a favorite of long standing with Jarrell; in fact, it appears in "The Ways and the Peoples" (*Blood for a Stranger*), one of the first poems in which Jarrell used fairy tale materials. It is obviously an image of transcendence, but transcendence that involves keeping the familiar, "mortal" body one has in life. It rejects the unfamiliar, inconceivable, incredible change to incorruption, immortality. Jarrell implies that such a retention of the living form might be a comfort to those who do remain alive, fearing the distintegration of the only form they have known (the "disassembling," "dismantling" process) even more than the lapse from consciousness. But for the "continually mortal," the effect is ultimately absurd.

> In my mind's eye
> I can hear a teacher saying to a class
> About the twenty-first or -second century:
> "Children, remember you have seen
> The oldest man that ever didn't die!"
>
> Woman, that is.

In "The One Who Was Different," Jarrell rejects the elegy's traditional reconciliation of life to death. The comfort of Christian promise does not work for him now, any more than it did in "Burning the Letters," as he looks at his dead friend, frustratingly odd in death as in life. Only something *different* will do for her.

Incongruity in death is the subject of still another poem, "A Well-to-Do Invalid" in which the poet-speaker tells of his resentment against the too-deliberately self-sacrificing wife of his invalid friend:

> She has never once said what she thought, done what she wanted,
> But (as if invented by some old economist
> And put on an island, to trade with her mate)
> Has acted in impersonal self-interest.

He has suspected her of nursing his friend at least partly in expectation of her reward at her husband's death—"all praise/ And understanding outside, and inside all insurance"—but the joke is on him (and on her, if his suspicions were well founded), for in the end it is she who dies, and the husband who is "up and talking, well with grief." The narrator is both ashamed and illuminated as to the nature of his friend's marriage and his well-being.

> As I realized how easily you'd fill
> This vacancy, I was sorry
> For you and for that pale self-sufficient ghost
> That had tended so long your self-sufficiency.

The plain, prosy style of this poem, and of "Next Day" and "The One Who Was Different," is buoyed up by the subtlety of the rhythm, which is anything but prosy. Nonetheless, it is a poetry, to use one of Jarrell's favorite Marianne Moore phrases, "in plain American that cats and dogs can read." Despite the skill with which the effect of simplicity is built up, it will seem to many readers too "easy" to be real poetry, and, in truth, the style does lack the excitement of poetry rich in imagery and figures of speech.

Jarrell's search for a way to make the real world and the real American language poetic seems to have been at a peak throughout *The Lost World*, but it was not uniformly successful. In the long run, the subject rather than the style seems to determine the quality of the poems. In general, I find that those poems like "Next Day," which so consciously strive for a contemporary setting and plain style, seem to have the least permanent appeal: sadly enough, since Jarrell obviously wanted them to show lasting human concerns in a particular, contemporary situation. In "Next Day," and to some extent in "The One Who Was Different," the wealth of local details tends almost to obscure the general theme. "Three Bills" is another example of this difficulty. Like "The One Who Was Different" and "A Well-to-Do Invalid," it gives the impression of being taken directly from life. Mary Jarrell confirms such an intuition in relating that the situation and much of the dialogue were overheard by her one morning in the Plaza Hotel in New York, just as the poem says. She recounted the episode to her husband before leaving on a shopping excursion, and on her return a few hours later Jarrell read her the poem he had made, substantially the same as it now appears. Surely he was right in seeing a possible poem in the unhappy human situation Mrs. Jarrell had observed, and his conception of the lonely, empty people as "bills," as "money talking," is illuminating. Yet, the speaker is essentially unresponsive to his subject; his being "sorry" at the end seems merely polite; and the dialogue about the Virgin Islands remains as meaningless in the poem as it had been in real life. A similar problem of response to the speaker and his subjects arises in "The X-Ray Waiting Room in the Hospital," where the concrete details—"my myelogram is negative," "I . . . ride back to my own room, 601"—puts the reader off rather than drawing him into the main concern of the poem, the patients' feelings of anonymity and invisibility as they wait for attention. Jarrell had treated the loneliness of the sick brilliantly in such poems as "A Quilt Pattern" and "In the Ward" by projecting the sufferer's fears and wishes into mythic patterns, using the actual surroundings merely as suggestive properties in the fantasy which revealed the sick protagonists to be extensions of ourselves, with our own latent fears and wishes. In "The X-Ray Waiting Room" the sick people are just plain sick, and their wish to be recognized individually gets lost in the busy-ness of the local color.

More successful poems in which Jarrell also uses old subjects in new ways are the two poems about art, "In Galleries" and "The Old and the New Masters." In the first, Jarrell moves wryly through art galleries, observing, in each of the poem's three stanzas, the attitudes of the museum guards toward the works of art in their charge. In the first stanza the guard in a prosperous American or European gallery is apparently as indifferent to the works of art as the visitors are indifferent to him.

> . . . He stands by God
> Being tickled by the Madonna; the baby laughs
> And pushes himself away from his mother.
> The lines and hollows of the piece of stone
> Are human to people: their hearts go out to it.
> But the guard has no one to make him human.

Such a guard, says Jarrell, "has a right to despair."

In the second stanza a different sort of guard appears: Italian, shabby, talkative, he shows the visitors the human details of the works in his charge.

> . . . he shows you that in the smashed
> Head of the crouching Venus the untouched lips
> Are still parted hopefully, vivaciously,
> In a girl's clear smile. He speaks and smiles
> And whether or not you understand Italian
> You understand he is human, and still hopes—

The visitor tips him "a dime's worth of aluminum" for showing the hopeful Venus of the Ludovisi Throne. The guard's interest and appreciation for the sculpture reveal his own humanity.

The final avatar of the museum guard is dumb; unable to speak, he evinces more than hope. "His gestures are full of faith . . ." With a magnifying glass he shows in a Pieta that "The something on the man's arm is the woman's/ Tear . . ." His action unites the visitor, the guard, and the figures in the painting in a moment of communion. The attendant's wonder convinces the visitor that "he guards a miracle." Unable to make any appropriate response to a miracle, the visitor gives the guard "A quarter's worth of nickel and aluminum." The poem captures very subtle nuances of our feelings of awe and inadequacy in response to the works of art that so often seem to us more human than human beings. The guards seem progressively more alive and human as they evince more involvement with the works of art. Jarrell uses the traditional rhetoric of Christian progression from damnation to salvation—despair to hope to faith—to express the progression from anonymity to humanity represented in the three guards. But the visitor as well as the guard must come alive to make the miracle happen. Jarrell uses the second person in referring to the viewer, and the reader readily identifies with the "you," seeing what Jarrell (and the guards) points out. The shallowness of our experience of both the guards' humanity and that of the painting or sculpture is gently needled in the closing lines of the last two stanzas. Subjected always to the proprieties of reality, we attempt to "pay" for "faith" with "A quarter's worth of nickel and aluminum." The speaker's attitude is not bitter, but cognizant.

"The Old and the New Masters" begins as a rebuttal to Auden's famous poem, "Musée des Beaux Arts." Where Auden asserted that the master painters recognized and portrayed mankind's general indifference to the sufferings of others, Jarrell contends that they express various attitudes. Auden's poem begins,

> About suffering they were never wrong,
> The Old Masters: how well they understood
> Its human position; how it takes place
> While someone else is eating or opening a window or just
>   walking dully along . . .

Jarrell paraphrases Auden only to deny his proposition: "When someone suffers, no one else eats/ Or walks or opens the window . . ." As evidence, he describes Georges de la Tour's *St. Sebastian Mourned by St. Irene*,[4] in which the four supplementary figures concentrate their attention, through various attitudes, upon the foreground figure of the martyred saint. The style and the disposition of the figures suggest an analogy with the crucifixion of Christ (though St. Sebastian lies on the ground and the figures consequently look down at him). Of this painting, Jarrell concludes, "They watch, they are, the one thing in the world."

---

[4] Jarrell had written of this beautiful Baroque painting in "The Age of the Chimpanzee," *Art News*, LVI (Summer, 1957), 34–36. The brief essay defends representational art against current enthusiasm for abstract expressionism.

Where Auden had written of a painting of the nativity, perhaps
Breughel's *Adoration of the Kings in the Snow*,[5] in which

> . . . when the aged are reverently, passionately waiting
> For the miraculous birth, there always must be
> Children who did not specially want it to happen, skating
> On a pond at the edge of the wood . . .

Jarrell chooses an earlier, more typical representation, van der Goes's
Nativity,[6] in which "everything is pointed . . . toward the naked/
Shining baby, like the needle of a compass." In the scene the attendant
human figures are represented by size according to their relative importance: big shepherds and patron saints; the donor medium sized;
his family small. Various points in time are presented simultaneously;
although the holy family and the shepherds are central in the painting,

> . . . far off in the rocks
> You can see Mary and Joseph and the donkey
> Coming to Bethlehem; on the grassy hillside
> Where their flocks are grazing, the shepherds gesticulate
> In wonder at the star; and so many hundreds
> Of years in the future, the donor, his wife,
> And their children are kneeling, looking: everything
> That was or will be in the world is fixed
> On its small, helpless, human center.

To van der Goes and de la Tour, suffering, or even the prefigura-
tion of suffering, is important, and everyone, sometimes every*thing*,
in the picture pays attention to it. But for other of the "old masters,"
such as Breughel, suffering and adoration both may be relegated to
the sidelines. Auden wrote of them,

> They never forgot
> That even the dreadful martyrdom must run its course

---

[5] Arthur Kinney, in "Auden, Brueghel, and 'Musée des Beaux Arts,'" *College
English*, XXIV (April, 1963), 529–31, identifies the painting as Breughel's *The
Numbering at Bethlehem*, although there is no one obviously "reverently, pas-
sionately waiting" in that picture.

[6] Sister M. Bernetta Quinn identifies this painting as *The Adoration of the
Shepherds* of the Portinari Altarpiece, of which Jarrell owned a reproduction;
see Quinn, "Randall Jarrell: Landscapes of Life and LIFE," 69.

> Anyhow in a corner, some untidy spot
> Where the dogs go on with their doggy life . . .

Icarus may fall, Christ be born and die, and life continue regardless of their agony. Jarrell calls these painters "the new masters," who "paint a subject as they please,/ And Veronese is prosecuted by the Inquisition/ For the dogs playing at the feet of Christ." In his too "realistic" representation of the guests and animals in the *Feast at the House of Levi*, Veronese presumably aimed at "truth"; but the Inquisition preferred its old "truth." The shift from spiritual, human truth to truth-to-nature culminates in truth to a mechanistic destiny.

> The earth is a planet among galaxies.
> Later Christ disappears, the dogs disappear: in abstract
> Understanding, without adoration, the last master puts
> Colors on canvas, a picture of the universe
> In which a bright spot somewhere in the corner
> Is the small radioactive planet men called Earth.

Auden's conception of "indifference" in the old masters and Jarrell's of "abstract understanding" in the new finally come to almost the same thing. Jarrell's poem is nearly three times as long as Auden's, and for the most part the extra length is used to present more elaborate descriptions of the paintings; where Auden was suggestive, Jarrell is detailed, as in his earlier poems that search out the moral center of visual art: "The Knight, Death, and the Devil" and "The Bronze David of Donatello." The subtle elevation of Jarrell's style in this poem befits the quality of the meditation. Like Auden's it is dignified without stiffness, beautiful without preciosity. The visual nature of the subject evokes Jarrell's great skill in developing a scene that is morally expressive, as in the passage describing the gifts brought to the infant in van der Goes's painting:

> . . . a sheaf of wheat,
> A jar and a glass of flowers, are absolutely still
> In natural concentration, as they take their part
> In the salvation of the natural world.

Of course, these inanimate objects would be still, in nature or in any painting (they might well be a subject for "still life"), yet there is a significance to their stillness in this particular composition, though not every eye could see it.

That Jarrell opts for de la Tour's or van der Goes's point of view is clear in the obvious enthusiasm with which he describes the two paintings, but also in his work in general. In the same way as these "old masters," Jarrell focuses his attention and love upon the hurt and helpless. His fervor is very nearly religious.

The remaining two poems of *The Lost World* that reconsider themes and images from Jarrell's earlier work are "A Hunt in the Black Forest" and "The House in the Wood"; both explore the psychological significance of the *Märchen*. "A Hunt . . ." is a revision of "The King's Hunt," which appeared in *Poetry* in 1948, but was not included in *The Seven-League Crutches* or *Selected Poems*. The poem relates the dream of a child, like "The Prince" (1947) and "A Quilt Pattern" (1950), in which the fears and forbidden desires of the waking hours work themselves out symbolically. "A Hunt . . ." represents the child's desire for revenge on authority; in the poem his personality is divided between a dwarf and a mute whose tongue has been cut out on order of the king, who probably represents a father. The dwarf is a sort of decoy and voyeur, leading the king to the mute's hut and then watching through the window as the king dies. The mute poisons the king, runs away briefly but returns to look in at the window, where he holds the dwarf up to see, too. In both the 1948 version and the *Lost World* version, the poem ends, "Their blurred faces, caught up in one wish,/ Are blurred into one face: a child's set face."

The dwarf and the mute, like the Good me, Bad me of "A Quilt Pattern," represent the two "sides" of the child's character. The mute, who has been punished, very likely for speaking evil (Bad me), actively avenges himself on the authority figure, but the more passive dwarf (Good me) shares the revenge vicariously by watching when the mute holds him up so that he can. The first two lines of the poem, except for the use of the third person pronoun, are the same as those of "The Prince." ("After the door shuts and the footsteps die,/ He calls out: 'Mother?' ") Perhaps they suggest that the child wishes to revenge himself on the mother for abandoning him to the night, as well as on the father. The revisions of the poem are minor, except for the excision of several lines describing the king's death, and the poem seems very close to the later poems of *Losses* and of *The Seven-League Crutches* in style as well as subject. "The House in the Wood" is a different matter. Although it utilizes the Hansel and Gretel story, its exploration of the basic pattern is from an adult's rather than a child's point of view. The two-line stanzas and the subject of the poem suggest that it may owe something to Möricke's "Forest Murmurs," which Jarrell translated and published in *The Woman at the Washington Zoo*. "The House in the Wood" is a modern poem, darker and psychologically more complex than Möricke's. The first half is highly allegorical, as nearly every image stands for an intellectual concept. The last part of the poem is a dream, utilizing the illogical, antiallegorical symbolism of the unconscious.

The houses of the first stanza represent the consciously controlled waking life of the speaker, which is civilized and domesticated. But "at the back of the houses there is the wood." The wood, as we might expect, is that obscure part of the personality, the imagination, a waking manifestation of the unconscious that emerges fully only in sleep. "Summer" is waking or life in the wood; in "summer" the wood of the imagination gives the speaker "sounds" or images for his "song," and "paths" or patterns of understanding. These patterns lead "to good/ Or evil: to the cage, to the oven, to the House/ In the Wood." Jarrell explains the significance of these images directly: "It is a part of life, or of the story/ We make of life." These images are close to our consciousness and conscience. We recognize and interpret them easily, partly because they have traditional forms. But the end of "summer" and the end of the day in the wood, like the nightfall in "The Märchen" (1946), present a less easily understood, less easily coped with aspect of the wood, because "each year is leafless,/ Each day lightless, at the last." At this point, "the wood begins/ Its serious existence." It is pathless, and any who would beat a track through it must do so at the risk of becoming lost. The speaker must once have forced an entry, for he knows what he will find if he goes as far as he can walk into the heart of the wood: the little house, so often found in fairy tales, but now his own. When he comes to the door of the House in the Wood, it opens to him; the story is not, however, the traditional one of capture and ultimate rescue, as in "Hansel and Gretel" or "The Robber Bridegroom," but a mysterious, ambiguous action whose plot and characters are distorted from any typical treatment of the motif.

"On the bed is something covered, something humped/ Asleep there, awake there—but what? I do not know." He senses that it is himself, though he also says he does not know who it is: "I look, I lie there, and yet I do not know/ How far out my great echoing clumsy limbs/ Stretch, surrounded only by space!" He feels enchanted, "numbed, wooden, motionless," as one so often does in nightmares; he hears sounds, "a high soft droning, drawn out like a wire," then "a scream like an old knife sharpened into nothing./ It is only a nightmare." Instead of waking, the sleeper drifts deeper into sleep, and at the very bottom of his sleep, he finds security, the cradling sleep that is death—not horrible, but peaceful and loving.

> Here at the bottom of the world, what was before the world
> And will be after, holds me to its black
>
> Breasts and rocks me: the oven is cold, the cage is empty,
> In the House in the Wood, the witch and her child sleep.

The dark mysterious witch-mother of "The House in the Wood" represents a new conception of the "wicked stepmother" of the Hansel story. In Jarrell's earlier treatments of the story, such as "A Quilt Pattern," the image represented the authoritarian side of the good mother, the side which seemed to capture and absorb the child as he sought individuation. Here the man wishes to return to the mother, whom he sees in her beneficent role, cradling him, rocking him to sleep. The image of death as a loving sleep Jarrell had used in "The Sleeping Beauty: Variation of the Prince" and in "The Black Swan." In the former, the prince lies down to sleep beside the princess forever, but ever separated from her by "Death's sword"; in the latter, the lonely little sister sleeps and dreams of transformation into a swan in order to be with her dead sibling. In contrast to these rather melancholy situations, there is a maternal—even incestuous—coziness in the image of the witch and her child sleeping, and a sense of reconciliation between the formidable mother and her unruly child, actually a grownup but dreamed back to childhood, where he can once again be soothed to sleep on a mother's breast. Perhaps an intermediate stage of the witch image is the anima-witch of "Jamestown," who is "Nature . . . wedded to a man."

Although it treats several old concerns of Jarrell's in some of his most characteristic images, "The House in the Wood" is closely related to several of the distinctly new poems of *The Lost World*. Sleep as a descent into the "woods" is the central image of "Field and Forest." The difficulty of maintaining an identity as one slips into sleep, into the forest, also appears in this poem, which combines some of Robert Frost's typical images and themes with Jarrell's own. Basically an epistemological poem, it is about how we know the world. "Field and Forest" begins by looking at the ground from an airplane, from which the land, field, and forest, are light and dark patches linked (or separated) by lines braided into a "net or web." The ordered, conscious world, and the chaotic disordered world are actually one, related as the lines and holes of a net. Though from the air "the fields have a terrible monotony" relieved only by the dark patches of the forest, the farmer on the ground would make all the forest into field if he could, "but it isn't worth it"; the forest is intractable, worthless so far as crop or stock producing is concerned. "Some of it's marsh, some rocks,/ There are things there you couldn't get rid of/ With a bulldozer, even—not with dynamite./ Besides, he likes it." He remembers its charms from boyhood, when "he had a cave there."

When at night the farmer takes off all the vestiges of civilized life, of knowledge and productivity—clothes, spectacles, teeth—and goes to sleep, he dreams or wishes himself back into the forest, to the cave.

> And there, curled up inside it, is the fox.
>
> He stands looking at it.
> Around him the fields are sleeping: the fields dream.
> At night there are no more farmers, no more farms.
> At night the fields dream, the fields *are* the forest.
> The boy stands looking at the fox
> As if, if he looked long enough—
>   he looks at it.

> Or is it the fox that's looking at the boy?
> The trees can't tell the two of them apart.

The merging of the boy with the fox is similar to the union of the witch-mother and her child at the end of "The House in the Wood" in that the supposedly antithetical elements have become indistinguishable as a result of the journey into the "wood" of the unconscious. In a sense the see-er becomes what he sees, and we are given to understand that he *has been* this thing all along, has been one with it in his imagination, without knowing it himself. Another poem in the volume, "The Mockingbird," develops the same idea in still another way, as it presents the mockingbird warring all day with "the world," the other birds and animals that invade his territory, then imitating all of them by moonlight. The real, phenomenal world is associated with the day, the illusion or imitation with the night, yet the imitation is so perfect it too has a reality, as dreams do. "Which one's the mockingbird? Which one's the world?" Jarrell asks in the last line of the poem. Which is real, the thing or the idea projected in the images of artistic creation? For the listener, the observer, it is sometimes difficult to distinguish, and perhaps not so necessary as we like to think, because both are ways of knowing, and both have a psychic value.

"The Mockingbird" is one of three poems from Jarrell's children's book, *The Bat Poet*, included in *The Lost World*. The other two, "The Bird of Night" and "Bats," are similar to "The Mockingbird" in their close description of the essential character of their subjects, owls and bats. The owl's shape, its soundless flight, its claws, beak, and eyes are presented as the features of death moving back and forth through the night, while "the night holds its breath." Like the world combated then imitated by the mockingbird, the owl has both an objective and a subjective reality to the observer. The bats present a different kind of perceptual problem: their appearance and behavior are contrary to what the observer expects from his own experience, and he is therefore surprised to find the bats' "real" life so similar to his own. The bat mother, for example, cares for her baby by careening through the air all night while he clings to her "by his thumbs and toes and teeth." She "sees" by hearing, and when she finally comes home, at dawn, she rests upside down. Yet "All the bright day, as the mother sleeps,/ She folds her wings about her sleeping child."

The Bat Poet is a story about a young bat who wants to write poems like the mockingbird's songs, and each of the poems he writes shows forth a different aspect of the psychological process by which the real world is changed into poetry. The book is one of those unusual children's stories that is equally amusing and illuminating to children and grownups: for children because it presents the grownup process of making poetry in the ever popular form of a beast fable, and to grownups because it presents old truths in an expanding perspective.

"The House in the Wood" depicts an allegorical descent into the unconscious, at the core of which the individual finds himself once again at rest beside his mother, seen as the witch of the Hansel and Gretel story. The ambivalent attitude of the child (and the child-as-father-of-the-man) toward his mother, evident not only in this poem but several earlier Jarrell poems, becomes in the two longest poems of *The Lost World* a central fact in Jarrell's exploration of the always dangerous, ever gratifying and necessary relationship between a man and woman. In "Woman," a funny, grudging panegyric to Everywoman, Jarrell probes the link between the wife and the mother who preceded her in the man's love. Like Proust's Swann, the man believes that the woman he loves is really not his type:

> But then, a woman never is a man's type.
> Possessed by that prehistoric unforgettable
> Other One, who never again is equaled
> By anyone, he searches for his ideal,
> The Good Whore who reminds him of his mother.
> The realities are too much one or the other,
> Too much like Mother or too bad . . . Too bad!

The man chooses a woman as "the best thing that this world can offer," then worries continually about the wisdom of his choice. Early in the poem, Jarrell quotes Freud's judgment on women's ethical sense, that their "superego . . . is never so inexorable, so impersonal,/ So independent of its emotional/ Origins as we require it in a man." Freud's indictment is itself a form of praise, for it implies a mercifulness, a generosity of sympathy in women that men's rigid ethical standards exclude. Woman is inconsistent, whimsical, immoral, even mercenary, Jarrell says, yet her gifts are transcendent, her faults are endearing, to the poet as to Freud.

Late in the poem Jarrell considers a woman's astonishing metamorphosis from a girl into a wife and mother. Each evening "she stands there in slacks/ Among the real world's appliances,/ Women, and children . . ./ This home of theirs is haunted by a girl's/ Ghost." But this domestic, maternal creature of the real world has also a mythic manifestation "many-breasted/ As Diana of the Ephesians, strewing garments/ Before the world's eyes narrowed in desire." Brought to Ephesus by Orestes—who had a lot of trouble with his mother—and Iphigenia as they fled Tauris, this legendary Diana demanded human sacrifice and yet was a fertility or mother goddess, and she seems the appropriate image for Jarrell's woman. To her he finally applies the epithet for Christ from the Moravian hymn, "O Morning Star," not blasphemously but lovingly.

The range of tone in "Woman" extends from the sublime to the absurd, reflecting the extremes and varieties of judgment and desire the lyric speaker feels toward his beloved, frustrating subject. The poem has a relatively simple structure, associational rather than logical, climaxing in the man's capitulation, after ineffectual struggles, to the love the woman gives so freely and unselfconsciously. The poem ends with his hope that his happiness with her may continue.

A more elaborate, more complicated treatment of a man's ambivalent attitude toward his wife is the longer poem (220 lines), "Hope." Structurally and in some respects thematically it is curiously similar to Jarrell's longest poem, "The Night Before the Night Before Christmas" (*The Seven-League Crutches*), and it also utilizes close temporal links with the commemoration of Christ's birth, taking place on Christmas Eve, at two in the morning. The earlier poem had traced the painful attempts of an adolescent girl to adjust to a world, personal and social, that seemed overwhelmed with death and suffering; this late poem follows a man's attempt to cope with a world that is filled with the object luxuries of modern life, peopled with a wife and son, a governess, a maid, and yet confusing and troubled, like that of the woman in "Next Day." The title, which points rather baldly toward the theme, Jarrell had used before,[7] but for a very different kind of poem; on the other hand, "Hope" would have been an equally appropriate title for "The Night Before the Night Before Christmas." Still like "The Night Before . . . Christmas," "Hope" includes among its poetic objects a squirrel which is a sort of pet to the child in the poem, though the squirrel is less important to the plot of the later poem.

A number of manuscript pages of this poem were received in the University of North Carolina, Greensboro, collection in December, 1960, under the title, "The Fir Tree." These include fragments up to line 84 in the finished poem. This title and the content of the fragments indicate a slightly different focus, even though the traditional symbolism of the evergreen Christmas fir tree *is* hope: basically, hope for transcendence. The speaker of the poem wishes to transcend not his mortality so much as the imperfect, ambivalent relationships he maintains with his family and his surroundings. The veiled wish for a simpler life appears in the opening lines;

> To prefer the nest in the linden
> By Apartment Eleven, the Shoreham
> Arms, to Apartment Eleven
> Would be childish. But we are children.

Presumably only the son has expressed a wish to be, or live like, a squirrel, yet the father returns to the notion with tacit sympathy several times in the poem. By normal standards, this family "has everything," a luxurious residence, complete with various *objets d'art*, among which the speaker, like Browning's duke, escorts the reader; the furnishings range from paintings and a harpsichord through a Kirman rug, an antique grandfather clock incongruously shaped like a large-breasted woman, to

> That? That is Pennsylvania Dutch, a bear
> Used to mark butter. As for this,
> It is sheer alchemy:
> The only example of an atomic bomb

---

[7] "Hope" (1948) appears on p. 111 of *The Complete Poems*.

> Earlier than the eleventh century.
> It is attributed to the atelier
> Of an Albigensian,
> Who, fortunately, was unable to explode it.
> We use it as a planter.
>
> We feel that it is so American.

These relics of civilized life do not make the people happy, as the title of the man's favorite television serial, "A Sad Heart at the Supermarket: The Story of a Woman Who Had Everything," indicates. Jarrell also used this title for a 1960 essay about the American obsession with buying and consuming things and people on the supposition, fostered by what Jarrell, à la Marshall McLuhan, calls The Medium, that such things will satisfy emotional needs. The use of "things" to fulfill spiritual longings is the ordinary outgrowth of man's double nature—material and spiritual—but it results in continuous frustration. The man in the poem sees that his wife is beautiful, and responds with the old Platonic notion that "Beauty is a good,/ It makes us desire it." The desire is inevitably translated into physical terms, but the speaker of the poem has had a dream about the elusiveness of physical satisfaction:

> I think of the God-Fish in a nightmare
> I had once: like giants in brown space-suits
> But like fish, also, they went upright through the streets
> And were useless to struggle with, but, struggled with,
> Showed me a story that, they said, was the story
> Of the Sleeping Beauty. It was the old story
> But ended differently: when the Prince kissed her on the lips
> She wiped her lips
> And with a little *moue*—in the dream, a little mouse—
> Turned over and went back to sleep.

The God-Fish amusingly burlesque the traditional sexual "symbols" of dreams and the fertility myths associated with the Fisher-King or perhaps that preserver-god Vishnu, whose first avatar was a fish. They are also, somehow, like the angel of God who appeared to

Jacob and wrestled with him all night before blessing him. These God-Fish tell a new version of one of Jarrell's own favorite stories, a version not so different from that in "Sleeping Beauty: Variation of the Prince." The sleeper does not wake but goes on sleeping; the prince's longing is not fulfilled, but postponed. The dreamer, waking, finds his wife asleep, and in a parody of Lady Macbeth's inability to kill Duncan, he cannot wake her to tell her his nightmare:

> I woke, and went to tell my wife the story;
> And had she not resembled
> My mother as she slept, I had done it.

This perception of his wife as his mother turns out to be the central intuition of the poem, a crux in the tense relationships of the family. The wife, sleeping, resembles the mother, fainted: a "recurrent scene" from the speaker's childhood, "a scene called Mother Has Fainted." The children, having arranged the mother's body as directed, wait for her recovery

It was as if God were taking a nap.

We waited for the world to be the world
And looked out, shyly, into the little lanes
That went off from the great dark highway, Mother's Highway,
And wondered whether we would ever take them—

And she came back to life, and we never took them.

The dominance of the mother when awake fills the children's lives, superseding their own wishes and concerns; it is only when she sleeps or has fainted that they begin to sense the possibilities of independence. Another manifestation of the wish to be rid of the mother occurs early in "Hope," when the speaker imagines his and/or his wife's mother whisked away on a space ship to "govern the happy people of another planet." Mother does not ever really disappear, for her image is resurgent in all the females that surround the narrator: his wife, the governess, the maid, even the clock.

Beside the omnipresent mothers, men are insubstantial figures.

> I have followed in my father's light, faint footsteps
> Down to some place under the sun, under the moon,
> Lit by the light of the streetlamp far below.
> Back far enough, down deep enough, one comes to the Mothers.[8]

The women are impatient with men; like Jarrell's Cinderella or the fisherman's wife in the Grimms' tale, they wish to go beyond these paltry things, their husbands, to become *Mothers*: to assume the role of governor or god.

> Do all men's mothers perish through their sons?
> As the child starts into life, the woman dies
> Into a girl—and, scolding the doll she owns,
> The single scholar of her little school,
> Her task, her plaything, her possession,
> She assumes what is God's alone, responsibility.

Even though his own wife seems to have disappeared into the archetype of the Mother, the speaker takes his hope from a vision of his son, who almost, but fortunately not quite, seems a replica of himself. "The next time that they say to me; 'He has your eyes,'/ I'll tell them the truth: he has his own eyes." If the son does not exactly repeat the father, perhaps the wife need not exactly repeat the mother. Perhaps some change in the pattern of family tensions will come after all. The danger of change, however, is that it may be for the worse: "You wake up, some fine morning, old./ And old means changed; changed means you wake up new." The hope, to wake up new, is the old wish for transformation, "to change, to change," even if only by equivocation. The man finally concludes that his notion that everyone in his house is a mother is perhaps simply an illusion, like the artificial whiteness of the fir tree, which is really "green . . . evergreen." If he can convince himself, convince his wife, that she is not like his mother, not a *Mother*, perhaps his life will change, will become satisfying: perhaps they can wake up new.

   Despite the fact that the poem provides an interesting vision of a peculiarly American situation, it lacks sustained emotional force. The

---

8 The allusion is to the "Mothers" episode in Goethe's *Faust*, Part 2, ll. 6173–6306.

speaker remains a shadowy figure, like his memory of his father, and his fixation on the archetype of the Mother is puzzling rather than illuminating to the ordinary adult reader who does not share Jarrell's assessment of women as Mothers, and is not convinced by the poem that he should. Even more than "The Night Before the Night Before Christmas," "Hope" seems diffuse; there is no clear link between the man's dissatisfaction with his material luxuries and his inability to keep his wife from turning into Mother, if, indeed, that is the central issue at all. It is too difficult to separate the dramatic speaker of "Hope" from the lyric speaker (presumably Jarrell) of "Woman." Is the reader to sympathize with or judge the quality of the man's life? Should we share or smile at his hope? The poem seems to ask for both kinds of response, but in what proportion or what specific instances it is difficult to say exactly. It offers too little real experience into which the reader might project himself and his feelings. It seems all setting and no acting, perhaps a result of the time and occasion of the poem: everyone but the speaker is fast asleep.

A poem which does offer the possibility of the reader's vicarious experience is "The Lost Children," one of the most beautiful and moving of Jarrell's poems. It is all the more remarkable in the circumstances of its composition: as I have noted above, the poem is based very closely on a written account of a dream of Mary Jarrell's and her subsequent meditation on the meaning of the dream experience. After hearing her tell of the dream, Jarrell had asked her to write it down, with comments, if she wanted. From her notes the poem was made. The only new content supplied by the poet comes in the last verse paragraph, and even here, the rainy-day game of hide-and-seek is obliquely suggested by Mary Jarrell's notes. Aside from changing the relationship of the two girls to the woman—in real life the dead girl was the daughter of Mrs. Jarrell's friend, not her own—Jarrell's work was the editing of the notes: rearranging the sequence, cutting discursive portions, sharpening diction, and in a few passages merely arranging the prose original into the blank verse of the poem. Some readers may regard such work as a kind of cheating in the sacrosanct poetic process, but as Jarrell's poem, "Jonah" (1948), reveals the lyric embedded in the four chapters of the King James Book of Jonah, so "The Lost Children" reveals the work of art embedded in the real experience of a woman who is not in the common sense of the word an artist. Thus Jarrell bears out Proust's assertion that the "life that is really lived . . . is to be found every moment in every man, as well as in the artist." [9] The artist's true work is "to get light on it," and this Jarrell emphatically does.

The dream of the "two little girls, one fair, one dark,/ One alive, one dead . . . running hand in hand/ Through a sunny house" that so delights the mother because it makes her feel that "somewhere, they still are," will remind many readers of Kipling's beautiful story, "They," which Mary Jarrell in fact mentions in her notes. "They" was a wish-fulfillment story for Kipling, who had lost a young daughter, a kind of conscious dream that like any parent's dream of "lost" children, whether dead or merely grown, embodies a wish to see and know them again. In "They," a man "finds" his own dead child among several who have returned to earth, to a beautiful Tudor home somewhere on the south coast of England, outside the ordinary realm of modern active life. The home is kept for them by a childless blind woman who loves them intensely though she can never get close to them, and only follows the sound of their play from room to room in a kind of hide-and-seek similar to that described in the last stanza of "The Lost Children." Kipling's story gave the dead children a place, an environment in this world where they could still exist, and its concreteness provided more comfort to the parent than the mystical promise of "everlasting life," which neither Jarrell nor Kipling seems to have found very helpful.

The poem uses the dream as a point of reference, a jumping-off place for contemplation of the changing relationship between a mother and her child, which begins with the mother's full possession of the baby inside her body and ends in the inevitable loss of possession as the child grows up. Each stanza after the first develops a new step in the parent's awareness of this changing bond. At first the mother knows the child "better than it knows itself./ You own it as you made it./ You are the authority upon it." When the child gets a little bigger, the mother knows "more/ About her than anyone *except* her." Even though the *person* lives, "Little by little the child

<hr />

[9] Marcel Proust, *Remembrance of Things Past*, trans. C. K. Scott Moncrieff and Frederick A. Blossom (New York: Random House, 1932), II, 1013.

in her dies./ You say, 'I have lost a child, but gained a friend.' " Still drawing on his wife's notes, Jarrell compares the early relationship to a game of follow the leader: as the child grows, she gradually tires of the game and refuses to play any more.

The fifth section of the poem is the longest, focusing upon the response of the mother to looking at a photograph album alongside the grown young woman who was once the fair child in the pictures. The reality of the children in the pictures is so great for the mother that she cannot reconcile those children with the daughter who sits before her; "I tell her foolishly, pointing at the picture,/ That I keep wondering where she is./ She tells me, 'Here I am.' Yes, and the other/ Isn't dead, but has everlasting life . . .'"

The physical details of the poem, culled and shaped from Mrs. Jarrell's account, form a catalogue such as every grownup remembers from his own or his children's youth, of incidents, things, experiences that make the past come alive once again each time they appear to the mind's eye, so that everyone says, with the speaker of the poem, "I *know* those children, I know all about them./ Where are they?"

The most baffling shock to the parent comes when she realizes that, to others, she is not even associated with her children.

> The girl from next door, the borrowed child,
> Said to me the other day, "You like children so much,
> Don't you want to have some of your own?"
> I couldn't believe that she could say it.
> I thought: "Surely you can look at me and see them."

The children seem so much a part of herself that she unconsciously believes they must also seem part of her to anyone who knows her, yet, of course, this is not true at all; even should the borrowed child know the grownup daughter, she could not really associate her friend with the now vanished child that only the mother herself remembers and knows.

The last eight lines strikingly summarize and intensify the feelings and perceptions developed in the rest of the poem. The image of hide-and-seek was perhaps evoked by Jarrell's recollection of the pursuit of the children in Kipling's "They."

> When I think of my dream of the little girls
> It's as if we were playing hide-and-seek.
> The dark one
> Looks at me longingly, and disappears;
> The fair one stays in sight, just out of reach
> No matter where I reach. I am tired
> As a mother who's played all day, some rainy day.
> I don't want to play it any more, I don't want to,
> But the child keeps on playing, so I play.

Thus the joy of remembering is coupled with the pain of loss; to remember the children is to remember that they are gone. Still, it is better to remember, and "The Lost Children" exquisitely captures the envelope of sensations and emotions that surround this wonderful, yet sad, experience of the mind and heart.

The need to remember one's own lost childhood lies behind the title poem of *The Lost World* and its companion piece, "Thinking of the Lost World," which brings the volume to a close. These two poems seem to gather together so much of what was most characteristic and best in the mature poetry of Randall Jarrell that it is tempting to regard them as culminating his work. Although they were actually not his last poems, and surely other major poems would have been written had he lived, they were the poems he needed most to write for himself, because in them at last his own life and his art coalesce. Commenting upon the two poems, Robert Lowell invoked Wordsworth and Rilke as Jarrell's fellows in presenting the child and his world.[10] Both are appropriate, but Proust, another of Jarrell's favorite writers, is even more intimately bound up in the creation of these poems. In her memoir, "The Group of Two," Mary Jarrell testifies amply to Jarrell's great love for Proust, and his intimate knowledge of *À la recherche du temps perdu*. But even without her account, we might deduce his attachment from the numerous allusions in his poems, the novel, and the criticism.

The earliest reference—to *Swann's Way*—comes in "Children Selecting Books in a Library" (1941), the last—again to Swann—in the posthumously published "A Man Meets a Woman in the Street." In "The Lost World," the influence of *À la recherche du temps perdu*

---

10 Lowell, "Randall Jarrell," in Lowell, Taylor, *et al.*, *Randall Jarrell, 1914–1965*, 109.

ranges from the almost joking parodies of Proust's famous madeleine episode from "Combray" (in Jarrell's taste of chocolate tapioca and his smell of eucalyptus from the Vicks factory in Greensboro, North Carolina, which take him back to Hollywood in 1925), through the treatment of an important character (the implicit comparison of Marcel's grandmother with Jarrell's great-grandmother, Dandeen), and, most significant, to the pervasive atmosphere of joy that envelops and permeates the memories recaptured by the poet. In fact, both of these poems about "lost" time, "lost" persons, are more truly about the recovery, through memory, of the quintessential spiritual beauty of the past experiences, a recovery precipitated, as in *Le temps retrouvé*, by sensory impressions.

Though Proust's influence is unmistakably behind the creation of "The Lost World" and "Thinking of the Lost World," the poems themselves are fully Jarrell's—perhaps more so, in a sense, than any other of his published works, since they deal explicitly with his personal life, the world of his personal childhood. Because for Jarrell the aesthetic form of his experience was not to be a multivolumed Proustian novel but a 308-line poem (with an 83-line sequel), none of Proust's formal strategies, except for the fundamental sense experience that evokes memory, was appropriate. For Jarrell, formal and stylistic modes worked out in nearly thirty years of writing poems about others' lives and experiences were naturally enough the aesthetic keys to recovering lost time. As in Proust, however, life and art— the *real*, external world and the *form* given to the internal, sensed and imagined world of the individual—are finally inseparable.

"The Lost World" is a triptych of poems focusing on different aspects of a theme: remembrance of things past. For Jarrell, the real part of the past, the lost world to be recovered, was that period he spent in Hollywood with his paternal grandparents and his great-grandmother: the Mama, Pop, and Dandeen of the poem. The title of the poem was, in 1925, the title of a film, based on a tale by A. Conan Doyle, about a group of explorers who find in a remote part of Africa[11] an enclave of prehistoric animals; with some difficulty they

---

[11] In Doyle's story the explorers go to South America and bring back a pterodactyl which, on escaping, merely frightens a few people before heading out over the Atlantic on its homing journey.

capture and transport one to London, where it escapes. Joe Franklin, in *Classics of the Silent Screen*, describes the outcome: "*The Lost World* was pleasantly off-beat and even revolutionary in its climax. The huge brontosaurus manages to outwit the stupid humans and escapes quite unharmed at the end—swimming happily up the Thames after having almost wrecked London." [12] The movie itself is alluded to only once, near the beginning of the poem, as Jarrell records seeing, on his way home from school, "a dinosaur/ And pterodactyl, with their immense pale/ Papier-mâché smiles, look over the fence/ Of *The Lost World*." The fantasy world represented by the movie is symbolic of the total imaginative experience of the poem in two ways: first, the world the grown man attempts to recover is his own prehistoric world, lost in the enclaves of memory, and the images he finds there are as overpowering emotionally as the "real" brontosaurus was to its captors; second, the blending of illusion with reality in Jarrell's lost world is, like the filmed dinosaurs, the result of an animating art, both the conscious art of the poem and the unconscious art of wishes working upon memory.

The title evokes not only a particular movie with a fantasy subject, but a whole other "lost world" whose magic is partly the ordinary magic of nostalgia, and partly the magic of Hollywood in the mid-twenties, then the exciting focal point of America's dreams. Unlike Proust's Marcel, who found his magic lantern disturbing in the long afternoons of "Combray" and who ridiculed "cinematographic realism" in *Le temps retrouvé*, Jarrell perceived the peculiar value the movie was to have to Americans: as the folk tales of the Black Forest provided escape from Necessity for generations of European children, the movies provided for at least two generations of Americans the fantasy life that enriches and makes tolerable things as they are. The fantasy of the film, *The Lost World*, derives its appeal from man's insatiable desire to recapture the past, and the child's fantasy in the poem, "The Lost World," makes us aware of the apparently endless ramifications of this desire.

Within the poem, as in the movie, there are two orders of being, the real and the fantastic, which interpenetrate. The first order is

---

[12] Joe Franklin, *Classics of the Silent Screen* (New York, 1959), 70.

represented by the grandparents, the eucalyptus tree, the boy's rabbit, Mrs. Mercer and her dog and electric car, the tall brown aunt, and the "real" lion whose dewclaw the boy keeps; the second order of being is the boy's interior world, in which he arms for battle, visits the cave of the Nibelungen dwarfs, makes a royal progress along Sunset Boulevard in an "enchanted drawing room," and worries about a mad scientist who might destroy the whole world from his laboratory "there off Sunset in the lamplit starlight."

The first section of the triptych, 146 lines long, brings together a cinematic montage of impressions from a child's life in Hollywood in the twenties, uniting a reality that is partly the fantastic world of film sets with the art-oriented fantasies of the child's private world. Achilles, Odysseus, Pitamakan, and the Admirable Crichton people the boy's world with a reality not much inferior to that of the actual people with whom he lives. In the phenomenal world "a star/ Stumble[s] to her igloo through the howling gale/ Of the wind machines;" a dog, "half wolf, half police dog," can play the piano ("play that he does, that is"); a boy and a woman and the dog can ride in a car that bears "yellow roses/ In . . . bud vases."

The title of the section, "Children's Arms," refers at first only to the "arsenal" of the boy's "real life" catalogued in lines 11 through 25: the helmet and breastplate soldered by the grandfather, the beaverboard shield, "the bow that only Odysseus can wield," the weed spears, a knife, his model airplane. The list of his armory is recognized as a

> . . . dead list, that misunderstands
> And laughs at and lies about the new live wild
> Loves it lists! that sets upright, in the sands
> Of age in which nothing grows, where all our friends are old,
> A few dried leaves marked THIS IS THE GREENWOOD—

Although the poem is presumably being narrated by the boy in the present tense, this passage and others like it serve notice that the real narrator is the poet, attempting, not always successfully, to project himself backward into the pastoral world of his youth, where he can defend himself with the weapons of his play. Not only this opening catalogue, but the whole first section of the poem, comprises a list of defenses against the vicissitudes of time and the outer world, for all the experiences and objects described, real, imagined, and mixed, also "arm" the child—and the backward-looking adult—against the loss that the world inevitably exacts from him. Thus Barrie's play performed by the older children—amazing not so much in its story, in which a butler proves his natural superiority to aristocrats, as in the fact that in the school production *children* run an island (ll. 50–52)— is part of the boy's "armor," just as the grandfather's stories of *his* youth in Shelbyville, Tennessee, are, or Mrs. Mercer's fabulous automobile is. The car has sensible characteristics of armor, of a sort, for behind the insulating, beautifying glass of its windows, as if in a protective aquarium,

> . . . We press our noses
> To the glass and wish: The angel- and devilfish
> Floating by on Vine, on Sunset, shut their eyes
> And press their noses to their glass and wish.

The strange inhabitants of this strange world, in which even the street names are suggestive in odd ways, respond to the magical protection of a fairy tale. Their wishes are not specific but generalized; the reader surmises that they do not wish for change as some earlier characters in Jarrell's poems did, but for continuation of the special, wonderful world through which they float unimpeded.

The middle part of Jarrell's triptych is the shortest, only twenty-six lines, and unlike the other two, which relate a whole series of randomly associated memories, it focuses upon a single image: the lady with the lion, already introduced in Part I (l. 54). The title, "A Night with Lions," may be a dark reflection of Proust's "Seascape, with Frieze of Girls" in *À l'ombre des jeunes filles en fleurs*, which, like "A Night with Lions," relates the awakening sexuality of its protagonist. Jarrell's dark lady is his tall, brown aunt, probably also projected in the tall girl with a wolf of the boy's dream in Part I, lines 60 and 61. She recurs as a dream figure in Part III, "Tall, auburn, hold[ing] her arms out, to unshackle/ The bonds of sin, of sleep," where she blends with the boy's image of the radio evangelist of the

"Four Square Gospel," Aimée Semple McPherson, whom she prov-
identially resembles. The aunt reappears undisguised in the companion poem, "Thinking of the Lost World." Though she is always
associated with the lion in the boy's mind, in the real world she does
not own the lion, Tawny, who appeared in *Tarzan* and at the beginning of countless films as the Metro-Goldwyn-Mayer lion. The boy
visits the lion with her, at the home of her friend. Both the lady and
the lion are a part of the growing boy's most important, most secret
fantasy, dark, dangerous and exotic, nurtured on tales or movies about
love and adventure in faraway wildernesses.

>   Now the lion roars
> His slow comfortable roars; I lie beside
> My young, tall, brown aunt, out there in the past
> Or future, and I sleepily confide
> My dream-discovery: my breath comes fast
> Whenever I see someone with your skin,
> Hear someone with your voice. The lion's steadfast
> Roar goes on in the darkness.

The woman is enveloped in the aura of the lion; she embodies for
the boy all the beautiful, wish-fulfilling women of his heroic dreams
and daydreams, while Tawny, in reality tame and bored in his
cage, is to the child still the preternatural jungle beast. In reality,
too, the tall brown aunt is a grownup friend who talks to the boy
"as grownup people do./ Of *Jurgen* and Rupert Hughes, till in the
end/ I think as a child thinks: 'You're my real friend.' " The section,
with its ominous yet appealing title, suggests a threat to the boy's
heretofore secure, protected existence; within him, even as he enjoys
the delicious fantasies evoked by the tall brown aunt and the lion, are
the seeds of change, of the growth that leaves the child's world behind, lost.

Part III, "A Street Off Sunset," takes the now mature narrator from
his present back into the past à la Proust, through a sensory experience
that bridges the years and projects the man once again into his youth.
No tea-cake or snatch of melody, it is the smell of eucalyptus that
carries Jarrell from the environs of the Vicks Vaporub Factory in
Greensboro, North Carolina, to the California of his childhood, to

the treehouse in the eucalyptus mentioned in Part I. "I feel its stair-sticks/ Impressed on my palms, my insteps, as I climb . . . . My lifetime got rid of, I sit in a dark blue sedan/ Beside my great-grandmother in Hollywood." The memories, like those at the beginning of "Children's Arms," are at first visual, this time from roadside advertising: the Van de Camp Bakeries' windmill, still a familiar shape in California; a "pink Sphinx," remnant of a movie set, gracing a realtor's front yard; advertisements for Allbran and a pancake flour, and for movies of *Salâmmbo* and *Robin Hood*. In the manner of a cinematic fadeout, these visual impressions dissolve into a scene in which the boy is reading in the company of his grandparents and Dandeen. His ritual of going to bed and arising is presented as sacramental, and as a counterpoint to the "amazing story" of a mad scientist "getting ready to destroy the world" which he reads with such excitement.

This final section, which is approximately the same length as the opening section, reinforces the threat of change hinted at in "A Night with Lions." The image of the mad scientist menaces the security of the boy's world, with its "ways that habit itself makes holy," for the interweaving of fantasy with reality that characterizes his environment makes it all the more difficult for him to dismiss the scientist as purely fantastic. The real world presents its threats, too: first, the inevitable loss of the great-grandmother, Dandeen. Though he loves her as a child can, though he recognizes that "it is miraculous/ To have a great-grandmother" whose own lost world is that of "The War Between the States," nevertheless he gets bored playing dominoes with her and forsakes her to feed and play with his rabbit.

> . . . As I run by the chicken coops
> With lettuce for my rabbit, real remorse
> Hurts me, here, now: the little girl is crying
> Because I didn't write. Because—
> of course,
> I *was* a child, I missed them so. But justifying
> Hurts too: if only I could play you one more game,
> See you all one more time! I think of you dying
> Forgiving me—or not, it is all the same
> To the forgiven . . . My rabbit's glad to see me . . .

The crying little girl is Dandeen, in an image that forcibly unites the abandoned old woman with her own childhood self, frightened by a Union soldier who put her on his horse (ll. 83–85). The boy Jarrell stayed with his grandparents in Hollywood only a short time, then moved back to Tennessee with his mother; hence the self-accusation, "I didn't write," an abandonment which parallels and intensifies his leaving Dandeen to feed the rabbit. But the memory of the rabbit supplants the remorse of the adult, and the narrator is again caught up into the stream of reminiscence. Jarrell, who delighted in analogies uniting his life with the lives or works of those he admired (he was elated to find that his birthday and Freud's were the same[13]), must have noticed that his experience of grieving Dandeen and his subsequent remorse closely paralleled Marcel's recurrent account of causing pain to his grandmother when she was near death, and his overwhelming sorrow some time later, described in *Sodom et Gomorrhe*. While the great-grandmother's demands leave the boy uneasy, the rabbit is "reassuring to a child," because it guarantees, "as so much here does, that the child knows/ Who takes care of him, whom he takes care of." Into this scene of security emerges Mama, the grandmother, taking the clothes from the line, entering the henhouse to choose a chicken for dinner. The demise of the hen which runs, already dead, "in great flopping circles" about her destroys the boy's complacency. Most immediately, he fears the death of the rabbit and pleads for his grandmother's word that she will never kill it; behind that, he fears the death and destruction of the whole idyllic world 'which, as the adult knows, was to be lost to him all too soon. The equivalence of love and fear remain fixed in his memory and judgment:

> . . . whenever
> I see her, there in that dark infinite,
> Standing like Judith, with the hen's head in her hand,
> I explain it away in vain—a hypocrite,
> Like all who love.

The concluding memory of "The Lost World" reestablishes the

[13] See Mrs. Randall Jarrell, "The Group of Two," in Lowell, Taylor, *et al.*, *Randall Jarrell, 1914–1965*, 278.

peace and safety undermined by the uncomfortable vision of death. In the evening, in that (formerly) "blue wonderland of Hollywood" the grandfather descends from his bus, haloed like some demigod by the setting sun, "a blurred nimbus/ Half-red, half-gold" that changes his "sober brown face . . . into the All-Father's"; Pop comforts the boy's anxieties about the mad scientist by calling the story "just play,/ Just make-believe." In 1925, of course, it was "just make-believe," but the stories, then as now, gave expression to children's and grownups' darkest fears of dissolution, fears temporarily assuaged by their deep wishes when, at the end of the tale, "the good world wins its victory over that bad man." The healing function of fantasy, long a familiar theme in Jarrell's poetry, lies at the heart of this exploration of memory. Although in a phenomenal sense the lost world is truly lost, because it no longer exists in physical reality, the love which the child had for it keeps it alive in the man's memory which, though it is "just make-believe" (being mental rather than physical, and past rather than present), has a powerful reality for his inner life. Consequently, he is able to re-create it, in poetry, with an atmosphere of miracle and a tone of joy.

"The Lost World," with its terza rima rhyme scheme and tripartite form, nods at Dante as Jarrell rediscovers the landmarks on his own spiritual pilgrimage into the past. Utilizing the time-scheme of a single weekend, with its following Monday, leaving out everything irrelevant to his "real" life, that is, school, church, household business, Jarrell's search for lost time focuses lucidly upon the interplay of fantasy and reality that marks not only his childhood in Hollywood, but every normal childhood. The Hollywood setting provides the link between the fantasies of youth and those of maturity, which are different in form and overt content, but similar in the basic need for security and love that impels them.

While "The Lost World" actually does recapture the past (as do the first six parts of *À la recherche du temps perdu*), "Thinking of the Lost World" deals more fully with the effort and the significance involved in the quest for the past. It is not simply another section of the former poem, though a knowledge of "The Lost World" is most helpful, even essential to our understanding of the images of "Thinking of the Lost World." As if to emphasize the difference in focus from "The Lost World," Jarrell shifted away from the formalistic rigor of terza rima to the more characteristic conversational free verse of most of his later poems.

This poem opens with another analogue of the madeleine incident from Proust: the poet tastes chocolate tapioca that reminds him of peanut butter, then of vanilla extract—false trails, such as Proust also encountered—then takes him "through time to . . . childhood." Curiously, he finds that middle age is much like "that calm country" of his youth. Returning to the physical scene of "The Lost World," however, he cannot find it. "The sunshine of the Land/ Of Sunshine is a gray mist now, the atmosphere/ Of some factory planet." The orange groves are gone, his eucalyptus tree, with its stairs and house, has been cut and burned for firewood long since.

But the memory is "better than ever," if only one could believe in it! Unable to relocate his lost world, he fantasies another one, an "undiscovered/ Country between California and Arizona," peopled by Indians, where all the images of his past continue to live (even though, as we know, Hamlet's "undiscovered country" was one "from whose bourne no traveller returns": the kingdom of death).

> . . . if only I could find a crystal set
> Sometimes, surely, I could still hear their chief
> Reading to them from Dumas or *Amazing Stories;*
> If I could find in some Museum of Cars
> Mama's dark blue Buick, Lucky's electric,
> Couldn't I be driven there? Hold out to them,
> The paraffin half picked out, Tawny's dewclaw—
> And have walk to me from among their wigwams
> My tall brown aunt, to whisper to me: "Dead?
> They told you I was dead?"
> As if you could die!

That this past does live in his mind is undeniable. The tall brown aunt appears again and again, in other women, disguised "as a mermaid puts on her sealskin." Even though all of those he knew then are dead, all gone, except in his mind, to him "nothing is gone," good or bad:

> The chicken's body is still going round
> And round in widening circles, a satellite
> From which, as the sun sets, the scientist bends
> A look of evil on the unsuspecting earth.

Now that he is aging, his beard turned gray, children call him "Santa Claus," and like having a great-grandmother in one's childhood, that "*is* miraculous." His own hands, now "brown and spotted . . . like Mama's," seem not really his. Like the mother of the lost children, he wonders where that child, his real self, is. Reaching out across time to a "shape in tennis shoes and khaki riding pants" that is himself, he draws back empty-handed.

> And yet . . .
> I have found that Lost World in the Lost and Found
> Columns whose gray illegible advertisements
> My soul has memorized world after world:
> LOST—NOTHING. STRAYED FROM NOWHERE. NO REWARD.
> I hold in my own hands, in happiness,
> Nothing: the nothing for which there's no reward.

This nothing is, quite simply, its own reward, and the memory fixed in poetry works in quite the same way as the mother's dream in "The Lost Children." It assures the dreamer, or the rememberer, that "somewhere, they still are." Like fairy tales, these memories enable the individual to transcend time and dissolution, and if one can manage to put aside regret for their being past and love them as a present reality, the result is "happiness."

The three poems, "The Lost Children," "The Lost World," and "Thinking of the Lost World," form a distinct group among the poems of Randall Jarrell's last volume. Although several of the other poems, "Woman" and parts of "Hope," in particular, develop new themes, these three stand apart from and go beyond the others in exploring territory Jarrell had not touched upon directly in previous poems. In a very special way they bring together the "real" world of things with the "real" world of the mind, no longer needing the masks provided in the early poems by myths or *Märchen*. In these poems, the individual's own reality becomes mythic and magical.

In one of his essays on Robert Frost, Jarrell praised Frost's achievement in writing a poetry that

> *is* like the world, "the world wherein we find our happiness or not at all," "the world which was ere I was born, the world which lasts when I am dead," the world with its animals and plants and, most of all, its people: people working, thinking about things, falling in love, taking naps; in these poems men are not only the glory and jest and riddle of the world, but also the habit of the world, its strange ordinariness, its ordinary strangeness, and they too trudge down the ruts along which the planets move in their courses.[14]

Jarrell himself wrote well of this world—not the same world in its minute particulars as Frost's—more urban, more modern, more neurotic, but equally American, and in its way equally real and important.

[14] Randall Jarrell, "To the Laodiceans," *Poetry and the Age* (New York, 1953), 68.

Conclusion

THE VIGOR SHOWN in the poems of *The Lost World* is very much present in the new poems already published in periodicals and the unpublished poems from 1964 and 1965 printed for the first time in *The Complete Poems*. Although none of the seven finished poems of the "New Poems" section, or the dozen-odd poems and fragments from Jarrell's last years in "Unpublished Poems," is among Jarrell's finest work, several, notably "A Man Meets a Woman in the Street," "Say Good-bye to Big Daddy," "The Player Piano," and "The Augsburg Adoration" are interesting and often moving. The first mentioned of these is a more personal treatment of the theme of "Woman" and "Hope" (1961): man's fascination with woman, his need for her love. Its plea, not for change but sameness—"May this day/ Be the same day, the day of my life"—poignantly exemplifies a change in attitude which had overtaken the poet in middle age. Recognizing the beauty and transitoriness of life as it is, and the illusory promise of change, which seldom satisfies our desires as we had anticipated, he now wants to hold onto what he has, even as he records its passing. As early as 1951, in "A Conversation with the Devil," Jarrell had jokingly reversed Faust's condition for giving up his life to "If ever I don't say/ To the hour of life that I can wish for: *Stay/ Thou art so fair!/* why, you may have my—/ Shadow." In "A Man Meets a Woman in the Street" the poet's wish to retain his happiness is desperately serious, though it is expressed playfully, in an elaborate fantasy of meeting a strange woman when it is really his wife he follows through the park. The atmosphere of the poem, washed in sunlight, reflected from the gold of the woman's hair and the champagne-colored sheen of her stockings and dress, and flickering in the leaves of the ancient, changeless gingko tree, effectively supports the man's desire that the day remain always just as it is.

"Say Good-bye to Big Daddy" is a very different kind of poem, but it is related to several earlier Jarrell poems, the elegies of *Losses*. "Big Daddy" Lipscomb, the well-known professional football player who died of an overdose of heroin, is remembered in life and in death: "Big Daddy Lipscomb, who used to help them up/ After he'd pulled them down, so that 'the children/ Won't think Big Daddy's mean.' " Dead now, this modern folk hero whom so many people watched, on television, and identified with, has become a vague image, a television ghost, "a NETWORK DIFFICULTY." The concluding lines are Jarrell's version of *sic transit gloria mundi*: "The world won't be the same without Big Daddy./ Or else it will be."

"The Augsburg Adoration" is another of Jarrell's explorations of contemporary men's responses to works of art, particularly the religious art of the past. More than any of his earlier treatments of this subject, "The Augsburg Adoration" blends the minute details of modern life—tourist life!—with the sublime attitudes of Christian art. As the gingko is the symbol of permanence in "A Man Meets a Woman in the Street," the sparrow, real and contemporary, or ancient and carven, or even metaphorical and exemplary—the sparrow whose fall is marked by God—is the unifying symbol of permanence in "The Augsburg Adoration." Of Jarrell's last poems on works of art, however, I prefer the following pithy observation from among the "Unpublished Poems."

Bamberg

You'd be surprised how much, at
The Last Judgment,
The powers of concentration
Of the blest and damned
Are improved, so that
Both smile exactly alike
At remembering so well
All they meant to remember
To tell God.

In spite of his general mellowing, Jarrell could still flare out with trenchant irony, as he proves in this epigram describing the tympanum of the Prince's Portal at Bamberg Cathedral.

The unfinished or fragmentary impression given by the unpublished poems written in the last year of Jarrell's life is testimony to his unfinished career, tragically cut short in October, 1965. With their publication, in January, 1969, in *The Complete Poems*, the sum of Jarrell's poetic work, including earlier poems he had left unpublished or uncollected, was made available for a total assessment. Leafing through this volume, just short of five hundred pages long, one is immediately struck by two things: first, how many interesting, moving, intelligent, and intelligible poems there really are in the first 350-odd pages, those devoted to the *Selected Poems* and the two subsequent volumes, *The Woman at the Washington Zoo* and *The Lost World*; and second, how shrewdly Jarrell himself was able to choose his own best and most characteristic work. Among the earlier poems in the "Unpublished Poems" section, for example, I found only one, "The Birth of Venus" (1952) which seemed obviously a superior poem; in fact, its exclusion from the self-selected canon is rather puzzling, particularly as it seems so polished. Among the poems collected in Jarrell's first four volumes but left out of *Selected Poems*, only "Orestes at Tauris" and perhaps one or two short poems seem as good or better than those Jarrell chose to represent himself. One wonders, too, if a second *Selected Poems* had been made, whether Jarrell might not have refined his choices even further.

As a critic, Randall Jarrell had an almost infallible sense of the important, lasting poems written by his contemporaries, and one of his chracteristic strategies in review and critical essays was to list the "best" poems by the writer in question. John Crowe Ransom, noting Jarrell's habit, in turn made his list of Jarrell's best poems in his memoir and eulogy of Jarrell.[1] Looking backward through the chapters of this book, I see my own list—in part but not altogether the same as Mr. Ransom's—cmerging. In presenting it here, I hope to point the way to some conclusions about Randall Jarrell's poetic achievement. As befits a study of this kind, it is an inclusive list, somewhat longer than Jarrell usually allowed his lists to become.

From the first separate volume, *Blood for a Stranger*, it seems to me that only "90 North" belongs with the best of Jarrell's work, though other strange and attractive poems appeared there: "Children Selecting Books in a Library," "The Blind Sheep," "The Memoirs of Glückel of Hameln," and "The Skaters." From *Little Friend, Little*

---

[1] Ransom, "The Rugged Way of Genius," 171.

Friend I would choose a larger number as among Jarrell's best: "2nd Air Force," "A Pilot from the Carrier," "Siegfried," "Absent with Official Leave," and "The Death of the Ball Turret Gunner." Other good poems in the volume are "Losses," "A Front," "The Metamorphoses," and "Mail Call." From *Losses*, the best poems seem to me "Lady Bates," "Eighth Air Force," "The Rising Sun," "Burning the Letters," "The Märchen," and, except for its last lines, "The Subway from New Britain to the Bronx." A second rank, very close to the first choices, would include "A Camp in the Prussian Forest," "The Dead in Melanesia," "The Lines," "A Country Life," "Jews at Haifa," "New Georgia," "In the Ward: The Sacred Wood," and "Orestes at Tauris." *The Seven-League Crutches* contains a number of very fine poems including "A Soul," "The Face," "The Knight, Death, and the Devil," "The Black Swan," "A Quilt Pattern," "A Girl in a Library," "The Sleeping Beauty: Variation of the Prince," and "Seele im Raum." From *The Woman at the Washington Zoo*, five poems seem to me outstanding: "The Woman at the Washington Zoo," "Cinderella," "Nestus Gurley," "Jerome," and "The Bronze David of Donatello," while three, "The Lost World," "The Lost Children," and "Thinking of the Lost World," outshine the others in the last volume. Here again, however, a second rank crowds the first: "In Galleries," "Well Water," "The Old and the New Masters," "Field and Forest."

Although, like the choices of any reader, mine are ultimately based on personal affinity, and I will have omitted some of others' favorites and included some not so popular, I do see the list as representative of all of Jarrell's major interests and poetic types. "90 North," the earliest on the list, might be said to foreshadow the central theme of nearly all Jarrell's mature poetry, as well as its characteristic techniques. The protagonist of "90 North" seeks meaning in human existence and finds pain. His diction is almost deceptively simple, his imagery drawn from literary allusion, popular culture, and the familiar strangeness of dream. Though grown up, he re-creates the child's perception of the quest for wisdom as a parable of adult experience. The verse form is rigorously organized, although in this particular instance the pentameter quatrains are unrhymed. A little story is told and its significance explained; the speaker is matter-of-fact, stoical in a predicament about which he can do nothing, for he has discovered the outrageous indifference of the universe toward mankind, the Necessity that moves men inexorably along the way into darkness and death.

In the war poems of *Little Friend* and *Losses*, the soldiers find that same wisdom in a different context: the world of the fighter planes and bombers, where the ball-turret gunner, Siegfried, the pilot from the carrier, the mother in "2nd Air Force," the wife who burns her husband's letters, the little Japanese boy, and the guilt-ridden speaker of "Eighth Air Force" learn to read suffering and death in their dreams and visions and in the elements of the world itself. Aside from dying and being resorbed into the elements ("The Subway from New Britain to the Bronx"), the only escape from the known Necessity comes through changes wrought by the imaginative faculty, in dreams ("Absent with Official Leave," "A Girl in a Library"); mythologizing ("In the Ward: The Sacred Wood," "Siegfried"); fairy tales ("The Sleeping Beauty . . . ," "The Black Swan," "The Märchen"); art generally ("The Knight, Death, and the Devil," "The Bronze David of Donatello"); or in the labyrinths of psychic disturbance ("Seele im Raum," "The Woman at the Washington Zoo").

The poems of the late forties and the fifties as a whole treat the antidotes for loss and pain in terms of imaginative experience that frees men's spirits to bear their lot "lightly, lightly." Jarrell's extensive knowledge of Freudian concepts of sublimation and compensation came together with his instinctive and learned responses to art—popular and sophisticated, international, interdisciplinary—in an extremely fecund period to produce many of his most hauntingly beautiful poems. The seductive quality of art as a remedy to the insufficiency of life never entirely lost its hold on Jarrell. Yet he shows plainly in his novel and his criticism, and in such poems as "A Conversation with the Devil," how well he knew that art has a very limited value for people like the girl in a library, the woman at the zoo and her counterpart Jerome, or Content ("The End of the Rainbow"), or those later protagonists in "Next Day," "The One Who Was Different," or "Hope"; and he became increasingly engrossed in their plight. In his later poems, especially, he tried to fathom their trouble, to penetrate the aura of loneliness and practiced indifference which isolates and insulates people from each others' pain: ironically, it is a pain that all men, of Necessity, share.

Like Wordsworth, Jarrell wanted to define and express the beauty and significance of ordinary life in a language actually spoken by men. Although a number of his attempts fail in the same ways Wordsworth's did, in a few poems it is probably not too much to claim that he succeeded better than his master; "The Woman at the Washington Zoo" and "Seele im Raum" would be two such poems. The quest for meaning and beauty in real life received its most serene fulfillment in "The Lost World," where Jarrell followed not Wordsworth but Proust; the result is an ecstatic vision that recalls Vaughan or Traherne as much as Proust. "The Lost World" seems to me to strike the tone of the late poetry as "90 North" had for the earlier work. Here, at last, Jarrell's quest culminates in a positive goal. Although the past *is* past, and Necessity impels us onward into oblivion, the individual can recapture through memory and fix in art the loveliness of human experience. In "The Lost World," as in Sherwood Anderson's "remembered" masterpiece "Death in the Woods," loss is transformed into sheer wonder. Other fine poems which record the affirmative thrust of Jarrell's late work are "Nestus Gurley," "Thinking of the Lost World," "The Lost Children," "A Man Meets a Woman in the Street," and "The Augsburg Adoration."

Jarrell's insistence on treating his themes of pain and loss in ordinary rather than heroic characters and in simple rather than densely packed language, has given rise to two main criticisms which are to some extent interdependent; first, that his poetry is childish and sentimental in subjects and attitudes; second, that its style lacks what James Dickey has called "*verbal* energy." [2] The child's consciousness is a territory explored by a number of the finest American writers of this century, yet Jarrell's use of the child's point of view does not require the sanction of a literary convention. Of the poems I have listed as Jarrell's best, it is true that many of the war poems utilize imagery of childhood in depicting the soldiers and their experiences. The poems are not finally about real childhood, however, but about the soldiers'

[2] James Dickey, "Randall Jarrell," reprinted in Lowell, Taylor, *et al.*, *Randall Jarrell, 1914–1965*, 40.

feelings of ignorance and helplessness that can only be compared to
the feelings of an abandoned child; the flyers, though adult, have
been figuratively born again into a world over which they have no
more control than a child has over his, and their education in this
new world culminates in knowledge only of death. Lady Bates was
a child, but her childhood was far from idyllic, and her future—to
have her hair straightened, to wait on someone else's table—hardly
satisfies even a childish dream. But she died; like the grownup soldiers,
like the old woman in "The One Who Was Different," or Greenie
Taliaferro; and to the universe her death, like all others, was a trifling
event. Again and again, in this poetry, the child's experience exemplifies and prefigures that of the man, but intensifies it with "the child's
peculiar gift for pain" that Jarrell recognized in the first version of
"Children Selecting Books in a Library."

Jarrell's poems evince his strong feeling about his subjects, but
feeling is not necessarily sentimental any more than an image of childhood is necessarily childish. If it is sentimental to be outraged at the
futility and inhumanity of war, to feel compassion toward people de-
prived of life and love for no good reason, then Jarrell is surely sentimental; however, in his best poems he presents the human situation
so fully and movingly that *not* to express his anxiety and love would
seem heartless. In the most painful of all his poems, "The Woman
at the Washington Zoo," the woman is surely self-pitying, but she
speaks from a life that is empty except for the constant anguish of
loneliness which is her only reality, and she does not ask for sympathy
—how pallid and useless that would be—but *change*: release from
her dreadful bondage.

One poem that seems rather vulnerable to the charge of sentimentality is one of the last written, "The Lost World," but only if
we mistake the poet's strategy. The idealization of boyhood in "The
Lost World" is an essential coordinate of a pattern of idealization that
fantasy—a child's fantasy, grownup literary and cinematic fantasy—
uses to enrich all lives. In exploring this idealization Jarrell is less childish and sentimental than intellectual and aesthetic; his approach to
the subject is by way of Freud and Proust. The child's world is
metaphorical as well as literal, and the metaphor is one of a series of
linked metaphors in the conceptual structure of the poem. In "The

Lost World" Jarrell embodies and expands a seminal insight about the relation of the movies to an individual's fantasy life that psychologists and sociologists of American culture have only recently begun to explore.

While the situations and characters of the poems in themselves warrant the expression of strong emotion, it is still necessary to testify that the poet has done more than arrive at "definition by ostentation . . . you simply point," as Jarrell's Gertrude put it,[3] borrowing from Wittgenstein. The rhetoric of the particular poem rather than its subject determines whether or not it is "sentimental"; the actual language must present what Eliot called an "objective correlative" to the evinced feeling. On this point critics have disagreed. Objections to Jarrell's style are difficult to answer categorically because in the less successful poems one may single out, as Dickey does in his essay, ineffective, even awkward or absurd lines and passages. I have referred a number of times to Jarrell's interest in creating a style that, like Frost's or Ransom's, would accurately but poetically reproduce the idioms and rhythms of contemporary speech. This ideal was difficult to achieve and hard to sustain, but the best poems are astonishingly convincing. Let some of them speak for themselves:

> In the turret's great glass dome, the apparition, death,
> Framed in the glass of the gunsight, a fighter's blinking wing,
> Flares softly, a vacant fire. If the flak's inked blurs—
> Distributed, statistical—the bombs' lost patterning
> Are death, they are death under glass, a chance
> For someone yesterday, someone tomorrow; and the fire
> That streams from the fighter which is there, not there,
> Does not warm you, has not burned them, though they die.
>   "Siegfried"

> Cowhorn-crowned, shockheaded, cornshuck-bearded,
> Death is a scarecrow—his death's-head a teetotum
> That tilts up toward man confidentially
> But trimmed with adders; ringlet-maned, rope-bridled,
> The mare he rides crops herbs beside a skull.
> He holds up, warning, the crossed cones of time;

---

[3] Randall Jarrell, *Pictures from an Institution* (New York, 1960), 178.

Here, narrowing into now, the Past and Future
Are quicksand.
                    "The Knight, Death, and the Devil"

Don't cry, little peasant. Sit and dream.
One comes, a finger's width beneath your skin,
To the braided maidens singing as they spin;
There sound the shepherd's pipe, the watchman's rattle
Across the short dark distance of the years.
I am a thought of yours: and yet, you do not think . . .
The firelight of a long, blind, dreaming story
Lingers upon your lips; and I have seen
Firm, fixed forever in your closing eyes,
The Corn King beckoning to his Spring Queen.
                              "A Girl in a Library"

    . . . this serviceable
Body that no sunlight dyes, no hand suffuses
But, dome-shadowed, withering among columns,
Wavy beneath fountains—small, far-off, shining
In the eyes of animals, these beings trapped
As I am trapped but not, themselves, the trap,
Aging, but without knowledge of their age,
Kept safe here, knowing not of death, for death—
Oh, bars of my own body, open, open!
                    "The Woman at the Washington Zoo"

    So, now, Lucky and I sit in our row,
Mrs. Mercer in hers. I take for granted
The tiller by which she steers, the yellow roses
In the bud vases, the whole enchanted
Drawing room of our progress. . . .

    · · · · · · · · · · ·
    . . . We press our noses
To the glass and wish: the angel- and devilfish
Floating by on Vine, on Sunset, shut their eyes
And press their noses to their glass and wish.
                              "The Lost World"

These passages, written over a span of twenty years, demonstrate
not only the flexibility of line and impressionistic vividness of which
Jarrell was capable, but a remarkable consistency of style: the skill-

ful use of verbs of seeing and motion, as well as of participles and other verbals; the series of descriptive phrases culminating in a broadened cadence; precision of image coupled with simplicity of diction; unobtrusive but sure control of the basically iambic meter; repetition with variation that both emphasizes an image and fixes it within a rhythmic pattern. The conceptual unit is almost never the single image—"a patient etherized upon a table"—but a composite scene—domes, columns, fountains, the caged animals, the lone female figure reflected in the savage eyes. It is not, perhaps, a poetry of "purely *verbal* intensity," but its music and the perceptions it realizes are inalterably poetic.

To examine the passages closely is to confirm their relationship, not to the "modern" poetry of Eliot, Auden, Tate, or Wallace Stevens, the poetry described and analyzed by Jarrell in the preface to "The Rage for the Lost Penny," but to the poetry of common life and language, the tradition of Wordsworth, Walt Whitman, and Robert Frost. (It is perhaps not coincidental that Wordsworth and Whitman were attacked for their "sentimentality" and flatness of style; Frost, too, has been disparaged for his simplicity.) Using many of their precepts and techniques, combining them, in his later poetry, with the exaltation of simple subjects he found in Rilke, Jarrell developed a poetry that reveals his life and time with a fidelity unsurpassed by any other writer, in prose or verse, of that life and time. Indeed, it is the prose writers who approach his work most nearly. The best of his war poems express the distilled essence of Ernie Pyle's sensitive and troubled but, to later times, distractingly detailed reports of World War II; his later poems embody with dreadful force the loneliness and frustration of modern life presented at greater length by the best short-story writers of his generation—Eudora Welty, Flannery O'Connor, Richard Purdy, and Peter Taylor.

Yet the poems are not stories, nor except perhaps for a few of the longest ones—"The Night Before the Night Before Christmas," "The End of the Rainbow," "Hope"—can we imagine them made into stories. The actions of the poems are not organized into plots; the time-schemes defy chronology; the rhetoric and rhythm do not belong to prose. One term from short story (and novel) criticism does seem applicable: Joyce's concept of "epiphany," the showing forth of the spiritual essence of a happening, a perception, a phrase. "Epiphany," thus defined, is the traditional business of lyric poetry; indeed, it is only since Chekhov and Joyce that the term has any marked application to narrative fiction. At his highest level, Jarrell works toward these moments of spiritual enlightenment which give the poems an autonomous aesthetic life that continues to refract its truth along the passages of memory.

Writing in the first shock of grief at Jarrell's death, Robert Lowell concluded his memoir of his old friend, "Now that he is gone, I see clearly that the spark from heaven really struck and irradiated the lines and being of my dear old friend—his noble, difficult and beautiful soul." [4] Reading through *The Complete Poems*, coming again upon those poems in which Jarrell's compassionate grasp of the moral importance of his subjects unites with the powerful poetic intelligence that made him also a fine critic, one recalls and affirms Lowell's statement. Jarrell's gifts were basically a far-ranging, inquisitive, continually testing intellect; a strong perception of the ironic incongruity of men's ideals with their way of living; a sure feeling for the moral and psychological crises men have in common; and a messianic vocation to show others what he learned and saw in the world. His limitations—some consciously self-cultivated—were a narrow scope, a too-dogmatic vision of human motivation and behavior, a sense of imagery and phrase that is only sporadically overwhelming. Because he wrote a relatively large body of poetry on a small number of subjects and themes, and perhaps because of a sometimes difficult public personality, as a lecturer and critic too certain in his own demanding standards, his poems have been erratically anthologized, erratically praised and blamed for both virtues and faults.

Jarrell's is not finally a poetry of the academy, but of the people. Since the people, as Jarrell wryly knew, do not generally care much for poetry unless, like Frost's or Sandburg's, it is promulgated as a national cultural heritage, with the poet himself playing the role of National Grandfather, Jarrell's poems have not yet received the audience they intrinsically merit, an audience somewhere between academe and the popular culture. These readers may be "too few," as Jarrell once plaintively wrote, but they exist, and their numbers

---

[4] Lowell, "Randall Jarrell," in Lowell, Taylor, *et al.*, *Randall Jarrell, 1914–1965*, 112.

may well become larger as American affluence gives more people more leisure in which to despair or, hopefully, to live. Represented by his best work, and read side by side with the best poems of his contemporaries or even that brilliant generation of poets which precedes his in Anglo-American poetry, Jarrell's work requires no apology. His very best poems, some twenty or thirty-odd, chosen for the universality and truth of their subjects and the consistency and beauty of the treatment, will deserve a high place in American poetry of this century, in some measure because they record American life in this century so very well.

Like Walt Whitman, like Frost, Jarrell strove to present the America he saw. It is not the same America, of course; "America is hard to see," Frost once wrote; he might have added that it is continually changing its appearance. Jarrell's America is a nation of large towns and small cities, with suburban supermarkets and funeral homes; banks and zoological gardens; movie theaters and public libraries funded by the Carnegie Foundation. His Americans keep pets, shop for detergent or antiques, listen to the radio, fall asleep over their homework, visit psychoanalysts. When they go out into the country they do not know what to call things; when they went to war "in bombers named for girls, [they] bombed the cities [they] had learned about in school." They are educated massively, though probably not very well, and, especially in the later poems, they are self-aware, but neither education nor awareness can sustain them. Trying to define the essential qualities of Americans in *Pictures from an Institution*, Jarrell fell back on what

Marianne Moore has said about New York, that treasure-hoard which Americans lie with their tails around, growling at one another . . . "It is not the plunder but/ accessibility to experience." That said, almost, what I wanted to say about Americans. They had, so far, no armor against fate—for riches and bombers and empire aren't armor, but only fate. There was something helpless and noticing about Americans, a few Americans, which I liked; something happened to them, sometimes, and they looked at it and were at a loss, for long, for long. They did not understand it; and it takes a young and ignorant race not to understand something, when so many different ways of understanding it already exist.[5]

[5] Jarrell, *Pictures from an Institution*, 174.

In his poetry, Jarrell shows Americans trying to forge some armor against fate, generally under its other name, Necessity. The fabric of the armor, as we have seen, is dreams, or fairy tales, or more sophisticated art, or memory itself turning into art. That is an old armor to Europeans, Jarrell thought: so old that only Americans could still be surprised and bewitched by it, and learn from it.

"The world is everything that is the case": Jarrell often quoted, and even used as a title for one section of the *Selected Poems*, the enigmatic first proposition of Wittgenstein's *Tractatus Logico-Philosophicus*. He must have believed that poetry was at least as good a way as philosophy to understand that "totality of facts" Wittgenstein saw as composing the world. The progress of Jarrell's investigation of the world in his poetry suggests not only a methodical inquiry into the nature of things by means of one man's perceptions and intuitions, but an attempt to evaluate and concentrate on "what is important" ("The Old and the New Masters"). From his broad and deep reading in *all* kinds of writing—fiction, history, poetry, philosophy, psychology, criticism, anthropology, religion, popular culture from cars to football to fairy tales—he evolved one simple critical theory by which he measured his own poetry as well as that of others. His writing seems to ask always, both explicitly and implicitly, whether the poem tells truth about the world; whether it helps the reader see a little farther, a little more clearly the dark and light of his situation. His theory, which is not really theory but just clear-sightedness, reflects Jarrell's own great capacity for responding enthusiastically to many different kinds and styles of art and life, and it gives his mature poetry as a whole an extraordinary sense of that "accessibility to experience" he recognized as characteristic of the American consciousness. His work affirms the dignity and worth of individual human efforts to understand and change themselves and, if possible, the world. Even though he sets these efforts in his own particular time and place, their impulse is timeless, universal, and transcendent. The world of Randall Jarrell is a world that does not get lost.

Biographical Note

RANDALL JARRELL was born in Nashville, Tennessee, on May 6, 1914. His parents were Owen and Anna Campbell Jarrell, both native Tennesseans. The family moved to California, settling in Long Beach, when Randall was very young. His parents separated in 1925, but when his mother and younger brother went back to live with the Campbell family in Tennessee, the boy remained in Hollywood with his paternal grandparents. Late in 1926 Randall Jarrell rejoined his mother in Nashville, where, soon after, he modeled for the Ganymede of the full-scale concrete replica of the Parthenon in Centennial Park. While attending Hume Fogg High School, from which he graduated in 1931, he was active in dramatics, playing in school productions of "The Chocolate Soldier" and "The Trumpet Major." Although he was to have gone into his uncle's candy business, the family soon recognized his boredom with the business course in which he enrolled, and his uncle, Howell Campbell, sent him instead to Vanderbilt University.

At Vanderbilt he majored in psychology, graduating in 1935 with a B.S. degree, but in the meantime he had come under the sway of John Crowe Ransom in the English department and had edited the literary magazine. Although the Fugitive Movement was in its waning days by then, a number of its members remained active in Nashville, at least off and on; besides Ransom, Jarrell knew Robert Penn Warren, Allen Tate, and Donald Davidson well. He returned to Vanderbilt for graduate work in English, but when Ransom went to Kenyon College in 1937, Randall Jarrell followed, as an English instructor. He finished an M.A. at Vanderbilt in 1939, writing a "new critical" thesis on A. E. Housman under the direction of Donald Davidson. At Kenyon, Jarrell continued his friendship with Peter Taylor, who had also followed Ransom from Vanderbilt, and he formed what was to be a lifelong attachment to Robert Lowell, another drawn to Kenyon by Ransom.

After receiving his M.A., Jarrell accepted a position in the English department at the University of Texas in Austin, where he met, and married on June 1, 1940, Mackie Langham. During this period, his first two collections of poetry, "The Rage for the Lost Penny," in New Directions' *Five Young American Poets*, and *Blood for a Stranger*, were published. Soon after Pearl Harbor he enlisted in a ferry-pilot training program in Austin, but failing to qualify he became a private in the Army Air Force. He served as a Celestial Navigation tower operator for a short time at

Chanute Field, Rantoul, Illinois, and then, until the end of the war, at Davis-Monthan Field in Tucson, Arizona. His second independent volume of poems, *Little Friend, Little Friend*, appeared in 1945.

Having been awarded several poetry prizes, he was given a Guggenheim Post-Service Fellowship in 1946. At that time he was poetry editor for the *Nation*, a position in which he matured his natural bent for criticism. After a year of teaching at Sarah Lawrence College he returned to the South in 1947, accepting a position at the Women's College of the University of North Carolina in Greensboro. Except for visiting appointments and his tenure as poetry consultant at the Library of Congress (1956–58), he remained at Women's College (now University of North Carolina, Greensboro) all his life.

Losses was published in 1948, and in the summer of that year Jarrell made his first trip to Europe, teaching at the Salzburg Summer Seminar in American Civilization. It was an experience that bore fruit in a number of his most memorable poems and translations, as did subsequent visits in 1959 and 1963. *The Seven-League Crutches* appeared in 1951, followed by a volume of criticism, *Poetry and the Age*, in 1953, the novel *Pictures from an Institution* in 1954, and *Selected Poems* in 1955. In 1951 Randall and Mackie Jarrell separated; they were divorced in the autumn of 1952. At a writers' conference in Boulder, Colorado, in the summer of 1951, he met Mary von Schrader, and they were married in California late in 1952.

Randall Jarrell received the National Book Award in 1960 for his book of poems and translations, *The Woman at the Washington Zoo*. A second collection of his essays, *A Sad Heart at the Supermarket*, was published in 1962. Also in the early sixties, Jarrell composed his three children's books, *The Gingerbread Rabbit*, *The Bat Poet*, and *The Animal Family*. In 1963 he was awarded a second Guggenheim Fellowship.

He was hospitalized for a nervous breakdown in February, 1965, but was well enough to return home in May. He was teaching again the next fall, until, on the night of October 14, 1965, he was struck and killed by an automobile in Chapel Hill. His last volume of poems, *The Lost World*, appeared in December of that year.

Since then, a number of volumes have been issued under the supervision of Mary von Schrader Jarrell: *Complete Poems* (1969); a translation with notes of Chekhov's play, *The Three Sisters* (1969); and *The Third Book of Criticism* (1970). Still in preparation are a children's book, *Fly by Night*, and a translation of Goethe's *Faust*, Part I. Approximately a third of the Jarrell manuscripts were donated in the poet's lifetime to the Walter Clinton Jackson Library at the Greensboro campus. The remainder of the Jarrell Archive is in the Berg Collection of the New York Public Library.

Selected Bibliography

Books and articles by Randall Jarrell

Jarrell, Randall. *The Animal Family*. New York: Pantheon Books, 1965.

_____. *The Bat Poet*. New York: Macmillan Co., 1964.

_____. (ed.). *The Best Short Stories of Rudyard Kipling*. Garden City, Hanover House, 1961.

_____. *Blood for a Stranger*. New York: Harcourt Brace and Co., 1942.

_____. *The Complete Poems*. New York: Farrar, Straus & Giroux, 1969.

_____. *The Gingerbread Rabbit*. New York: Macmillan Co., 1964.

_____. *Little Friend, Little Friend*. New York: Dial Press, 1945.

_____. *Losses*. New York: Harcourt, Brace and Co., 1948.

_____. *The Lost World*. New York: Macmillan Co., 1965.

_____. *Pictures from an Institution*. New York: Alfred A. Knopf, 1954.

_____. *Poetry and the Age*. New York: Alfred A. Knopf, 1953.

_____. "The Rage for the Lost Penny," in *Five Young American Poets*. Norfolk, Conn.: New Directions, 1940, pp. 81–123.

_____. *A Sad Heart at the Supermarket*. New York: Atheneum Publ., 1962.

_____. *Selected Poems*. New York: Alfred A. Knopf, 1955.

_____. *The Seven-League Crutches*. New York: Harcourt, Brace and Co., 1951.

_____. *The Woman at the Washington Zoo*. New York: Atheneum Publ., 1960.

About Randall Jarrell

Adams, Charles M. *Randall Jarrell: A Bibliography*. Chapel Hill: University of North Carolina Press, 1958. Supplement in *Analects* I, (Spring, 1961), 49–56. [See Shapiro entry in this section for works after 1960.]

Alumni News, University of North Carolina, Greensboro, LIV (Spring, 1966). Memorial issue for Randall Jarrell. Memoirs and tributes by Peter Taylor, Adrienne Rich, John Berryman, Allen Tate, Marianne Moore, John Crowe Ransom, Stanley Kunitz, Robert Lowell, Eleanor Ross Taylor, L. Richardson Preyer, Robert Penn Warren, Mrs. Ran-

dall Jarrell, Charles M. Adams, and former Jarrell students Jean Farley
White, Ineko Kondo, Pamela Pfaff, Angela Davis, Heather Ross Miller,
June Cope Bencivenni, Jo Gilliken, Alma Graham, and Bertha Harris
Wyland.

Analects. University of North Carolina, Greensboro, Literary Magazine.
I (Spring, 1961). Special issue on Randall Jarrell. Essays by Michel
Benamou, Nathan Glick, Glauco Cambon, Richard Fein, Sr. M. Ber-
netta Quinn, Inigo Seidler. Supplement to Charles M. Adams' *Randall
Jarrell: A Bibliography* (1958).

Ciardi, John (ed.), *Mid-Century American Poets.* New York: Twayne
Publ., 1950.

Cowley, Malcolm. "First Blood," review of *Blood for a Stranger, New
Republic,* CVII (1942), 718.

Humphrey, Robert. "Randall Jarrell's Poetry," in Ray B. Browne and
Donald Pizer (eds.), *Themes and Directions in American Literature:
Essays in Honor of Leon Howard.* Lafayette, Ind.: Purdue University
Press, 1969, 220–33.

Lowell, Robert, Peter Taylor, and Robert Penn Warren (eds.). *Randall
Jarrell, 1914–1965.* New York: Farrar, Straus & Giroux, 1967.
Essays by Hannah Arendt, John Berryman, Elizabeth Bishop, Philip
Booth, Cleanth Brooks, James Dickey, Denis Donoghue, Leslie A. Fied-
ler, Robert Fitzgerald, R. W. Flint, Alfred Kazin, Stanley Kunitz,
Robert Lowell, William Meredith, Marianne Moore, Robert Phelps,
Sr. M. Bernetta Quinn, John Crowe Ransom, Adrienne Rich, Delmore
Schwartz, Maurice Sendak, Karl Shapiro, Allen Tate, Eleanor Ross
Taylor, P. L. Travers, Robert Watson, Mrs. Randall Jarrell.

Quinn, Sister M. Bernetta. *The Metamorphic Tradition in Modern Poetry.* 2nd ed. New York: Gordian Press, 1966.

————. "Randall Jarrell: Landscapes of Life and LIFE," *Shenandoah,*
XX (Winter, 1969), 49–78.

Shapiro, Karl. *Randall Jarrell.* (A lecture presented under the auspices of
the Gertrude Clarke Whittall Poetry and Literature Fund, with a
bibliography of Jarrell materials in the collections of the Library of
Congress.) Washington, D.C.: Library of Congress, 1967.

Index